To Paul,

With best wishes,

AGAINST THE CURRENT

'Bon courage!'

Mike Bodar

AGAINST THE CURRENT

Au revoir to corporate life and *bonjour* to a life afloat in France!

MIKE BODNAR

Matador
9 Priory Business Park,
Wistow Road, Kibworth Beauchamp,
Leicestershire. LE8 0RX
Tel: 0116 279 2299
Email: books@troubador.co.uk
Web: www.troubador.co.uk/matador
Twitter: @matadorbooks

ISBN 978 1784625 382

British Library Cataloguing in Publication Data.
A catalogue record for this book is available from the British Library

Printed and bound by CPI Group (UK) Ltd, Croydon, CR0 4YY
Typeset in 11pt Aldine401BT by Troubador Publishing Ltd, Leicester, UK

Matador is an imprint of Troubador Publishing Ltd

For Liz, my Number One, and for Catherine, Karis, James and Yasmin who never questioned what we were doing.

The cartoon on page 158 is by the very talented Merrily Harpur. *Merci beaucoup* Merrily.

*In memory of Jeremy McCall
and Gillian Wood*

PROLOGUE

'Do not, do NOT, let go of that rope!' I yelled to Liz as she heaved back on it, trying with all her might to hold *Liberty*'s bows from swinging further into the current. She had wrapped it once round a guardrail on the *quai*, but it wasn't enough, and the rope was slipping through her grip.

'I can't hold on, there's not enough rope,' she screamed back. I pulled harder on the stern rope, but could feel it too dragging through my hands as the rear of the boat wanted to follow the bows out into the river. By now the bows were about five metres out from the *quai* and the stern about three. The current was winning. 'We're losing her!' I shouted. '*Pull!*'

But the bow swung out further. And yet somehow the stern seemed to have paused, almost as though it needed to make up its mind what to do. It was the pivot on which the rest of the boat would at any moment completely swing round, the current taking control and pulling the ropes out of our hands.

For the diners at the riverside restaurant on the opposite bank it must have been a tug of awe, but we could see *Liberty* crashing into the other craft moored behind us further along the *quai*, then being swept away down the Rhône to collide with one of the giant hotel boats or a bridge support. She would heel over, the green waters of the river surging through her hatches, and within minutes she'd be gone.

Despite heaving with all my might it had hardly any impact. We were, after all, fighting ten tonnes of steel. There was only one thing left to do. I let the rope go, ran to the edge of the quayside, and leapt...

A map of France with some of the key locations mentioned in the book. Although not to scale, to give you some idea the straight-line distance from Paris to Aigues-Mortes is 604 kms or 375 miles.

For images go to: www.againstthecurrent.uk

CHAPTER ONE

It would be fantastic to begin this book by saying that boating had been in our blood since we were born; that we were brought up by sailing parents, and were weaned to the snap and crack of sails in a stiff offshore breeze, our nappies hung out to dry on the backstay.

Or that Liz's maiden name of Cook could be traced directly back to Yorkshire's famous son, and that exploring, navigating and staying off cannibals' dinner menus were an inherent part of her DNA.

Sorry to disappoint. Despite having genuine Yorkshire connections, Liz's maiden name is, sadly, just coincidental. Until this adventure, spending a week on a narrowboat in England with some fellow cider- and lager-drinking Oxford students was about the lengthiest single experience she'd had of things nautical, except for a few forays in a rubber inflatable off the south coast to go scuba diving on shipwrecks. (Oh, and she did once hitchhike from Oxford to London with some fellow students all dressed in full scuba gear – including flippers – for a charity fundraising event. Oxford eh?)

Despite her paucity of boating experience or knowledge, Liz was at least prepared to learn and explore, so in that respect she did have some commonality with Captain Cook, and for the purposes of this crazy adventure, an attitude of devil-may-care, boldly-go, let's-just-do-it was all the qualification she needed as far as I was concerned.

I can perhaps claim a slightly closer affinity with water, though still nothing so substantial as to qualify me for having what might be called a solid background in sailing, and certainly nothing so useful as any sort of maritime training.

The most that could be said is that with a captain as a father, I did at least know the correct names for the sharp and blunt ends of a vessel from an early age. Plus, I grew up in Liverpool, England, at a time when the city's maritime and mercantile status was still strong. My mother worked at the Pier Head in the Cunard Building for HM Customs and Excise, processing ships' cargo manifests, and meeting future husbands. And of course as a lad I travelled on the famous ferry 'cross the Mersey many a time (though 'ferries' is more appropriate – there were a few of them).

You may be wondering why then, since my father was a captain, he didn't formally introduce me to boating, and guide me through the tricky currents and tides of maritime skills and knowledge so that I could, at the age of 13, jump on a yacht, take a bearing from the stars, and sail boldly towards the distant horizon.

In short, my parents divorced when I was just four years old, so although he was indeed a fully-qualified seafarer, I saw him only briefly on those occasions when he was in port, when he had the agreed 'access' to see me. Instead of taking me boating however, he preferred to whisk me by taxi into central Liverpool to buy me new clothes, and to try and introduce me to yucky foreign foods such as Hungarian sausage.

I agreed freely to the taxi rides (a real treat as we didn't own a car) and I quite liked shopping for the clothes, but drew the line at the sausage, much to his dismay. Maybe that lack of adventurous spirit on my part put him off encouraging me towards a nautical career. If I was reluctant to steer a piece of Hungarian sausage into my mouth then I was unlikely to be keen to steer a boat anywhere; I guess that was his thinking anyway.

But that's not to say I didn't get some maritime opportunities, even without his presence or guidance. One of my earliest boating experiences (if not my very first) was as a young child – I'm guessing I was about six – when I was taken on an outing to New Brighton, a seaside 'resort' on the Liverpool Bay entrance to the Mersey, known for its promenade, fresh sea air, and typical English seaside entertainments: fairground rides, dodgems, a miniature train, pinball machines, amusement arcades, fish and chip stalls, and a boating pond, at which my Auntie Doll hired a rowing boat for me.

I didn't have a natural aptitude for rowing – I just went in circles – but I distinctly remember the shouting and yelling that finally pierced my brain, and I have a clear picture of turning round in the little boat to see what all the fuss was about.

On the shore my Auntie and others were screaming, 'The baby! The baby! Get the baby!' It sounded like a script from a Punch and Judy show. I had no idea what they were talking about, until I saw a man wade into the water and pull out a bedraggled heap of what looked like discarded clothing, but was in fact an infant.

I recall feeling a bit slow on the uptake, chagrined at not being able to control my rowing boat with any degree of dexterity, and feeling embarrassed that I was unable to play any meaningful part in the rescue. I may have even worried about the health of the infant, but can only remember my own shame at the time. A policeman came along, presumably having been summoned by bystanders, keen to find the hero who he said should get a medal for saving the child's life. I'd have liked a medal, but unfortunately didn't deserve it.

I have no memories of rowing a boat after that until probably ten years later, half a world away in New Zealand on a park lake, but in the meantime I did enjoy a few more bigger sailing experiences, such as crossing the Irish Sea on the overnight ferry to Dun Laoghaire, travelling to the Continent on the cross-Channel ferries, and occasionally visiting one of the ships my father was skipper of, when he was in port in Liverpool to discharge or take on cargo. We once even sailed from Ireland to Liverpool on one of his vessels. I was pleased to discover that I was a good sailor, with never a hint of sea sickness. Force eight in the Channel? Bring it on!

Thanks to my Mum's involvement in the shipping scene I had pictures of ships on my bedroom walls, some of them travel posters from travel agents and shipping lines like Thomas Cook (still no relation), P&O, and Cunard, and they always seemed so exotic. Ships sailed to far-off lands, over the horizon and away from grimy Liverpool, to sunnier climes. I envied those passengers who could afford to go on such journeys, but at the age of 11 I had few thoughts of joining them, and even fewer of ever owning a boat. I was more worried about passing the 11-plus exams.

Meanwhile, at that same time 200 miles south, Rachel Elizabeth Cook was born in Bridgend, Wales. She was, unbeknown to me, to become my wife, my navigator, my Number One, and that we would, some decades later, buy a boat and cruise through France together. We would survive snowstorms, breakdowns, and boardings by armed maritime police. We would lose control of our vessel, and reel in horror as we inadvertently rammed lock gates, threatening to close the Canal du Midi for weeks.

But all that excitement was in the future and out of sight, as of course the rest of your life usually is when you're still a child.

Anyway, while Liz was still having her nappies changed, I was trying to come to grips with Latin, French and (ugh) Maths at my high school, Tower College. We would grow up blindly unaware of each other for the next forty years or so, leading completely separate and diverse lives, marrying, having children (that is, marrying other people and having kids with them) but slowly and inexorably moving towards each other on convergent paths.

But in 1965 there was certainly no hint that one day in the future we'd be walking together down a pontoon in a marina in central-eastern France looking for a boat to live on.

CHAPTER TWO

'It smells a bit,' Liz said, as we looked around the stifling cabin. 'Yeah,' I agreed. 'Needs a lot of work as well. Too much work. Let's carry on.'

We emerged from the dank and stuffy cabin onto the deck and looked around. Boats were everywhere, tied up in neat rows along the floating pontoons. Above, the sun beat down relentlessly from a clear blue sky. It must have been around thirty degrees Celsius, but inside the boats – most of which were unmanned and locked up with no windows open – the temperature was more like forty. Choosing a boat was going to be hot work.

I'd been here in Saint-Jean-de-Losne (pronounced like 'lawn' only a bit shorter) a few weeks earlier with my long-time friend Shaun from the UK, to check out the boat sales scene and to narrow down a few options before Liz arrived from New Zealand.

Now here she was with me in central-eastern France, looking over some of the boats I'd selected for further investigation. This had been a much looked-forward-to destination because here there were many, many boats for sale, and it was a popular spot with boaties in general.

That's because Saint-Jean-de-Losne lies at a confluence of the Saône River, the Canal de Bourgogne, and the Canal du Rhône au Rhin. It's a convenient place to get to by boat, road or rail. It's also midway-ish between the Mediterranean in the south and France's northern boundary with Belgium, and not far from the mustard capital of Dijon. Some say it's France's premier inland port, and it has the added bonus of full facilities, from dry-docks and cranes to marine chandlers and moorings. So here we were, eager beavers, salivating over boats.

The key part of our Grand Plan had long been to buy a boat and live on the French canals and rivers for a year while exploring France at an escargot's pace. Liz and I had trawled the Internet to see what was for sale in France, and what our money might buy. There were some tantalising possibilities, and our projected budget of around €40,000 seemed viable. We were excited.

It was during this preliminary research that we identified Saint-Jean-de-Losne as our prime destination, a perfect place to go and kick some hulls. Now we were doing just that, and with all the boats here in real life laid out before us, with bright yellow *à vendre* signs on them, we were somewhat overwhelmed.

As well as the asking price, each For Sale sign included the boat's year of manufacture, and its dimensions. In the brokerage office a display board with photos gave even more information, such as how many cabins each vessel had, what it was made of, how many it could sleep, the engine size, and so on.

In our minds we'd visualised buying something older, perhaps made of wood, with tons of character. Something that could sleep at least four people and preferably six; that had adequate deck space for those lazy lunches or al fresco dinners in the lovely warmth of French summer evenings. We saw ourselves exploring the rivers and canals through the seasons of a full year, heading south for the winter to escape the cold, and exploring the southern Canal du Midi, and the Canal Latéral à la Garonne towards Bordeaux, before heading back north in late spring.

It was romantic, ambitious, and it was all about to change.

Not that there was any shortage of craft to choose from; Saint-Jean-de-Losne is home to two busy boat brokerages, but we quickly discovered that what looked charming on the Internet was – in reality and close up – tatty, peeling, scruffy or in need of complete overhaul. Some boats looked like they would have taken a further €40,000 to renovate, and we didn't want to spend either the money or the time doing that.

'No, too much work,' we agreed again and again as we looked around the boats. 'We want something we can set off on straight away, something we can be confident in,' I said. Liz concurred, and made notes in a notebook so that we'd remember the details and what we thought of each boat.

Actually, let me expand on that, because it doesn't do justice to the scene, or to Liz. When I say 'notebook,' I really mean spreadsheet. Liz, rather like other superheroes who prefer to keep their true identities secret, is – unbeknown to the general world – Process Woman. She doesn't have a cape or mask, but when it comes to logical thinking, making comparisons, highlighting features and faults, and reaching cogent conclusions, she spins into Process Mode, without needing to get changed in a phone box. She doesn't need gimmicks like a shield or sticky web strings either, but give her a PowerPoint display and it's wise to duck for cover. If she had anything in her utility belt it would likely be four felt-tip pens, a pie chart and an Excel spreadsheet.

This all stems, she will tell you, from having been a policy analyst by profession for a number of years. And there's another similarity with superheroes; if someone asks Clark Kent, 'Hey, aren't you Superman?' he would simply say 'No, you're mistaken. I'm just a mild-mannered reporter.' Liz, like Clark, has discovered that if anyone asks what she does for a living and she replies, 'I'm a policy analyst,' her enquirer quickly drifts away to find someone more interesting to talk to, such as a second-hand car dealer. Or insurance salesman.

This suits Liz, who prefers to stay out of the limelight. 'You keep forgetting I'm an introvert,' she reminds me frequently.

'I don't like being the centre of attention.' And I do forget, because I see her as a bubbly, fun person, a bit Out There, and not afraid to be Off The Wall. Hell, I mean here we were: she'd just resigned from a good job, had agreed to selling our lovely newly-renovated New Zealand home, and had moved half a world away to live with me on a boat. That sounded like an extrovert to me.

But no, apparently not. For example, if we go to the *boulangerie* together for croissants and a baguette, I'm the one that has to go through the door first. If we walk into a bar for a glass of wine, same thing: I must enter first. Why? Because, she says, she's shy.

'I *am* shy!' she's just said, reading over my shoulder.

Maybe she is – the jury is still out on that one, though the defence puts up a solid argument – but I do know she is a logical and clear thinker. Which is why she was in charge of making notes on each boat we looked at, checking them against our criteria, and scoring them so we could easily identify our favourites. Thank God you're here Process Woman! And just in time!

No seriously, there *was* a need for urgency in deciding which boat to buy; it was already August, and September would herald the start of autumn, so not only did we want the right boat for us, we also wanted to be casting off as soon as possible. As you know, we'd dreamed of finding something older, something with charm, and a bit of history; a bit like me really. It would be both practical and elegant (ditto), and gorgeous, and cosy (…), but time was against us, and we had only three days before we were due to go to England and prepare for the arrival of our possessions from New Zealand. We also needed to get Yasmin – Liz's 16-year-old daughter – organised for her boarding school in Yorkshire. Our schedule was full of Things To Do, and we had multiple lists, but top of everything was: Buy A Boat.

The broker we spent most of our time with was very casual about allowing us to go on board the *à vendre* boats; there was no sales pressure, and in fact all he did was give us the keys and tell us to look around, which we did. Most boats were unattended, their owners absent, which we liked because it meant we could take our time, explore every nook and cranny, open cupboards, sit on the couch and imagine ourselves living there, lift the carpets and floors, check the condition of the hull (at least on the inside), see if the bilge was dry, and generally have free unfettered access to each craft we saw.

The boats on offer ranged from converted former commercial barges over a hundred years old to sleek modern gin palaces no more than two or three years of age. Online, it was the older ones that had initially appealed to us, those that most people imagine a canal barge should look like. One of our favourite types was the *tjalk* (pronounced – roughly – chall'k), of Dutch origin. These boats were long and low, with a graceful bow that curved upwards, and sometimes a tiller at the stern rather than a conventional helm. They had a lovely shape and a good displacement, which was one of the criteria we had to take into consideration.

Why displacement? Okay, quick lesson: the French canals are not deep – sometimes no more than about 1.2 metres – so if your craft's hull extends 1.5 metres below the water, you're in for a potential grounding. We needed a good grounding in boats and boat handling, but not that sort.

In French, we learned, the extent of a boat's hull underwater, the draft, is called the *tirant d'eau*, so we wanted our boat to have a *tirant d'eau* of preferably no more than 1.2m. As well, we were warned by Keith, a very experienced canal boating friend of ours, that it's equally important how tall your boat is, because many of the canals have low bridges. If your boat can't get under them, well, all you can do is turn around and go back the way you came. We wanted Access All Areas in France, so to add to the *tirant d'eau* criterion was the *tirant d'air* – the measure of how high a boat is above its waterline. Liz's logical process brain was going to be busy. The more we saw of the boats for sale the more complex our list got.

With specific criteria of budget, depth and height, construction material, and of course character, it was relatively straightforward to eliminate many of the boats on offer – they were either too expensive, the dimensions or layout were wrong, or they were made of the wrong material (for us).

Then Liz had a change of heart about buying an old boat. 'I'm not keen on buying anything older than me!' She declared. So that ruled out a few more.

We walked up and down the pontoon, noting a number of possible candidates, but not realising we'd already walked past and ignored the boat that we would eventually buy.

But in examining the various craft, we also came to understand a bit more about them. For example, there were a number of ex-hire boats for sale. Made of fibreglass (or 'GRP' for those who want to show off their knowledge) these make especially good canal boats because they've been designed exactly for the express purposes of travelling in shallow water and under low bridges. They're well laid-out inside, and often have two bathrooms, or at least two WCs. One we saw even had a full-sized bath. They commonly have ample deck space for sitting out, sunbathing or entertaining, and – because they are designed to be rented out to people who likely don't know the first thing about boating and who couldn't tell a barnacle from a binnacle – they are usually fitted with an all-round rubber fender, for playing bumper boats.

But for us they lacked character; for all their practical points, the ex-hires looked just a bit too utilitarian. Some had only an interior steering position too, which we thought was a shame, as we envisaged steering from up top in glorious sunshine, the breeze in our hair and a glass of Chablis to hand. And sometimes the helm wasn't just inside but positioned right up towards the front, and we'd been warned by Keith about this.

'The thing with a forward steering position,' he told us sagely, 'is that you have ninety percent of the boat behind you, and you can't always see what it's doing, especially when you're manoeuvring in a tight situation.'

Process Woman reached for her utility pen and added 'no forward steering positon' to our list. 'And avoid tight situations,' I noted mentally.

Meanwhile, back on the pontoon our search slowly continued in the sweltering sun, when suddenly we saw a New Zealand flag flying from one of the boats for sale. Not only that but the owners were actually aboard, so we stopped to say 'G'day,' as you do.

Mark and Paula were old hands at this boating lark; for a long time they'd been coming to France each year for a few months' cruising, but now they were selling their ex-hire boat – the *Anna Marie* – to buy something bigger. In fact they'd already bought their new boat; she was moored a few metres along the pontoon, and Mark was busy transferring boxes of stuff from the *Anna Marie* to the new craft.

Paula enthusiastically showed us around the *Anna Marie*. 'We're well-known locally as The Party Boat,' she said, indicating the spacious stern deck. 'Crikey we've had some good fun on here, and you'd be surprised how many you can get on board!' Her enthusiasm was infectious, but there was a potential issue.

'We've already had an offer on her,' she told us. She and Mark were asking €49,000, and she said that a Frenchman had recently made an offer of €47,000. 'But who knows?' she laughed, waving her arms dismissively. 'This is France… anything could happen!'

It dawned on us that we knew nothing about the boat-buying process in France, so we asked her about how it worked and how long the offer had to run before it became unconditional. She threw back her curly blonde head and laughed some more. 'Who knows? This is France!' she said again. 'It could be two weeks, three weeks… anyone's guess.'

Which didn't help. She said we were welcome to top the offer. We said we'd think about it, and thanked her for showing us over the boat.

As Liz and I walked back down the pontoon, deciding that we'd seen enough for the day, we reviewed the *Anna Marie*.

'Very clean and tidy,' I said.

'Good space,' Liz remarked. 'And two cabins.'

'But made of GRP. Still, I like the stern deck area, opening off the salon (we'd already learned that on a boat you didn't call the main room a 'lounge'…) which would be great for entertaining. But what was all that about the offer, and how long it takes to settle? I mean, have they accepted it or what? Are we actually allowed to gazump?'

Liz didn't have an answer, and I was just bewildered, so we headed back to our accommodation somewhat confused about things. Oh, and when I say 'accommodation,' I mean of course a boat.

CHAPTER THREE

For the three days we'd set aside to find our perfect floating home, Liz and I obviously had to stay somewhere local, and what better place – given the circumstances – than on a boat.

Jubilant, however, was a lot more than that. In fact, she was a luxurious floating bed and breakfast hotel, conveniently moored a short walk from the marina where we were focusing our search.

Built originally for the sand and gravel trade in Belgium in 1937, *Jubilant* showed little evidence of her former occupation, other than her overall shape and size, which suggested a robust utilitarian history. She was just over 38 metres long by five metres wide, and in her younger days would have had either multiple holds or just one large hold between the wheelhouse at the stern and the bow. Tarpaulins or sliding steel covers would have protected her cargo.

Today, under the ownership and management of hosts Steve and Helen, there was still a wheelhouse, but the rest of *Jubilant* had been beautifully converted into luxurious accommodation, with three double cabins with *en suite* bathrooms, and a large (46 square metres!) red-carpeted salon with plush furniture and a huge dining table. There was air-conditioning and central heating. The boat could accommodate a maximum of six guests, who also had access to a lovely teak deck up top, with tables and steamer chairs, and a large umbrella to provide welcome shade.

We knew two of the guests currently on board, as it was they who'd recommended *Jubilant* as a great place to stay. I'd known Keith and Hilary for over thirty years, having met them in New Zealand where they'd ended up after driving their Land Rover half way round the world from England. (This was deliberate by the way, not the result of a roadworks diversion off the M25.)

They'd subsequently returned to England to live, and for over twenty years Keith had operated a narrowboat hire company based in Stourport, Worcestershire, where the River Severn, the River Stour, and the Staffordshire and Worcestershire Canal all meet.

It's a pleasant part of England, and Keith's boatyard was a busy place, with his hire boats always either in preparation for a voyage or being serviced following a hire, or of course nowhere in sight since they were out cruising the canals.

As a result, there wasn't much he didn't know about boats, and having him on tap in Saint-Jean-de-Losne was, for us, a major bonus. With all his hire boats now sold and the business closed, Keith had focused his attention on just one vessel that he'd built specifically for he and Hilary to use to explore the French waterways. And yes, we can partly blame them for our decision to do the same; their blogs from France as they cruised the canals and explored charming little villages had whetted our appetites over the previous year or so.

Their boat, a Dutch barge called *Picton* (so-named because it's the small town in New Zealand's South Island where they lived in the mid-70s) was presently in the Saint-Jean-de-Losne dry dock so that Keith could recoat the hull with antifouling paint. Meanwhile he and Hilary, like us, were staying on board *Jubilant*, looked after with enthusiasm and panache by Steve and Helen.

After a shower to wash away the sweat of the day's boat-hunting, Liz and I joined our friends on deck where we shared a bottle (or was it two?) of French bubbly in the balmy early evening. We told them all about the various boats we'd seen, and how confusing it was all getting.

Keith wasn't sure about the purchase process in France either, or whether we were legally allowed to gazump the offer on the *Anna Marie*. His experience was based solely on buying and selling boats in England, which is also where he'd fitted-out *Picton* before sailing her across the English Channel. But he did agree to come and have a look at some of the ones we'd shortlisted, and give us the benefit of his experience.

Liz and I reviewed our criteria list, and wondered whether we were being too strict on ourselves. Was there something we should compromise on, something that would better enable us to find what we were looking for?

The answer was yes, but we just weren't sure what it was. We were fairly definite about some things – we still wanted to find something with character, in good condition, and ready to go. But we were uncertain now whether our resolve to buy something only made of wood was too restrictive. The *Anna Marie* was ticking quite a few boxes, but she was made of GRP. Those who own steel or wooden boats disparagingly call such craft 'plastic boats,' and we wanted to have some street cred within the boating community, not be lumped in with hire boaters. Call us snobbish, but…

And then there were some other practical considerations. Keith recommended buying something with a single engine and propeller rather than twin engines. 'With the canals being shallower at the edges it's better to have one prop in the middle than one either side,' he advised. That seemed sensible, and it helped rule out a boat we'd seen online in the south of France that we'd initially been keen on. Anyway, pure logic dictates that one engine is likely to mean only half the problems of two. You didn't need to be Process Woman to work that one out.

(Okay, okay, before you argue; yes we do understand that two engines can also get you out of trouble. Obviously if one breaks down then to have a fully operating second engine would be an advantage. We could debate this forever, but let's not!)

We were definitely resolved to finding something with a length of at least ten metres – preferably a bit more – two separate cabins (with the main cabin having an island bed if possible – one that gave access from either side), good heating, a decent bathroom with shower, WC and hand basin – and if possible two WCs (or 'heads')… and of course room on deck for that all-important lounging and entertaining.

Oh, and the appropriate *tirant d'eau* and *tirant d'air* to allow us to cruise any or all of the French waterways, plus a flybridge or at least on-deck steering position. Things such as a galley and salon we took for granted. Perhaps most importantly, it had to be something we knew we could live comfortably on for at least a year; after all, this was to be our home for a while.

And then we got some bad news from England, yet news that ultimately would help us buy a boat. But first let's take you back to our original Grand Plan.

The plan was that after selling our property near Wellington in New Zealand and paying off our mortgage we'd bank what was left, the fund that would subsidise our next move in life.

We would then find an apartment in one of New Zealand's holiday destinations, put a deposit on it, and promote it as a holiday let. The rental income would take care of the new mortgage, leaving us unencumbered to start The Adventure overseas.

Next – with Liz still to finish her job – I would say goodbye to her and our grown-up kids in Wellington, all of whom were flatting and living lives of their own, and would head off to England and then France to begin the boat-search in earnest. (Remember how I always have to walk into a room ahead of Liz? Same rule applies to countries...)

Liz meanwhile would finish up her work and then follow with daughter Yasmin some weeks later, by which time I'd have a shortlist of possible boats to consider, one of which we would buy. Simple.

We would install Yasmin in her new school – she'd been lobbying to finish her high school education in England so she could go to university there – and then Liz and I would move onto our new boat and sail off into the sunset. Fade up romantic theme music, cue end credits. (Bill Nighy as Mike, Drew Barrymore as Liz.)

Easy-peasy, in principle. But you know what they say about the best-laid plans etc. In fact we never did find a suitable apartment to buy in New Zealand – we simply ran out of time – so Plan B was to buy a modest property in England instead, but this time pay for it in full, tenant it, and watch the rental income roll in subsidising our new boating lifestyle.

Did I mention that thing about best-laid plans? Sigh. The first part of the Grand Plan had gone well; we sold our property without too much difficulty, pocketed the balance, and while Liz and Yasmin stayed in an apartment in Wellington I high-tailed it to England where I put Plan B into action and started looking for a property to buy. I found one, made an offer, which was accepted, and went ahead and organised a survey.

The survey came up trumps, I paid the bill, and instructed the lawyers in my best Jean-Luc Picard voice to 'Make it so.' Then my mate Shaun and I took off on our motorbikes to France for a few days to look at boats, and try out our French in a few bars and cafés. Meanwhile Liz and her daughter were finally making their way to Britain via Hawaii, San Francisco and Washington. It was all coming together.

There was also already a family French connection; Liz's parents lived in France and had been there for over twenty years, having retired to a lovely rural part of the country in the south-east, not far from Grenoble. This was where Liz and Yasmin were initially heading, and it was after Shaun had headed back to England that I met up with Liz at her parents' place.

Which is how she came to be with me looking at boats after I'd ridden back up to Saint-Jean-de-Losne on the motorbike with her on the back. Now you're up to date.

So, back to the bad news. Half way through our research at Saint-Jean-de-Losne we got a phone call from the real estate agent in Merseyside to say that the house we were buying had been withdrawn from sale. Basically, the vendor had changed her mind, which, under English property law she had every right to do.

'That shouldn't be allowed,' I whinged. 'We've paid over £300 for a survey, and she just changes her mind!'

Liz was equally disappointed. 'I know. But that's her prerogative I guess. It's not like New Zealand. We'll just have to move on.'

We certainly weren't going to be moving in.

We reviewed our options, and decided we would have a second go at buying a property in Merseyside, but maybe not outright. Plan B was still alive, but we realised we were going to have to bump up our boat budget if we were to find something that matched our increasingly complicated criteria, especially a boat on which we could simply turn the key, start the engine and cast off.

So next day the search continued.

When I'd been here some weeks earlier with my mate Shaun we'd found a boat for sale called *Reina*. She was a 'Pedro' model, a Dutch-built steel cruiser rather than a traditional barge, but I quite liked the look of her, and the asking price was about right for our budget.

However, the owners, Felix and Penny, had said they'd be leaving Saint-Jean-de-Losne shortly to go cruising up the Saône. This was a good thing, because it told me that *Reina* was in decent working condition, and still being used on a daily basis. She was, presumably, the sort of boat we could be handed the keys to and set off in.

Penny had given me their contact details, so Liz and I phoned and tracked them down to a small town on the Saône called Gray, not far north of where we were. That's one of the lovely aspects of inland boating: you don't travel very far each day, so we knew they were unlikely to be any great distance. We decided to hop on the motorbike and follow them.

The French countryside is a pleasure to ride a bike through – motorised or pedal-powered – so we set our navigation device to avoid major roads and autoroutes. This meant our electronic guide took us down narrow lanes and along twisty roads, some actually going right through farmyards. *('Keep right.' 'Turn around when possible.' 'Wave to the farmer.' 'At the next cow, turn right.')*

We passed fields of *tournesols* – sunflowers – standing to attention with their faces dutifully facing the sun, though within a few weeks as autumn arrived they'd be hanging their heads as though in shame.

We don't know much about French farming, but it's obviously taken very seriously, especially when you consider the investment in agricultural machinery. The roads were busy with tractors, threshers, trailers, and combine harvesters – it was harvest time – and all the machinery looked brand spanking new. Mudguards gleamed, cabin windows shone, and most of the farm vehicles looked like they'd just been driven out of the showroom rather than through fields and farmyards.

Every time we spotted a tractor or harvester coming our way I'd feel Liz's knees clench against me as she gave a squeak and mentally willed us to be thin and streamlined enough to get past without running off the road and ending up in a ditch. At least we were on a bike and not in a car, otherwise there were multiple times where we'd have found ourselves having to reverse to let the farmer pass. (*Wave clenched fist when possible.*)

Actually the French farmers were all very considerate, and we made it to Gray without incident, parked the bike and easily found *Reina* moored in line with a few other boats along the town's *quai*. Felix and Penny welcomed us aboard, and Liz had a look around. Like me she was quite taken with the boat; it was a good size, had two cabins, a nice salon and reasonable galley area, and we could visualise ourselves and our friends sitting on deck in the sunshine. She looked to be in quite good condition too (the boat, not Liz. Although…).

But. There's always a But, and in this case it was the shower. There wasn't one.

'So how do you wash?' Liz asked. Penny gave a dismissive toss of her head and said, 'Oh we just swim in the river!'

Hmmm. Okay. That didn't wash with us, as we wanted to live aboard for a full year, and neither of us relished the idea of swimming in a river in mid-winter. Or for that matter in any of the canals at any time of the year. Liz said to me later, 'Sod that! The only water I get into is a fully-heated spa pool or a bath; there's no way you're going to get me in a river, even in summer!')

However, there was always the option of installing a shower in the existing bathroom area, but would that be possible in the short time we had before we headed off on our adventure?

We shelved that problem and concentrated on the next aspect of *Reina*: a river trial. Felix offered to take us for a short jaunt up the Saône. He started the engine, Penny cast off the ropes, and *Reina* moved out and into the gentle current. Felix turned the wheel to port, increased the throttle, and with a satisfying growl *Reina* picked up speed and headed upriver, like a horse that's just been given the heels and knows it's okay to gallop.

The town of Gray and its moored boats slid past, and very soon we were on our own, mid-stream, with green trees on either bank, a pleasant breeze blowing, and from the bows the lovely sound of water breaking as the boat ploughed ahead.

At last we were on a boat on a river in France! Admittedly it was someone else's, but it was actually moving and not just tied up at a mooring. It felt alive, and I was beginning to think that maybe we could quickly get a shower installed after all, or even rig up a solar version, with one of those black bladders that absorb the sun's warmth and heat the water.

Felix let me take the wheel and encouraged me to do a 360-degree turn mid-stream, which I did. He showed me how to throttle up and down, and how to put the engine into reverse, warning me to always pause after engaging neutral and before moving the throttle back into reverse. 'Otherwise it can make a big clunk... not good!'

We cruised along, chatting about boating and the *Reina* in particular, then turned the boat around and headed back to Gray. As we approached the *quai* once more we suddenly heard a shout; it sounded like someone was yelling '*Liz!*' And it was. Turning to the source of the yell we discovered a man waving furiously from one of the moored boats. Liz said, 'Oh my God, it's Wynn!'

Small world that it is, here we were having come about 18,000 kilometres from New Zealand, only to bump into one of Liz's former work colleagues. Wynn and his wife Anne are part-owners of a boat called *Waiheke*, and every year they come to France for a couple of months to cruise the canals. And here they were in Gray!

Felix kindly brought *Reina* alongside *Waiheke* so we could say hello, and I was pleased to see how manoeuvrable the boat seemed. We told Wynn we'd come back and see him shortly.

After tying up the *Reina* we thanked Penny and Felix for taking us for the introductory cruise and told them we would do some serious thinking. They seemed very relaxed about selling the boat and we didn't feel under any pressure, which was nice.

And then we were climbing onto *Waiheke* with lots of hugs and handshakes as Wynn welcomed us aboard and explained that his wife Anne was at the *supermarché*, and would be back shortly. Wine was poured, and we toasted the surprise encounter.

'You know, it's funny,' said Wynn as we sat in the salon. 'I saw the *Reina* go by and I thought, "That's the sort of boat that Liz and Mike would probably like," and then next thing there you are already on it! Amazing!'

Amazing indeed. And although Wynn – and Anne when she arrived – had welcomed us on board *Waiheke* as friends, it was also nice to be able to pick their brains as mariners, about boats and boating, especially since *Waiheke* was an ex-hire boat, a 'plastic' boat.

What we learned, or rather had reinforced for us, was that she was well-laid out, bright and airy. Wynn and Anne had enjoyed many a summer cruise on her, and were co-owners with another Kiwi couple, a type of partnership we were to discover is quite a common feature of boat ownership in France. It's a good concept, and spreads the costs of maintenance and winter mooring, while still enabling two or three months' cruising every year per couple (well, depending on how many investment partners there are).

We brought Wynn and Anne up to date with our research and told them of our plans to head south down the Saône and Rhône once we'd found a suitable boat.

'That's out of our league,' Wynn said, chuckling. 'I'm not

sure we'd have the power to cope with the Rhône. We tend to stick to the canals!'

In fact, most hire boat companies restrict use of their boats to the canals for that very reason, with the main rivers usually off-limits. So this highlighted for us that we would need a boat with enough engine power to cope, and that maybe some of the ex-hires we'd seen at Saint-Jean-de-Losne could now be ruled out.

We climbed back on the motorbike, waved farewell to the crew of *Waiheke*, hoping to be able to return the on-board hospitality at some stage, and rode back to base to make a decision. Tomorrow was to be our last day in Saint-Jean-de-Losne; we had a shortlist of boats, so now it was time to see if any of them would actually be The One.

CHAPTER FOUR

With Keith in tow we returned to the broker's main sales pontoon, and with multiple sets of keys in hand, set about showing him those boats we'd been considering.

We sat in the salon of a Dutch barge called *Dorothée*, which had a classic shape and a heritage feel, yet was actually no more than about 12 years old. Inside however she looked much older, and the chipped and tatty yellow-painted interior had the feel of faded parchment in need of careful restoration.

Keith flipped through the boat's records which had conveniently been left aboard. 'Ahh, that explains it,' he said. 'This has been a multiple-owner boat – bit like a timeshare really – and the problem with these is that very often there's nobody actually in charge; no single owner to look after it, which means sometimes the maintenance can slip.'

The asking price was high, and we could also see we'd be spending quite a bit of money to get the boat looking how we wanted it. We struck a line through *Dorothée* and moved on.

In the next boat Keith lifted the floor. The engine looked a bit grimy, and there wasn't much space around it – if we ever needed to work on the motor we'd first need to find a nearby circus and engage their contortionist. The bilge looked dry enough, but Keith got on his hands and knees and reached in under a panel and brought out a handful of flaking rust. 'Always worth checking the bits you can't see,' he remarked. We nodded sagely, relieved to have him with us.

Mark and Paula were still aboard the *Anna Marie*, so since we had Keith with us we asked if we could all come aboard for one more look so that our learned friend could give us the benefit of his wisdom. Once again we were welcomed with enthusiasm.

Had there been any progress with the Frenchman's offer, we enquired? 'No,' laughed Paula, and then added (yet again) 'But this is France!'

Liz and Keith flipped through the vessel's log book and papers while I walked the length of the boat to the bows and back. At one point I paused where I thought the deck felt a bit strange underfoot, a bit spongy, and I saw Paula watching me.

Walking back along the pontoon, and past the only other ex-hire boat we'd considered, I mentioned the spongy deck. Liz clicked her fingers. 'Ah, yes! In the receipts there was one showing they'd paid €6,000 for osmosis treatment!'

'That doesn't sound too good,' said Keith. 'But it's not uncommon with GRP boats, they can absorb water, and it can be expensive to fix.'

I think it was at that point that Liz and I started to rule out buying a plastic boat, even though Wynn and Anne and their partners didn't seemed to have had any issues with osmosis on *Waiheke*. It was the last time we were to be on board the *Anna Marie*.

After learning that our house purchase in Merseyside had fallen through, Liz and I had decided to increase our boat-buying budget, but we were disappointed to find that this didn't result in a big increase in potential boats. It seemed that even upping our limit by a further €20,000 wasn't going to do the job. We would have to further review our criteria and see what else we might be able to compromise on.

Which is how we came to be on board a boat called *Liberty*. An 11.4-metre Dutch-built steel cruiser, she was everything we thought our boat wouldn't be like. She was a gin palace, a sleek white motor-cruiser, with a get-up-and-go attitude about her. No rustic wheelhouse, no tiller, no carved prow, and no colourful history (as far as we knew). She wasn't the sort of vessel that had ever been pulled along the canals by horses, or had carried grain or coal in those sepia days of old.

She also had only one cabin, and was for sale at more than double our original budget. But, as it turned out, she was the boat for us.

'This is nice!' remarked Keith as soon as he stood in the middle of the salon and looked around. It was the first hint of enthusiasm we'd heard from him, and we felt encouraged.

We'd probably walked past *Liberty* six times or so during our boat search – she just wasn't the sort of thing we'd been considering, especially with having just a single cabin, and being out of our price range. But after we increased our budget we also looked at what else we might be able to compromise on, and decided it would be… Can we have The Envelope please? It's… (Fanfare): The Second Cabin! (Audience goes wild. Friends go, 'Boo!').

Call us mean-spirited, but we reached the conclusion that for more than ninety percent of the time it would be just the two of us on board. If we did have visitors to stay they would likely be very occasional and for short stays, so why were we bending over backwards to find a boat with two cabins? Many vessels had perfectly acceptable alternative sleeping arrangements, including *Liberty*. In fact she was advertised as being able to accommodate six people.

'Six?' Liz asked, looking around. 'Seriously?' Well, maybe. If there's one thing we'd learned about boat design it was that boats have an amazing ability to accommodate things: equipment, spares, food – and people. Every bit of available space is accessible or convertible, and in *Liberty*'s case the

U-shaped banquette in the salon could convert into a bed large enough to easily sleep two adults.

As well, down in the bows for'ard of the galley – where in many other boats there would be two single bunks angled together towards the sharp end – there was a quirky round table cocooned in an equally circular banquette. We discovered that the table could be lowered, and that shaped cushions, like segments from a nicely-sliced round of *Brie*, could be placed on top to create another sleeping area, in this case a round bed large enough for two grown-ups to sleep together like two croissants in a basket (cosy!), and definitely roomy enough for a couple of kids to stretch out in. We wondered (briefly) where we might buy round sheets.

So quirky was this accommodation/dining area that we instantly nicknamed it The Bond Lounge, because it looked like something a secret agent hero might enjoy.

Keith meanwhile had lifted the carpet and the flooring to expose the 110-horsepower diesel engine below. It looked clean and new, with no signs of oil or grime. It was surrounded by acoustic baffling which could be slid out to open up the entire area, which included the fuel and water tanks, multiple batteries, various pumps, the heating system, and the bilge.

Everything looked clean and dry, and Keith made more positive cooing noises. There were no handfuls of rust to be had here. We replaced the floor panels and carpet and poked around *Liberty*'s cupboards and other storage areas. In the wood-lined cabin was an island bed – a double – which was hinged and could be lifted up to expose further storage beneath. There were also two wardrobes.

The bathroom included a WC, hand basin and proper shower area – not just a 'wet-room' like some of the boats we'd seen.

In the salon the banquette was large enough to seat six around a central coffee table, and there was an interior helm as well as the one up on the flybridge, which meant we would be able to steer the boat from inside on days when the weather precluded being up top.

'It feels homely,' said Liz, echoing my thoughts exactly. 'Good condition,' murmured Keith. Back out on deck we could easily picture ourselves enjoying lunches and dinners, and although the aft deck wasn't a huge space, the lockers with squabs on them plus other deck chairs meant we would be able to sit four in relative comfort, and maybe even six if needed. There was even space for a table.

And, it looked like *Liberty* came fully-equipped with everything we'd need to just start the engine and head south. On the bows covered in a tarpaulin were two bicycles. In the lockers there were power leads, hoses, buckets and all sorts of tins and canisters of boat cleaning stuff. Down in the galley there was a full set of crockery, cutlery, mugs, glassware and cooking implements. There was a fridge, a gas hob and a microwave.

And, in the salon there was one particular object that seemed to say, 'Pick Me! Buy Me! Sail Me Away!' It was a table lamp, on the shade of which was a representation of an antique map of New Zealand as drawn by Captain Cook. Add to that a Welsh flag fluttering in the breeze (remembering that Liz is Welsh by birth) we needed no more persuasion. The boat seemed to want us, and we wanted *Liberty*.

Back at the brokers we asked about the possibility of getting her out onto the Saône for a trial run and Nicholas our sales person willingly allocated Max, one of their staff, who we arranged to meet a couple of hours later at the boat. In the meantime Liz, Keith and I looked into the pros and cons of buying a vessel like *Liberty*.

Unlike Process Woman, who legend has it was once bitten by a Logic Spider and has since been possessed of superhuman reasoning powers, I am Heart Man. Having avoided all clear logical thought my entire life, and having been born an emotionally-driven Gemini, I am the sort of person who makes their mind up based entirely on the question, 'Does this *feel* right?'

Liberty certainly felt right to me, especially after I accepted our reconfigured criteria. Admittedly she was nothing like the boat we'd imagined buying; instead she was a canal-, river- and even sea-worthy cruiser, but even at almost twenty years-old she looked to be in really good condition, had most of the attributes we wanted, and most importantly she satisfied Process Woman's spreadsheet mind.

The fact that Keith, with all his years of boating experience, was visibly enthusiastic was, for us, another major tick of the boxes.

And so, a short while later we were on the flybridge with Max, whose English was excellent. He explained the starting procedure, and we were pleased to hear the engine roar into life at the turn of the key.

Keith immediately went and peered over the stern and said, 'Good; there's water coming out.' I asked what he was talking about and he pointed to the exhaust pipe hole just above the waterline. 'The exhaust is water-cooled, so you want to see water coming out of it. If there isn't any it will overheat. But that looks fine.' I shook my head; we had such a lot to learn.

Max put the boat into gear, eased us away from the pontoon, and guided *Liberty* out through the busy marina and out onto the Saône. He turned left, and we burbled past Saint-Jean-de-Losne's quayside to head north, in a repeat performance of *Reina*'s cruise earlier at Gray. Once clear of the local moored boats our temporary skipper pushed the throttle forwards.

Liberty responded well and surged ahead nicely, with no increase in vibration or any excessive smoke from the exhaust. Max talked us through the various gauges, told us the same thing as Felix about always pausing between forward and reverse, and then he offered the helm to us. Liz wasn't keen to take it, but me? Try and stop me!

So there we were, on a nice sunny day standing on a flybridge in control of a cruiser that broke all the rules of our proposed purchase, but at that point we didn't care. I think even Process Woman had thrown logic overboard and was running on adrenalin. She was certainly smiling.

Keith continued to give off positive vibes as the short shakedown cruise continued, and then, all too soon, it was over and we were nosing back under the bridge and into the marina again. I gave Max the helm, not being keen to accidentally ram any of the boats, or damage *Liberty*, or – especially – make a complete ass of myself in full view of the marina's more experienced boat owners.

Max made manoeuvring the boat seem easy, and the tight squeeze returning her to the mooring was no problem for him. I was envious, realising that when you watch someone who knows what they're doing it always looks easy, but in reality it rarely is. We helped tie up (not actually knowing how to do that properly either!), the engine was switched off, and the exhaust burble died away, but our minds were still buzzing. The short jaunt on *Liberty* had been flawless, she was fully-equipped – even to having spare fan belts, fuses and oil filters – she was in good condition and required no obvious work from us, she was comfortable, well laid-out and homely. But the asking price was more than double our original budget.

We thanked Max, and he locked *Liberty* up and headed back to the office. Liz and I posed for photographs beside the boat, and then talked through everything with Keith, who after the cruise remained buoyant.

It was our last day in Saint-Jean-de-Losne; the next day we were to head off on the motorbike back to Liz's parents, and our boat searching opportunity would be over. Either we bought now, or postponed the whole adventure.

We decided to make an offer.

We watched Nicholas as he spoke on the phone in perfect English to *Liberty*'s owners in Wales. They had answered the call almost immediately, and we were thankful that there was only a one-hour time difference between France and the UK.

Nicholas told them he had 'interested buyers' and gave the man in Wales our offer, considerably less than the asking price. Nicholas covered the mouthpiece and said to us, 'He is asking his wife,' and smiled.

Then we were hearing Nicholas saying, 'OK, I will be in touch again soon, Goodbye.' He turned to us and said, 'So, you have a boat!'

We sagged in our seats with relief. In a matter of minutes we had signed the contract, paid a deposit, and nominated a pick-up day – Friday 13 September. Not the best of days if you're superstitious, but what could possibly go wrong between now and then?

For the people in the brokerage it was just another day at the office; if they were ebullient about having just made a sale (and a hefty commission from the vendors) they didn't show it. Nicholas processed the paperwork, informing us that he would also need to get the contract signed by the Welsh owners, 'But that should be no problem.' We shook hands and headed from the cool air-conditioned comfort of the office into the blasting heat of the day.

We hugged and laughed, and said, 'We own a boat!'

We met up once again with Keith and Hilary to tell them the news. Their own boat, *Picton*, had finally been released from the dry-dock and they'd moored a little way along the Canal du Bourgogne. We'd originally intended to head back to Liz's parents' house this day but Keith and Hilary kindly invited us to stay an extra night on board with them, for which we were very grateful.

So, over a celebratory drink or two (or possibly more...) we talked of our intentions once we returned to take over *Liberty*, and they told us their plans now that the antifouling was all done on their boat. They would be heading south also but would have a head start on us. They'd be going exactly the same route though (the mighty Rhône being the main north-south waterway in France) so we hoped to catch them up at some stage. In the meantime we all promised to keep in touch, and we thanked Keith yet again for his welcome input. We'd learned a lot about boats and boat-buying in a very short time; the next stage would be an even steeper learning curve – coming to terms with being actual sailors, and owning and living on our own boat.

Frustratingly, that would have to wait for about a month because we now had all sorts of other things to take care of.

CHAPTER FIVE

The next day and the days following were a whirlwind of activity. Liz and I loaded up the bike and bidding farewell to our hosts, as well as to Steve and Helen on *Jubilant*, we set off south, and a smooth ride on the autoroutes to the small village of Chatte where Reg and Kate – Liz's parents – lived nearby.

They'd been there for over twenty years, and their converted farmhouse looked out over a pleasant valley of trees, with a view to the west over rural fields and forests. It's a peaceful spot, and always a nice one to arrive at after a long hot day's drive, or in this case ride.

Yasmin seemed non-plussed when we told her we'd finally bought a boat, but when you're 16 and not remotely interested in boating I guess we shouldn't have expected anything else. She'd already informed us that she had absolutely no intention of ever staying on it anyway, and without a proper second cabin she was likely to stick to her resolve.

Kate and Reg were more interested to hear about *Liberty*, but were also curious as to what we were going to do, how we were going to survive, what plans we had for future income and work, and was it really wise to have sold up in New Zealand, 'abandoned' the other kids, and left secure paying jobs to go and buy a *boat*?

They were valid questions, although not all easy to answer, and certainly not to their satisfaction. 'Well, it's all part of the adventure,' we said, hoping we sounded convincing. 'We're not planning on living on the boat for ever, and we do intend to buy a property in England so that we still own some bricks and mortar. And we'll be a lot closer to you than we were in New Zealand.'

Our defence seemed compelling and Liz and I were quite relaxed about everything, but we were to discover that this wasn't the last time the wisdom of our decisions would come under scrutiny.

'And what about Yasmin in boarding school?' The interrogation spotlight was unwavering. 'She'll be OK,' we asserted (hoping this was correct). 'It's where she wants to be so she can springboard on to a UK university. It's all part of her plan too.'

Back in New Zealand we were fairly certain there were a few people we knew who shared similar misgivings about the whole adventure, especially those who have what you might call 'Rainy Day Syndrome,' which is basically the principle that you don't frivolously waste money – you invest it, save it, secure it in some way so that when you retire in your sixties you will have a 'nest egg.' *Then*, when it's safe, you can go adventuring and take risks, but only then. Until that time you stick to your annual holidays and long weekend mini-breaks. And save, save, save.

Boring. Sorry, but we know of people who took that approach, and who, in their sixties were comfortably off and ready to finally take the plunge, only to see one of them die before they could do it. Conversely we also know of people who have thrown caution to the wind and left New Zealand to spend an extended period living the high life in Europe or the United States. In both cases the people concerned took their young children. And they were very glad they did, because within a few months of returning from their 'frivolous' adventures, the women of both couples learned they had cancer. A few months after that they had passed away.

But what a legacy of great memories those silly reckless trips bequeathed, and what relief for the husbands and children left behind, who had such wonderful holidays to remember, rather than forever regretting they never did it.

We had therefore also decided to be reckless and silly before it was too late, and in fact we didn't think we *were* being that frivolous; we had a reasonable financial safety net, and would be keeping close tabs on Yasmin. The older kids back in New Zealand – Catherine, James and Karis – were all flatting and either in tertiary education or work, so had already flown the nest. That's not to say we didn't miss them or care about them, of course we did. We'd talked through our plans with them before leaving and we had their support and endorsement, maybe even their admiration (not sure on that one!).

So we patiently explained to Reg and Kate how we would manage and what our plans were, though it didn't seem to convince them.

And then of course there were the terrorists.

It turned out that moving from our base country – even back to the UK where we were both born – was also not without its trials and interrogations (as I had already discovered, having arrived early), something Liz and I were to experience repeatedly in the coming weeks and months. And it's all because of Osama Bin Laden.

The thing is, post-9-11, the terrorists won. They have cost countries all around the globe billions in increased security at airports, rail stations, shopping malls and in city centres. They have increased paranoia levels to record highs. Where they have struck successfully they have also cost lives and heartache. We all suffer from terrorism to some degree.

Take money laundering for example. Because terrorists and other criminals need to move large amounts of money secretly, it means we're all now guilty until proved innocent. Banks and other institutions today want absolute proof that you are who you say you are, you live where you say you live and that your money is legally yours and not someone else's.

That you do actually *live* somewhere is perhaps the most vital requirement. This, we discovered, has become a major point in establishing your credibility in the UK, and, from what we hear, now in New Zealand also. Possibly it's been standard practice in other parts of the world for years, but it was certainly new to us when we arrived 'home' to England.

Essentially, the currency of credibility is now a gas bill. Or an electricity bill. Or rates demand. Any utility bill or bank statement will do as long as it's got your name and address on it, as it 'proves' you live at that address.

But we had a problem; we didn't really live anywhere. We had sold our property in New Zealand, left the country, and having arrived in England we were 'of no fixed abode.' Our friend Shaun had kindly put me up from the day I arrived, and had allowed me to use his house as my 'home address' for the purposes of establishing myself. This was very generous of him, and I feel he deserves a mention in dispatches, if not a medal. Especially when the debt-collecting heavies eventually arrive on his doorstep looking for me.

Anyway the point is that UK society, and bureaucracy in particular, was suspicious of us because of our circumstances, and we frequently found ourselves sweating under interrogation, with the onus being on us to prove we were who we said we were. There was even one occasion when I'd booked and paid for a rental car online, and went to pick it up with my passport and new UK driver's licence in hand.

The snotty youth behind the counter went through confirming the reservation with me and then, just before handing me the keys, asked me for a utility bill or bank statement.

'Why?' I asked.

'Our policy is that we have to have proof of your address,' he replied.

'It's on my driver's licence,' I pointed out. (It was too, though it was Shaun's address)

'But our policy is that we need to see either a utility bill or bank statement with your name and the address on it.'

'But what if I'm just a tourist, here for three weeks?' I asked, smugly thinking *Gotcha!* But no.

'Then we'd need to see your return ticket.'

I went into meltdown, something I do rather well, and said his job was on the line and that he was refusing to honour a contract I had with his company. They had, after all, already taken my money online. He continued to trot out the 'It's our policy...' line, without apology. I was furious.

To cut a long story short I phoned another rental company, asked if they'd accept my licence and passport as ID, whether they needed anything else (they didn't) and within twenty minutes was sitting in a nice shiny rental car. Weeks later I received an apology and a refund from the first company who said the guy behind the counter had been out of order. I hoped he was out of a job.

I was very thankful that I still had an English bank account dating back to the mid-80s, as it meant we didn't have to try and open one – a very difficult process when you don't live anywhere and have no regular income. So for the purposes of establishing ourselves as credible human beings with genuine identities I arranged to have paper bank statements sent to us at Shaun's address near Liverpool, not because we like wasting trees, but because we wanted to be accepted as genuine members of English society. Which, dammit, we were!

Anyway, enough of that sort of rant for the moment. The point is we were getting a bit tired of having to justify ourselves.

So let's get back to France, where it was time to leave Reg and Kate's. Liz was taking Yasmin via Paris to the UK, and I was to ride the motorbike back, there being no room for three of us on the machine.

I strapped on my leather pants, boots, motorbike jacket and helmet, and started sweating immediately. The weather was still fine and hot, and while I much prefer riding in good weather, this was really too hot, with little prospect of cooling down while on the move since the bike was fitted with a full fairing to protect me from the weather. Which is great in the cold and rain.

But with the weather so nice I could hardly complain, so I set off and was soon hurtling along the French autoroutes at a decent speed. The limit is generally 130 kilometres per hour – reduced to 110 in wet weather – so the countryside raced by. Autoroute is just the French name for motorway, but in France they are so much better than the English motorways, with very few road works, less traffic, and much better road surfaces. They are, however, expensive, and to avoid tolls you have to take the slower 'N' or 'D' roads.

It's swings and roundabouts really; the French motorways take you quickly past, or even right over, quaint towns and villages, while the less major roads often go straight through them, so if you want to experience the lovely French countryside then minor roads are the way to go. But you need to have plenty of time up your sleeve. For me, in this particular case, I just needed to get back to the UK as quickly as possible, though it pained me to have so much beauty pass by in a blur.

Spookily though, there was one particular stretch of autoroute where I had a weird feeling that I'd somehow ridden through an invisible barrier and into another dimension. All of a sudden I noticed I was the only vehicle on the road; the countryside either side was devoid of human life – no tractors, harvesters or Gauloises-smoking farmers – and the road ahead and behind was eerily deserted. I swooshed into a long curving tunnel, the guide-lights of which added a futuristic '*Tron*' feel to it, and opened the throttle in the sheer exhilaration of having the place – maybe the whole of France – to myself.

I shot out of the tunnel and back into bright sunshine, with still no one in sight. It got to the point where I was seriously beginning to wonder whether I had in fact crashed and died some distance back, and that this spooky empty road was The Other Side, and was actually a gentle introduction to the fact that I was dead. Soon I would see a *péage* in the distance, with multiple lanes and toll booths, and above each an illuminated sign. One would be an LED symbol of the Pearly Gates, and another a bright red triple-pronged devil's trident.

The nightmare would begin when the Pearly Gates machine would keep rejecting my credit card, and I'd be forced instead to go to the trident one, where I would be granted immediate and free access. It would be all downhill from there.

I was jolted out of my fantasy when, finally, a little Citroën appeared on the opposite side of the road, driven not by a man with pointy red horns but a very ordinary Frenchman, smoking. After him came more vehicles, and soon I found myself being overtaken on my side of the road too. The illusion was over; I was alive, and the world had returned to normal, but I decided the toll was worth it for the entertainment value of having had an empty road to myself.

I stopped at Bourges for the night, continuing on to coastal Caen the next day, and finally found myself on the cross-Channel ferry to Portsmouth, where I stood on deck and looked for boats and ships on *La Manche*. I had read of people who had taken some very small boats across the Channel – including canal narrowboats, which are absolutely not designed to go to sea – and was keen to see if I could spot any adventurous souls doing likewise. Instead all I saw were some large cargo ships in the distance, and a few trawlers nearer, but nothing unusual.

Keith had sailed *Picton* across a couple of years previously, having engaged the services of a professional skipper. Much of the crossing had been in the dark, and the skipper had – at the start of the voyage – stood with Keith in the wheelhouse and said, 'See that light over there? Keep heading for that. I'm going below for a kip.'

And so Keith was left in sole charge, heading unwaveringly for the distant light that was Calais. The contract captain rejoined him in time to pilot the boat into the harbour, and once he was satisfied that Keith was okay, disappeared with a cheery wave and went back to England. Keith's wife Hilary meanwhile had taken the train. 'No, there's no way you'd have got me on the boat going across the Channel!' she told us in her lovely lilting Welsh accent.

But the point is that if you pick the weather carefully, are well-equipped, and – preferably – have a fully-qualified skipper aboard, then you can cross the English Channel in a small boat, even one not designed to go to sea. Oh, and you do have to let your insurance company know what you're doing too, just in case.

Liberty was, apparently, suitable for the sea, but Liz and I had no plans to do anything ocean-going, except – just maybe – taking her out for twenty minutes into the Mediterranean when we got that far south, but only if the weather and conditions were suitable. It would be a shame not to.

But that little dream was still some weeks or months in the future; for now it was back to the reality of jockeying for position on the English motorways as I headed north in the rain, squeezed between lorries and goods vans cascading curtains of spray over me. I was once again sweating in my motorbike jacket, but this time it was nothing to do with the sunshine.

And so we came to something of a hiatus in our plans; keen as we were to set sail and begin our new life afloat, we still had to take care of a multitude of details in the UK, not least of which was finding another property to replace the one we'd recently lost.

CHAPTER SIX

B ack at Shaun's, and while Liz and Yasmin were still on their way, I set about looking for a replacement property in the local area. There was no shortage and it seemed to be a buyer's market, but rather like the boat, what we wanted was something that didn't need a lot of work doing to it (or in fact any), so that we could quickly rent it out.

So, while Liz and Yasmin made their way via Paris and the Eurostar to London, I spent a lot of time on the Internet and on the phone to real estate agents, arranging viewing appointments. It wasn't nearly as much fun as looking at boats.

I picked up 'the girls' from London (in the rental car that I managed to hire without a gas bill!) and finally, two months after I'd left New Zealand, we were all together in England. The following days became a blur as I showed Liz some of the properties I'd shortlisted and she showed a distinct lack of enthusiasm for most of them.

'You seem to forget,' she said patiently, 'that one day we might actually have to live in whatever house we buy, and none of the ones I've seen particularly appeal to me as a home.' She was once again in logic mode, which I was thankful for, I guess. No, really, I was. I think.

We did find one that seemed like a good deal and a reasonable fit, perfectly placed for local transport, shops, schools – and pubs, though that was just a bonus. We made an offer which was accepted by the vendor, and then guess what? The very next day she changed her mind and withdrew it from the market. We were reminded of Paula on board the *Anna Marie* when she was telling us about the boat-buying process: 'Who knows? This is France!' – only now it was us thinking, 'Who knows about buying a property here? This is England!'

We were grumpy; this business of being allowed to change your mind at the drop of a hat was making us very uneasy. In New Zealand, if you have an offer accepted on a property, you sign and it is basically binding to both parties; the vendor cannot easily back out from the deal, and neither can the buyer. A deposit is paid and accepted, and a few weeks later the balance is paid and the deal is done. Here in England we were quickly learning that the process was a lot more, well, 'fluid' seems to be the word, which made the whole thing unsatisfactory. Even the real estate agents agreed it needed reviewing.

We were disillusioned, but had to push on with other arrangements. We took Yasmin over to Yorkshire and introduced her to her new school, Liz's alma mater. Yorkshire is famous for all sorts of things; Yorkshire pudding, for example, the Brontë Sisters, the Yorkshire Dales and Moors, and of course the legendary gruff nature of Yorkshiremen in particular. (There's a saying: you can always tell a Yorkshireman – but you can't tell him much!)

But the other thing that's as local, resilient and as tough as a Yorkshireman's attitude is the ubiquitous dry stone wall. For over 5000 years people in this part of the world have been building walls out of hand-shaped stones, using only gravity and what's called 'an educated eye' to construct them.

Traditionally, mortar or cement are not used; the stones are merely stacked according to their size, shape and weight, topped off usually with a row of upright narrower stones. (To say 'merely' is not doing the process justice though; there's a lot more to the skill than just stacking.)

Luckily, earthquakes are relatively unknown here, so freestanding walls don't need to survive that sort of shaking, though they do need to be strong enough to resist the butting and shoving of sheep and other beasts, the often-strong winds, and temperature extremes from the depths of bitterly cold winters to the occasional scorching hot summer.

The fact that many of the walls in Yorkshire today have been around for hundreds of years prove they can do that, and it was pleasing to see so many of them still in use as boundaries, despite a modern trend to larger acreages.

Anyway, we left (not abandoned) Yasmin at her new school, warning her that her Kiwi accent would be something of a novelty and that she might want to consider adopting a more local dialect, but she resisted the suggestion vehemently.

'No! I'm not going to speak any differently to how I do now,' she responded. 'I'm proud to be from New Zealand!'

We believe that's called stone-walling.

Back in Merseyside we had another issue: our personal effects from New Zealand were due to arrive any day and we needed to think about how and where we were going to store them. There wasn't much – about three square metres of cardboard boxes and trunks – but there certainly wasn't going to be any room on board *Liberty*.

Instead we'd thought that if we bought a property with a nice dry loft, or a spare room, or even a garage, we could lock all our stuff away in there until we needed it later. But, as you know, we weren't having much luck buying anything. And then we came up with a bright idea, in fact what turned out to be a bright *red* idea: a van.

In a relatively short time we found a not-too-old Ford Transit. Since it was a vivid red and we were going to be living in France for the foreseeable future, we nicknamed it 'Van Rouge.'

Lucky we bought it when we did because just a few days later we got the call to say our stuff had indeed arrived at the shipper's depot in Wembley, so Liz and I headed south in Van Rouge to collect it, hoping that in fact the vehicle would be big enough to accommodate it all. We had watched our possessions being packed up some months earlier in Wellington, and had a vague idea how much space they took up, but now, heading down the M1 we were a bit nervous. What if it didn't all fit in? Would we have to buy a roof rack and a tarpaulin, and tie-downs? How could we secure stuff on the roof from thieves and vagabonds?

But thankfully we had the help of Krzysztof. This friendly giant Polish man took a look into the van's interior after we'd backed it into the loading bay at the depot, and in response to our concern about limited space he shrugged, saying, 'Is okay.' And then he was grabbing cartons and trunks from the container that had spent about two months at sea, and was passing them to us in the van. We stacked them as we thought best, but Krzysztof had other ideas, and frequently folded himself into the back of Van Rouge to rearrange our packing. He was a man of few words, but infinite patience, and had a keen eye for fitting the cartons together in a way that maximised the space available. His assembly skills were formidable, and we suspect he was probably Poland's Tetris champion.

The container emptied, the van filled up, and finally it was done, though Liz and I found ourselves sharing the front seat with two boxes that just wouldn't fit in the back, but at least we didn't have to buy a roof rack. We thanked Krzysztof for his help – we were both knackered but he'd hardly broken into a sweat – and drove to Liz's sister Louise's house in a nice rural area not far from Newport Pagnell, home of Aston Martin motor cars. It could also be said it's not far from Milton Keynes, but whenever we'd say that to people they would look at us aghast and go, 'Eew! Milton *Keynes*?'

So it's close to Newport Pagnell; nobody says 'Eew' about that.

In Louise's front room Liz and I set about opening everything we'd picked up and decided how to prioritise it all. This meant repacking the van, not because we were dissatisfied with the Polish workmanship, but because we knew that a certain percentage of the cargo was merely packaging, and we reckoned we could reconcile the number of boxes with some judicious reorganising. This was a good exercise for us because we were soon to discover that space is always at a premium on a boat – unless you're wealthy enough to own a super yacht – and being able to stow things neatly and in a prioritised manner was something we would have to get used to.

It worked, helped also by Louise kindly agreeing that we could temporarily leave some artwork and some of Yasmin's less-essential things at her place, and so it was in a much less cramped van that we were finally able to catch the ferry to France where we would pay the balance owing on *Liberty*, cast off and sail away into the sunset.

CHAPTER SEVEN

I s it sailing or is it cruising? Or just boating? What was it – what verb – that we were going to do once we took over *Liberty*?

We only mention it here to get it out of the way, because there are some people who will argue to their dying breath that it is impossible to 'sail' a motor cruiser such as we were buying, and that the term 'sailing' is reserved only for those vessels with, in fact, sails. Like yachts.

Liz, with her logical bent, you would think might agree that to sail a boat it needs to have a sail, but you'd be wrong. We both felt that the terms 'sail' and 'sailing' fell naturally to the tongue when we told people of our plans; we were going to sail through France at a snail's pace ('snailing'), soaking up the scenery, the history and the language.

It's true that we would also be cruising, along the canals and rivers, so we figured the terms were interchangeable. And anyway, we would later come across yachts on the Canal du Midi as they traversed the country from the Atlantic to the Mediterranean, but of course they were doing so by running their motors because the bridges are too low to have masts up, and the canals are certainly too narrow for tacking. So we decided that if sail boats could motor along the canals then we could sail along them.

We don't want to get bogged down in the subject, so let's just say that if you go to P&O's website for their cross-Channel ferries you will find they advertise up to '46 sailings a day'. And that's with massive engines and not a sail in sight. So there. Stick that in your funnel.

And so we battled the horrendous English motorway traffic south to catch the ferry back to France, all the while looking forward to the more peaceful and sedate travelling to come.

We had a couple of deadlines to meet also. The most important was that Ross and Julia, some very good friends from New Zealand, were due to join us on board *Liberty* around the third week of September, and we hoped they could sail (there's that word again!) with us part way down the Saône over a few days. They would be our first guests, and we were looking forward to sharing the experience with them. Little did we know then that we would end up almost killing them.

The second deadline was purely seasonal; just as we'd be taking ownership of *Liberty*, most other boat owners would be tying up for the winter, having completed their cruising for the summer. Some would be getting their boats craned or cradled out of the water to be put 'on the hard' for the next six months or more, and we wondered how many others might be doing what we'd planned – sailing all through the winter down south where it would be warmer. All we knew for sure was that we wanted to get underway!

After the ferry crossing we swapped over to the other side of the road, rouged our way east through France and eventually arrived back at Saint-Jean-de-Losne. Although we knew *Liberty* was bobbing at her mooring awaiting our arrival we had another priority... get to the *supermarché* to buy some celebratory Champagne and lunch, and then go to the boat brokerage to do whatever final paperwork was necessary and get the keys.

We got to the office minutes before they were due to close for lunch (everything shuts in France around midday; we learned just to go with the flow – *c'est normal!*) but Nicholas was expecting us and within minutes we had signed the papers for transfer of ownership of *Liberty* to us. He handed us the log book, the all-important keys, a small brass plaque of France for us to attach on a boat wall somewhere, and a fire blanket.

We took our backpack with bubbly and lunch and found *Liberty* at her new temporary mooring on Pontoon E, among many other pleasure craft, some securely tucked up for winter, others with washing drying in the warm sunshine, like a sort of domestic bunting declaring that the owners were aboard. This pontoon wasn't full of *à vendre* boats – this was a normal working pontoon.

We opened up our boat (*our* boat!), opened the Champagne and sat on the deck in the sun. Within minutes we had met our nearest *voisin* – Erica – German, sixty-something, weather-beaten and with a wheezy laugh – as well as another neighbour, a Swiss woman opposite from the boat *Gobi*. Her name was Helga, and she quickly advised us that she had been on board for at least twenty years, and Erica for 26. They seemed pleased to see us, which was nice. A warm welcome, plus we had our first proper conversations in French.

Lunch on the aft deck was simple… baguette, ham, salami, cheese, but all the more tasty for the location. *Liberty* is a cruiser, with the high aft deck doubling as the cockpit, meaning we had a nicely-elevated view over the marina.

Then it was time to properly explore inside. *Liberty*'s owners had left everything – not just the pots, pans, crockery and cleaning stuff, but also all their personal decorator items, many with a nautical theme but nearly all dreadful tat, in our opinion. Liz quickly declared that it was all going, if not overboard then maybe to be given away to other boaties. Or a charity shop.

We posed for selfies in the Bond Lounge. Sitting there drinking the rest of the Champagne we examined some of the 'tat' including two vases which had paper stuffed in their tops. When Liz removed it we discovered what looked like ashes inside. Aaargh! Were these vases… or funeral urns?! Hopefully not, though I suggested perhaps a ceremony on deck and burial at sea might be appropriate, just in case.

A quick reconnaissance of the boat revealed that everything was as it had been when we'd first looked at the boat a few weeks back, except that the two bicycles on the bow had disappeared. Something we need to follow up, since the contract specifically said the boat came complete as is.

Returning to the van we grabbed our suitcases and started to make the boat our home, filling wardrobes and cupboards and shelves with our personal items, and clothes creased from long weeks of foldedness at sea.

During a pause I spotted a new boat arriving at the end of the pontoon so decided to demonstrate my nautical spirit and help them moor, for which they seemed grateful. The fact that I wouldn't know a danfort from a fairlead didn't seem to worry them, but of course they didn't know I didn't know.

Later we discovered we had no water on board – something else to follow up – but a woman from a boat further along showed me where the taps were on the pontoon and helped me get *d'eau* into a container I'd found on board. Mr Helga (Helga's husband, also Swiss, but nameless so he shall take her name also) seeing me filling the container warned me against 'ze chlor' in the water. 'Sometimes too much chlor,' he said, then left to continue wandering up and down the pontoon dispensing advice to anyone who would listen. I sniffed the water but couldn't detect chlorine or anything else.

Having emptied our suitcases and organised cupboards we decided a French siesta was in order, followed later by more Champagne on the deck. Well, this was the start of the adventure – a day worth celebrating!

The cloud increased and the temperature dropped a bit, a reminder that summer was drawing to a close and all sensible people should be battening their craft for winter hibernation, not drinking bubbles and beginning an odyssey.

Mid-pontoon a lovely large boat cruised in, flying a Kiwi flag. It moored, and we suddenly remembered the New Zealand flags we'd brought with us and decided it was time we declared some identity also, so we attached a silver fern to one of the flagpoles, and put an 'NZ' sticker on the stern. The previous owners, having Welsh connections, had left their Welsh flag flying too, which we decided to leave for the time being in acknowledgement that Liz was technically Welsh even though she lived there for only a few months.

Helga and Erica strolled past later, Erica with a dog. I asked her its name and she wheezed, 'Giorgio...' (another wheezy laugh) 'Giorgio... *Armani!*' Gales of laughter (from her).

Down below once more, and time to establish our mariner status... well, one of us at least. I was now officially – though self-declared – Captain Bodnar, the second to carry the title in my family. That's stretching it a bit really, since although my Dad was a captain, initially on freighters and latterly on oil tankers in the Persian Gulf, he was fully and properly qualified. Whereas I had no qualifications whatsoever, but apparently a boat must have a skipper, and Liz was quite happy for me to take on the role.

So, to add a dash of *je ne sais quoi* I had with me a captain's hat (a replica, not one of my father's unfortunately), and I got this out and attached a Russian naval badge to it, thoughtfully brought back for me from Moscow by Shaun. So I became the new skipper of *Liberty*, complete with official captain's hat, purely for formal occasions of course. Later we were to discover that to be seen wearing such headgear on the canals or rivers sets you apart, but for all the wrong reasons.

That night, our first on board, we retired to what we already had begun calling the 'stateroom' and found the bed to be up to the Goldilocks Standard: not too hard, nor too soft, but Just Right. After all the celebratory bubbles we slept very well, and missed the sinking boat.

CHAPTER EIGHT

The next morning Helga was in a state, rambling on about being woken up around midnight by flashing lights, the police running down the pontoon, and (we think) *les pompiers* – the fire brigade. Apparently they were rushing to save a boat from sinking in the marina, in fact right at the end of our pontoon. But we'd snored blissfully through the drama and missed it completely. Helga pointed to the boat at the centre of all the action, but as it seemed to be properly afloat we just smiled and mimed relief by wiping our brows. She muttered something and grumbled her way back onto her boat.

Before we could find out any more details as to what causes a boat to sink at its mooring, Monsieur Gerard turned up as arranged by the boat brokerage, on the dot of 9am. This short, sweat-marinated Frenchman – called 'Captain G' on his business card – then spent the best part of the next two hours showing us the technical details of *Liberty* – every fuse, valve, pump, filter, switch and knob.

Despite the wafts of body odour, magnified by the confined space of the engine compartment in particular, he appeared to be a nice man, but spoke hardly any English. In fact, it should be said, none at all, but between us we muddled through, with me using lots of sign language, pointing and raised eyebrows, while Liz made copious notes.

It helped to a degree that I had grown up tinkering with motorbikes, and later cars, so I knew an oil filter from an alternator, but I had no experience of diesel engines and certainly not one installed in a boat. But most of what Monsieur Gerard was pointing to I recognised, and some of what he said we think we understood. He used the word *nettoyage* a lot, which I knew meant 'cleaning,' and it seemed that he was telling us it was important to keep the various filters clean, and to check them regularly.

Another word he used a lot was *technique*, but since it means in English what it says in French I was at a loss as to what he was trying to say. However he seemed to always tap the side of his nose when he used the word, so maybe he was warning me that to blow my nose in the confined space of the engine bay required a certain *élan*. I shrugged, which always seems to be the accepted thing to do in France, and he continued to point at various bits and pieces.

I looked at Liz frequently as she jotted notes and mouthed, 'Did you get that?' to which she would silently mime, 'Think so.' I hoped so, since her comprehension of French was better than mine, and I figured that between my knowledge of engines and hers of French we should be okay. *D'accord*, I would nod to Gerard, and he seemed pleased.

In the process of the boat exploration and pulling lids off secret compartments (with M. Gerard blissfully unaware of showing off his 'builder's crack' every time he stuck his head down a hatch) we found all manner of things we'd been wondering about, such as the missing canvas Bimini top for the fly bridge, and the elusive bed plank (which converts the banquette in the salon into a bed), so that was all good.

We also discovered a lonely front basket for one of the bicycles we didn't have. Captain G lifted every bit of flooring and even hauled up our bed for access to hidden panels. Bewildering, but at least we knew what lay beneath, even if we didn't really know what all the levers and pumps were for.

The upshot of this was that we weren't confident of sailing anywhere for fear of something going wrong. Safer to stay here a bit longer, we decided, and maybe wait until those more experienced mariner friends of ours (Keith and Hilary) arrived back from up north the following week so that Keith could give us further benefit of his experience and knowledge.

Meanwhile, with our exploratory and technical tour of *Liberty* at an end, Monsieur Gerard brought out a sheaf of papers, some explaining a regular maintenance schedule, and some for us to sign acknowledging that he had shown us everything in detail. We suspected this was in case *Liberty* sank that night at her mooring, and that he would be completely absolved of blame and not have to appear in court.

We said multiple *mercis*, and a couple of *au revoirs*, and then Gerard climbed down off *Liberty* and headed off home, which wasn't far away – in fact only about twenty metres since it transpired he lived full-time on board his own boat just along from us on the same pontoon. His was an old red one with vegetables growing in pots at the stern. His tomatoes had died though, he explained with a look of pain crossing his face… something to do with either a lack of water or the wrong water, we're not sure. '*Technique!*' I felt like telling him, tapping my nose. Or maybe, 'Too much chlor!'

It was nice to know he was a neighbour; even though we were the new kids on the block the sense of community here seemed strong, and we were already enjoying 'knowing people,' and having passers-by on the pontoon wish us *bonjour* or *bonne soirée*. If we were eating – even if only cheese and crackers – we would be politely wished *bon appetit*.

Erica and Helga regularly greeted us, but Giorgio Armani remained suspicious and barked furiously every time we climbed on or off *Liberty*. He showed none of the class or style his name suggested. We also suspected him of stealing a bath towel we'd left to dry on the stern railing overnight, but unfortunately it seems more likely it actually fell off and into the marina. Being a sort of murky green colour it must have blended well with the water before sinking to the bottom, since there was absolutely no sign of it. We hoped it wouldn't wrap around our propeller when we finally ventured out.

We went back to the *supermarché* and bought more supplies for the boat. The previous owners had left a good supply of cutlery, but curiously only one fork, and while Liz and I enjoy dining together we draw the line at sharing a single implement. There are limits.

And so that evening we cooked our first proper meal on board: stir-fry Thai chicken. Lovely, and very cosy sitting in the Bond Lounge to eat it. And thanks to Monsieur Gerard's poking around we'd also found the quadrant squabs that help turn the dinette seating into a round bed. Not that we were in any hurry to try it out; we decided to leave that for some future guests.

As evening fell we went up top for a last gaze around before retiring. Looking at other people's boats you could gauge their commitment to life afloat according to what they had on board. Bicycles said they were voyagers who liked to explore where they stopped. Dogs, we figured, meant the owners were serious sailors. And washing hanging out shouted 'we are aboard' more than any flag could. Unlike underpants drying in the breeze however, flags do at least identify the crew's origin, which would come in handy later, and would also be a good test of our knowledge of nationalities, not being vexillologists.

Often it seemed the tattier the boat the more likely it was to be a live-aboard. *Atlantique*, Erica's barge next door, had seen better days. The wheelhouse was covered with a black plastic tarpaulin. Paint peeled, rust showed through, and on the superstructure there was evidence that someone had once started to sand back the paint ready for renovation work, but got no further.

Those boats that were tucked up for winter were obvious by the canvas covers fastened over their windows, with everything stowed away, ropes knotted and secure, and items on deck covered with tarpaulins. Inside you knew they had drained water tanks and pipes against freezing. For the next six months they would sit cocooned until their owners returned for the following year's boating season.

The visual feast of the marina apart, we discovered all the different specific boat-related sounds also: pumps, bow- and stern-thrusters, diesel engines idling, and the hollow sound of footsteps on the pontoon as someone walked along to their boat… comforting sounds that say life is going on around you.

Glimpsed through some boat windows we could see the flicker of televisions. Many vessels had satellite dishes on their roofs, and we'd even found one on *Liberty* in the compartment under our bed, but had decided we were in no hurry to try it out. Watching television wasn't what we'd chosen to live on a boat for, even though *Liberty* came complete with a flat-screen TV. We had decided our evenings and spare time would be best spent learning French, or reading, researching our routes or blogging about our journey. (Later we would end up watching quite a lot of French TV, and would even feature on a Channel 4 programme in the UK. But that was a while away yet.)

For the time being we were just pleased to be finally living on our own boat, and looking forward to starting our adventure.

We retired to the stateroom for our second night on board, which, because of where we were moored, wasn't much different than sleeping in a bedroom at home. We may as well have been on land as the boat was wedged firmly in between the pontoon and the other neighbouring boat (empty), plus being a marina there was very little water movement, so no swells, no rocking, and no real sense of even being afloat.

The master bedroom was cosy, but the close confines of *Liberty* were taking some getting used to. Banged elbows, knees and heads are common dangers on small boats (as we'd already discovered) but we figured we'd get used to it. The headroom was good though, and even Keith, who is just over six feet tall, had no problem standing up.

Despite the neighbourliness of the marina we looked forward to setting off south for sun and warmth, escaping the oncoming autumn and winter, and cruising gently through Languedoc-Roussillon, the Midi-Pyrénées, and Aquitaine towards Bordeaux on the east coast.

Next day we were to learn that maybe that wouldn't be such a good idea.

CHAPTER NINE

After a night of heavy rain we woke to a leaden sky, with the clouds promising more rain to come. It was another reminder we were leaving our departure late.

Mr Helga, who spied us slowly emerging on deck, asked about our plans, but creased his brow and shook his head when we told him. He warned us that even going south we wouldn't escape the cold of winter.

'You should stay here!' he advised, gesturing to the other boats around us. 'Zough in vinter zere can be sick ice on ze pontoons.' Liz and I glanced at each other and he quickly added that this was a rare occurrence.

'And by now ze suzzern marinas vill all be booked solid,' he said. 'Your only chance of a vinter port will be one of ze Mediterranean sea ports, and zey are very expensive.'

Obviously some challenges awaited us, but we weren't going to be put off zat easily.

Anyway it was Sunday morning, *Dimanche*, and since the boat had proved to be nicely watertight we weren't too worried about the glowering sky or more rain, though ice wasn't something we wanted, unless it was in cubes, tinkling in a glass.

We both assumed that because we would be heading south and would be going just that bit closer to the equator that winter would be less noticeable, maybe even benign and balmy.

We certainly hadn't considered that the southern marinas would be 'booked solid.' Again we assumed that with being close to the Mediterranean, boats on the Canal du Midi would continue to sail. But some of what Mr Helga had said turned out to be true and we would soon be in for a reality check.

In the meantime there was a lot to be happy about. We'd found our boat, it was well-equipped and ready to go, we had bought books with detailed maps of the inland waterways so we'd know where to go and what to expect, and above all we were in France!

As Francophiles we'd both been really looking forward to spending some quality time in the country. Improving our French was high on our list of Things To Do, and although almost everyone we'd met in the marina (apart from Monsieur Gerard and Erica) had spoken English to us, we were enjoying hearing colloquial French in the town.

Dimanche, for example. It's a lovely word. In fact French is lovely to listen to, even as a casual non-understanding bystander. It's nice to hear locals speaking in their sing-song cadence. French to me always sounds like a language of permanent surprise, disbelief, and delight.

But just how much daily French we got involved in depended it seemed on what sort of shops we went into. The supermarkets for example are no different to those in the UK or New Zealand – just shelves and shelves of goods already priced, and checkouts where your items are scanned with the total shining brightly on the top of the till. There is no need for conversation, no need even to ask '*C'est combien?*' and we quickly discovered that a visit to the *supermarché* wasn't going to improve our French much.

The *boulangerie* was a little better, but not much. However it seems compulsory in France to bid *bonjour* to everyone in the shop as you walk in, if for no other reason than they all say it to you as you come through the door. It's charmingly polite. But again, other than asking for your *deux croissants* and a *baguette*, the opportunity for conversation is minimal.

We set off in Van Rouge to the not-too-distant city of Dijon to see if we could fulfil the list of things we still needed on board, and to buy a couple of replacement bicycles. Our Sat-Nav told us Dijon was 45 minutes away and called us meanies for avoiding the toll roads. Well, maybe not, but I always felt a bit cheap when the stern voice warned us, 'Toll Roads' and we chose not to take them.

But that was a good thing as the route took us through back-country roads and even down an un-named lane that looked like it would become a mud track at any moment. As it happened it led us though a nice little place called Tart de Haut, which had us on the lookout – though we never did see her – for the 'High Tart' herself. (On the return journey we actually went through Low Tart, but she was also busy, possibly generating more business through cheaper rates, the scamp.)

Anyway, it was during this short outing to Dijon that I was introduced to another aspect of French life that was somewhat less charming than having other shoppers say *bonjour* as you walked in the door: unisex toilets.

Need I say more? Yes, I need. The first disconcerting thing about strolling into the loos at the Toisin D'Or shopping mega-mall was the pretty 18-year-old girl waiting just inside, possibly (hopefully) for a friend to come out. I don't know about you but this had an instant and suppressing effect on my need to go, as did the row of men's urinals in full view of any female walking past to the cubicles. But what can you do? When you gotta go you gotta go. This presumably was the embodiment of the *Égalité* that went along with *Liberté*, and *Fraternité*.

Anyway, that little adventure was all over in a couple of shakes, though the pretty girl was still there when I left. Our eye contact was slightly awkward, and just that wee bit too prolonged.

The good news is she didn't summon the *gendarmes* and Liz and I managed to buy a couple of bikes, having established with the brokerage that those on board when we first viewed the boat were never intended to be part of the sale. Well, we think that's the case. When I went to the brokerage to enquire as to the whereabouts of the *velos*, Nicholas was on holiday, and I had to deal instead with the elegant Amandine, who looked like she had just stepped off the cover of *Vogue*. She spoke very little English, and when I enquired in halting French about the missing bikes she rattled off some rapid response that seemed to explain either that a) they were never included in the deal, or b) they had mysteriously *disparu*. She shrugged her elegant shoulders, presumably indicating that nothing could be done and she needed to get back to her modelling.

Either way we were *sans velos*, which was annoying and frustrating. We hoped our command of French would improve beyond *boulangerie*-basic over the coming months so that we could better manage situations like this. Not that we were completely helpless, but for best effect Liz and I needed to work as a team.

I hadn't been particularly good at French at school, though I had undertaken an adult continuing education course in conversational French some years later, and – importantly – I'm quite good at mimicking accents. So it turned out that I could communicate relatively well, to the point sometimes where locals would believe I *could* speak the lingo; my problem was I couldn't understand a word they said in reply.

Liz on the other hand is very good at understanding rapid French, and will usually catch the main phrases. 'It's context,' she explained to me. 'If you know what they're talking *about* then you just listen for key phrases, and get the drift.'

That was easier for her than me though, plus her vocabulary is more extensive. I much preferred talking than listening, and would relish any opportunity to 'become French' by adopting all the nuances that go with the language – the long drawn-out ums and errs (more errs actually), the shrugs, the tilt of the head, and the musical cadence of the sentences themselves. I would make a good French waiter. *Oui monsieur, errrrrr nous avons les vins errrrrr magnifiques!*

So, when we were together we could get by quite well. I would speak, Liz would listen, and then she'd tell me what had just been said.

But the day I'd enquired about the bikes she wasn't with me and so we still don't really know what happened to them. What we do know is that we ended up having to pay €300 for new ones. Still, we would now have the means of going to the shops and exploring local towns and villages at stopovers on our way south.

The next day we felt we were starting to settle into what passes for domestic routine, even to the extent the previous night of watching a DVD on the telly. (I know, I know, we said we wouldn't…)

This morning we'd awoken to a slightly cooler temperature – yet another hint of things to come – so we turned on the warm-air heating to try it out. It worked a treat, and nicely warmed the whole boat through the vents in the stateroom, salon and galley.

Looking around the boat, and using all its cupboards and drawers, we were constantly amazed and delighted by the lateral thinking that goes into boat design. Lateral, horizontal and vertical thinking really, as every spare centimetre of space is put to some good use. Just as well, as we discovered we were well on the way to filling all the nooks and crannies with our stuff. But you have to admire the sheer cleverness of boat design. It must of course apply to any cramped spaces that double as living quarters, whether a motor home, caravan or the International Space Station. Space, at a premium, the final frontier.

Another quaint piece of domesticity in the marina was the daily broadcast from 'Radio Station *Gare de L'eau*' at 0930 on the VHF radio, channel 77.

It's not a radio broadcast that would win any awards or attract a huge audience because it's basically a morning rally-round (in English) of those local boaties who want to stay connected. That particular morning's session was conducted by Sandy on board a boat named *Liberté*, the French version of our own boat. As we discovered, the formula for each broadcast is essentially the same: she first of all finds out who's listening with a sort of roll-call, followed by a call for anyone who might need assistance or advice, and then there's an opportunity for everyone to share information or offer goods or services.

The broadcast also acts as a community notice board, and that morning we learned of a weekly 'boating ladies' coffee meet-up in the café opposite the main church in town. I thought Liz would be sick overboard at the thought, her not being a coffee morning type and a self-confessed introvert, but surprisingly she wanted to go along.

'This is my new life,' she explained. 'I want to do new things, and not just be the "old" Liz. And it would be good to go and meet people, maybe make some connections.'

When she got back she was a little disappointed that there had been only two others there, and that the bar the meeting was held in was a bit of a dive. 'But it was nice to meet Sandy and Jackie,' she said. 'Sandy's the one who does the broadcasts and organises activities like bike rides, and Jackie and her partner have bought here and are trying to sell their aluminium boat.' In fact we'd looked at it briefly when we'd been searching, but it didn't tick enough of our boxes.

While Liz was busy being new and making connections, I occupied myself filling the twin water tanks on *Liberty*, swabbing the decks, working out how to attach the rest of the Bimini top to the flybridge (needed Liz's help for that I decided) and then brushed up on my French irregular verbs in the salon. Especially so I could explain to 18-year-old girls in toilets, 'Excuse me, I am here to have a quick wee. Please avert your pretty eyes…'

CHAPTER TEN

As I wrote online the next day, '*In this blog: Naughty Jack goes swimming, Mike and Ross drink beer, we all nearly die, and* Liberty *flees the nest…*'

Yes, at last, we set sail on *Liberty*, but only on a short 'shakedown cruise'. Not wanting to place ourselves in danger, we waited to do this until our Kiwi friends Ross and Julia arrived to stay on board as the boat's first 'guest guinea-pigs.' Mean of us? No, practical, because if during the maiden voyage something went wrong then we needed to know that if we shouted, 'All hands on deck' that we would actually *have* a few hands.

I picked up R & J in Van Rouge from the local station – they were mid-way through a six-week European tour – and delivered them to the boat. They said nice things about *Liberty* and didn't seem fazed by the idea of being first to try out the convertible banquette bed, though we softened and offered them the stateroom for the duration of their visit. Well, it seemed only right given they had two large suitcases, and we figured if anyone should be the first to try out the more makeshift sleeping arrangement in the salon it should be us.

Mid-morning we all went into town to the weekly Book Swap, a regular ex-pat boat people get-together, another event that we'd heard about on Radio *Gare de L'eau*. It turned out the book swap was actually a whole mini-library, beautifully organised into different language sections, and with a wide range to choose from, from bodice-rippers to boating manuals.

The event also included an opportunity to pick the brains of local experienced sailors including Polish Mike, who owned two boats, a brace of MG cars and a scooter. He was 83, and with thirty years' experience afloat he was regarded as the boat guru in these parts. He was a lovely man.

In fact he boosted our confidence when he gave us the welcome news that we would almost certainly find moorings down south, especially on the Canal du Midi between Sète and Toulouse, plus it would, he assured us, be warmer than Saint-Jean-de-Losne… exactly the sort of optimistic forecast we needed to hear.

After a quick visit to the *boulangerie* for sticky tarts it was then back to the boat for a glass of Champagne to celebrate Ross and Julia's arrival. Any excuse.

And then, finally, finally – *at last* (about time too, we hear you say) – we took *Liberty* out for the first time on our own, albeit just a short jaunt of two hours in the afternoon. We didn't do anything more adventurous than go out onto the Saône, where we tootled upstream for an hour, turned around (the bow and stern thrusters are great for turning on a sixpence, or a centime or whatever France uses now) and returned. Not the most exciting of voyages, but a necessary gentle introduction.

It was nice and sunny when we started but from half way it rained, though that didn't spoil the thrill of being out on our own boat. Backing *Liberty* into her mooring between a pontoon finger and the other boat next to us took some doing but with much stopping and starting and over-use of the bow- and stern-thrusters I managed it in the end. Having Ross and Julia aboard was a bonus as they were able to help wrangle ropes, and fend off when I was in danger of colliding, plus the French couple from a boat called *Tranquil* also helped, and kindly gave me a round of applause when I finally wedged *Liberty* in.

The boat performed well except we couldn't get the inverter going so that's something we needed to address. (For the non-technical it's the electronic thing that enables you to get mains power-equivalent from the boat's batteries when not connected to shore power) We decided it was likely to be more of a fault with our understanding of it than with the system itself (and so it turned out).

Engine-wise it was a flawless voyage, and we didn't sink – which is just as well because despite being otherwise well-equipped we discovered there were no life jackets on board. (Liz went to the brokerage and bought one the next day, but was horrified at the cost. 'I wasn't buying two at that price!' she told me. I wondered which of us would have to swim in an emergency. I suspected it wouldn't be her.)

So anyway, first sailing uneventful. Long may it stay that way, we hoped.

In order to balance Liz's trip to the a boat-ladies' coffee morning, Ross and I went to the male equivalent: Boys' Beer at the *Bar de la Poste*, where the marina's expat male boaties gathered weekly to swap boating stories, advice, and enjoy a pint or two of ale.

There we met Ray and Joe, both living on Dutch tjalks, Ray's dating to about 1890. Joe's boat was, by comparison, a youngster having been built in 1905. Both vessels were made of iron and were very solid. In fact, Ray's boat spent the Second World War completely underwater where it had been deliberately submerged so that the occupying Germans couldn't use it. He made its salvage and recovery sound like an easy job but in reality it must have been a major project.

As in so many bars and restaurants, the *Bar de la Poste* encouraged dogs, with the barman's own canines – two spaniels – being accorded the special privilege of being allowed to lie on the tables. This encouraged us to woof down our beer.

Despite the chauvinist nature of the gathering (Lucy from the boat *Kiwi Rose* popped in to introduce us to her husband Max, but then quickly ducked out saying, 'I'm not a man so I'm not supposed to be here!') there was an excellent community feel, and some great boating stories.

It was during this session that we learned that boating is widely acknowledged as an expensive hobby, and that the word BOAT actually stands for: Bring Out Another Thousand.

Later, back on board as we sat down to another stir-fry, followed by some yummy French cheeses supplied by Ross and Julia, the boat's gas alarm started blaring.

We turned off the gas supply to the cooker – about the only practical thing we could think of doing – and after lots of farting around with the alarm it finally stopped and after multiple resets was quiet, showing nothing untoward on its small digital readout.

All remained peaceful until just before bed when it seemed to detect more gas. Was it perhaps the ripe blue cheese, we wondered? Or the hot sweet chilli sauce? The hot air we'd been talking? Hard to say, but we couldn't personally detect anything wrong, couldn't smell anything (other than cheese) and so we convinced ourselves that we didn't seem to be in any danger and assumed the alarm to be faulty.

Blissfully unaware of the genuine danger that lurked below, Julia and Ross retired to the stateroom, while Liz and I assembled and tried out the convertible salon bed, which turned out to be surprisingly comfortable. As we dropped off to sleep we noticed how quiet it was now that the wind had dropped.

Two-twenty in the morning and the gas alarm suddenly shrieked loudly. Liz leapt out of bed, did all the right things, turned off the gas again, and checked everything while I selfishly continued to sleep, or at least tried to (the lingering effects of the earlier chauvinistic gathering, you understand) but again there was no obvious culprit. Ross and Julia chose to ignore the alarm, assuming we (meaning Liz) were in full control.

The rest of the night there were no more alarms and we awoke to bright sunshine. As we lazed under the duvet we could hear the owner of Jaques, the little white terrier, who some weeks back had almost jumped into the water in the dry dock as it was filling to enable Keith and Hilary's boat to exit. He'd been fascinated by the swirling water, and seemed very keen to investigate further. While we'd watched his antics from *Picton*, his owner, a bow-legged Frenchman with flat cap, had berated him, 'Jaques! Jaques! *Non! Arrêtez! Jaques!!*'

Jacques seemed disappointed that he wasn't allowed to jump in and chase the whorls and eddies, and we felt a bit sorry for him.

But this morning as we lay in bed we heard Jacques' owner in the distance yelling at him once again, this time with increasing desperation, obviously trying to dissuade the dog from doing something – presumably diving into the marina – but it was obvious he failed. It was very funny. The shouting crescendoed into a wail of dismay as (we assumed) Jaques lived up to his Cousteau name and dived in. 'Jacques! Jacques non! *Jacques!* Oh Jacques, non, *non, noooon!*'

It was difficult to understand the stream of French invective that followed but Jacques was clearly in trouble, and possibly banished to the car, his morning walkies terminated.

Meanwhile our gas alarm mystery remained, and we added it to the list of things to follow up with Keith, who along with Hilary and two friends from England was due to return to Saint-Jean-de-Losne that day on their boat.

The regular morning VHF Radio *Gare de l'eau* forecast a nice day, so in lovely warm sunshine we decided to set off once again on *Liberty*, this time to meet *Picton* up-river. Using the bow thrusters we gracefully pirouetted midstream when we met Keith and crew, took photos of each other's boats, and sailed in tandem back to Saint-Jean-de-Losne. There was something special about cruising along with another boat whose crew you knew. It added a degree of comfort and companionship.

And, pure coincidence, at one point there were three Kiwi-flagged boats in view of each other, each crew waving enthusiastically at the sight of a silver fern or Southern Cross flag.

Picton entered the Bourgogne Canal lock and we moored back at our pontoon, a much more elegant return than the previous day's dodgem display. This time we reversed in beautifully – if very slowly – without any bumps, grinds or embarrassment, and without need of help from other boaties. But you know what they say about pride and falls; there were certainly a few falls ahead, but at that moment I felt like I was qualified to wear the Captain's hat.

A pleasant lunch at a restaurant overlooking the river with *Picton's* expanded crew followed, and we gleaned more information from Keith about what we needed to do before setting off on our odyssey. He explained we needed to get a *vignette*, like a registration sticker on a car, which shows the waterway authorities that your boat is properly paid-up and therefore entitled to use the locks and cruise the rivers and canals.

Most of the French waterways are run by the *Voies Navigable de France* – the VNF – and the fees you pay for your registration go towards the maintenance of the canals and locks as well as the manning of locks where required. Or womanning of the locks, in some instances. We discovered there was a VNF office in town so buying our *vignette* should be straightforward.

Our timing was out for taking Ross and Julia with us for the start of the planned voyage south as we still weren't ready to leave, but they seemed happy enough to just be on board, and had they come south it would have meant we'd have had to try and find a stopping point close to a railway station so that they could easily continue their European trip. We all agreed it seemed simpler to stay where we were for the moment, and to be honest Liz and I were quite glad of the extra time to become more familiar with *Liberty*, and tie up the remaining loose ends.

So, at the end of their brief stay I dropped our Kiwi mates back at the station, where they caught the train south. Their journey would be a lot quicker than ours. It had been lovely having them aboard as our first guests, though at that stage we were still unaware how close we'd all come to being injured or worse, and just how serious a situation it had been.

Back at the boat I decided to do some exploration in the engine bay. There was a bank of batteries – eight in all – which Monsieur Gerard had tried to explain to us. We knew that two of them powered the bow- and stern-thrusters, one was for starting the engine, and the others were our domestic supply for when we weren't plugged into shore power.

I discovered two batteries were low on electrolyte, maybe even dry, so at the nearby boat chandlers we bought some demineralised water for topping-up, along with some more of the all-important French canal and river guide books (*guides fluviales*) which itemise absolutely everything you need to know about your journey and the waterways.

Then we went to the VNF office to buy our *vignette*, which turned out to be very expensive. We discovered it would actually be cheaper for us to buy a full year's registration than to purchase *vignettes* month by month. But Madame was closing for lunch and we felt pressured to make a decision, so we left with just a one-month vignette which would see us through to the last week in October, by which time we hoped to have survived a good portion of the Rhône and be in Avignon.

There was still one more important item to be taken care of before we set sail though, and that was to take Van Rouge a half-day's drive to Liz's parents where we'd arranged to park it in safety for the winter.

As we drove south on the autoroute we had no idea that the two batteries I had topped up below decks on *Liberty* were heating up, in fact bubbling, and beginning to vent explosive hydrogen sulphide gas.

When we arrived we found 83-year old Reg roped to a tree on an almost vertical bank behind the house cutting scrub. I can only hope I'm as fit when I'm that age, or if not, then at least wealthy enough to employ skilled arborists. We persuaded him off the dangerous slope and Liz and I set to work cutting back the remainder of the offending scrub and small trees.

The rest of the weekend was spent attempting to re-roof the carport where we would be parking Van Rouge, and deciding which of our possessions would be better off stored in the house rather than the van. We were very grateful to be able to leave the vehicle in a safe place, and it was the last piece of the jigsaw we needed to slot into place before we could begin the voyage proper.

We returned the following Monday morning by train to *Liberty*, but during the evening once more were confused by the gas alarm sounding. Again our investigations showed nothing untoward, but the problem was we weren't looking in the right place. Liz was more worried than I was; while she was convinced we had a gas leak, I still thought the alarm was probably faulty, especially in the absence of any evidence.

But the next day we were presented with more evidence than we wanted. As we returned from a shopping trip a German woman from a nearby boat said, 'Vile you are avay, your phone on board it is going beep-beep-beep!'

We thanked her, somewhat bewildered that we hadn't actually left a phone on *Liberty*, but as we opened the door we were hit by a wave of sulphur. It smelt just like Rotorua, New Zealand's famous geothermal area, on a bad day. Think rotten eggs and you'll get the picture.

Once more we checked the gas supply – nothing – and then I lifted the floor panel beneath which the batteries are stored, only to be greeted by acid bubbling out of two of the batteries and gas venting through the caps… very dangerous and highly volatile hydrogen sulphide gas. One spark and *Liberty* could have exploded.

We quickly opened all windows and hatches and went up on deck. Obviously something had gone horribly wrong, but what? I knew I hadn't overfilled the batteries and I had used the proper demineralised solution.

We rushed to the brokers for advice and they seemed appropriately concerned, sending two of their guys in overalls to investigate. These men, Philippe and Thierry, took one look and quickly vacated the boat, saying that the batteries were too hot and dangerous to work on and would need to cool down. They must have done something to render then safe, maybe they disconnected them, because after a while we were allowed back on board. They said they'd be back the next day to check on the situation.

Liz had a told-you-so look on her face, and I had to agree that I hadn't taken the situation seriously enough. The gas alarm was, after all, a safety device. But silly me had assumed that with no obvious gas leaks, and with the engine not running to produce any exhaust, the alarm must have been at fault.

The next morning Philippe and Thierry were bottoms up and heads down in the engine bay as they poked around the battery compartment. They finally identified the problem as being a battery cell that had deteriorated, which caused the other cells in an adjoining connected battery to overcharge, heat up and almost boil. We were, they said, very lucky not to have suffered an explosion. The venting hydrogen sulphide gas was very dangerous, and even a slight spark could have had disastrous results.

Ross and Julia meanwhile had narrowly escaped a nasty situation as the blaring alarm must have detected gas escaping from the deteriorating batteries even while they were with us.

Anyway, our French saviours removed the offending batteries and replaced them with brand new sealed ones, which we hoped would solve the problem and – at last – enable us to get on our way the next morning, two days late and many Euros lighter. (We later learned that buying bog-standard truck batteries can save a lot of money. If only we'd known.)

Liberty seemed like an inappropriate name for a boat that was having some difficulty escaping.

A South African, an Australian and an Englishman walk into a bar. Sound like a joke? Well, actually it was amusing. There I was at another Boys' Beer get-together sitting this time outside the *Brasserie L'Amiral* in Saint-Jean-de-Losne, chatting as we had the previous Wednesday about all things boating. There weren't many others there, and Madame Brasserie was very apologetic that they had almost run out of beer after an incredibly busy day.

I suspected this was due to the two boat-loads of Germans who'd arrived in port the evening before. There was no tangible evidence, but they're an easy target. Anyway we soon forgot about the beer shortage thanks to the local birds.

Outside the brasserie there were four large plane trees, and at this time of the evening the local bird population would come home to roost in them. This in itself was unusual as the French have, by and large, killed most living things in the name of *haute cuisine*, but somehow these delicacies were still living.

The birds were very noisy, chatting no doubt about the day's exploits, and where to find the best and bendiest twigs to build nests.

Monsieur Brasserie came out of the door and showed a little girl how to make the birds shut up by clapping twice. She tried her best, but although her claps had some effect it didn't shut the birds up completely, so he showed her how to slap the table instead, and the birds went completely silent! Not a cheep, not a chirp. Amazing.

It didn't last long though; once the *oiseaux* realised the noise wasn't actually both barrels of a shotgun, and that they weren't about to be served up as an *entrée*, they continued their chat, as did we.

That night we slept better knowing we had new non-fuming batteries beneath us, though Liz was once again up in the middle of the night to investigate a dripping noise in the hull. She's the sort of person who can't sleep if there's a faint regular noise of any sort, such as my snoring, whereas I can happily sleep through most things. She was, it turned out, also paranoid about us possibly sinking.

We knew we had some water in the stern tunnel beneath the propeller shaft – it had been there for a few days – but we were assured by Nicholas in the brokerage office that in 95% of cases it's due to water seeping in around the propeller shaft flange, and not coming in through the bottom of the boat.

As he pointed out very logically, all propeller shafts have to go through a hole in the boat, and keeping water from entering the hole is something all boating people have to manage. This seemed to involve ensuring enough grease is packed in the flange... something I resolved to find out how to do.

Anyway, it wasn't something Liz or I were going to fix in the middle of the night, and since it was a very minor drip we did our best to ignore it for the time being.

And besides, we needed to sleep because, finally, next day was departure day!

CHAPTER ELEVEN

We took care of the final admin stuff, which meant paying for our mooring, the electricity we'd used and – gasp – the work on the boat to find the electrical problem and install two new batteries. All this lent credence to the saying we'd learned earlier, that BOAT really does stand for Bring Out Another Thousand.

Our friend Shaun has a cruiser on the English canals, and in his cockpit is a plaque that also defines the word. It says: *Boat – [bōt] (noun) – A hole in the water surrounded by wood into which one pours money.*

Anyway, it was time to go. We said *au revoir* to Madame Erica and *au ruffoir* to Giorgio Armani, cast off in warm sunshine with a positive forecast, and glided out of the marina. (Surely the past tense of 'glide' should be 'glid', but seemingly it's not.)

We turned right onto the Saône with a sense of relief and headed south down-river into the unknown.

Well, not quite true. Having equipped ourselves with the waterway guides necessary for our trip we were left in no doubt what lay ahead; every turn of the river, every lock, hazard, signpost, limited speed zone, bridge, post, mooring place and duck is detailed on the guide map pages. OK, maybe not the ducks…

So in reality there were no surprises. On most rivers and canals there are even kilometre signs, called PKs – for *point kilométrique* – that are fantastic for identifying exactly how far you've travelled and where you are. You can also use them to accurately measure the average speed of your boat, simply by timing how long it takes to travel between them and doing some sums.

Combine the incredible detail of the river maps with the gorgeous calm and warm sailing conditions and we really started to relax. We passed a few craft coming our way, including a couple of large commercial *peniches* – huge barges carrying industrial cargoes – which reminded us that although we loved our *Liberty* to bits, we were small fry on rivers and canals that still carry behemoths such as these, and that we would need to keep our wits about us. And remember to look behind us every now and then to see what might be sneaking up.

Some of these boats were so laden with gravel or other heavyweight cargoes that they sat really low in the water, pushing a big bow wave out in front of them. The river looked like it would overflow at any moment, swamping the vessel and sending it to the bottom, but we soon got to realise that such sights were normal, and that in fact they weren't at all close to sinking. Still, an incredible thing to see if you've not witnessed it before.

And so we approached our first ever lock, at Seurre. (Not really our absolute first since we had both travelled on the English canals previously, but this was our first French one, and certainly a lot bigger than the English ones.)

Protocol dictates that you should advise the lock-keeper (*éclusier*) ahead of your arrival with details about your boat, its type, its name, whether you are heading upstream or down, and your expected arrival time – using the VHF radio on a specified channel, and all in French.

Having never done this before I was somewhat nervous, although I had worked out what I was going to say and had even written a script. Liz was very happy to leave all this to me, though to be fair she was also happy to be on stand-by to translate any answers we received.

The *guide fluviale* conveniently listed the number of the VHF channels to use for the different locks, so we selected the one for Seurre. Two kilometres out I tentatively pressed the transmit button and announced to the lock-keeper who, what and where we were and how long we would likely be, trying to sound as French as possible, with lots of *errrrs*. I took my finger off the button and we waited.

Amazingly the response came back almost immediately and without question that our arrival in ten minutes would be fine. Phew! So, a few minutes later we rounded a bend and there was the lock, with the 'traffic light' signals showing red and green, meaning the lock was in preparation mode. We pulled over to the side to wait for the double green lights that would mean we could enter.

Now you might think that the lock-keepers live beside their locks in quaint cottages with roses growing over the doors and with white picket fences out the front. That may be true of some, but not these on the Saône. These locks could hardly be called 'quaint;' they were huge and quite industrial, large enough to accommodate at least two of the giant *peniches* we had seen earlier. In fact, when the lock gates opened one of these monsters glid out, a titanic vessel that made our boat look like a dinghy by comparison. We watched in awe as it slid slowly by, its huge propeller churning the water into a boiling froth behind.

And then the lights turned green and it was our turn, so in we went, slowly, on tick-over.

The canal guide books have lovely illustrations showing how two crew members should handle the ropes and bollards in a lock, going up or down. We were '*avalant*' – going down – which meant the lock was full as we entered. According to the diagrams, one crew member (Liz) stands at the bow with a rope ready to throw round a bollard, while the second crew member (me) is at the stern, ready to cast a rope round the bollard nearest the stern.

This was all very well, except the bollards were so far apart we quickly realised that we were going to have to throw both our ropes around just one of them, so after some hurried reorganising, that's what we did. We were a bit tense, not having done this before, but it worked.

Why tense? Well, of all the challenges you can face with your boat, surviving locks is probably up there towards the top of the list, if not actually at the top. That's because there are so many things that can go wrong, mainly due to the fact that your boat either rises or falls according to which way you're going, and if you make a mistake with the ropes you can be in serious trouble.

For example, at the Seurre lock we were descending. The theory behind having your ropes around the lockside bollards is that you can have some control over your boat as the lock empties, and by holding the ropes firmly you can prevent the boat moving around too much as the water swirls around you. But, if you make the mistake of actually tying your rope round a bollard, 'making fast' as we nautical types say, then you are in very real danger of having your boat hang on the rope, tilting horribly as the water level drops. In the worst scenario your boat would be left hanging on the side of the lock, the rope would likely snap, and the boat would smash down to the water below, probably throwing you into the lock, from where you would get a water-level view of your vessel sinking.

So, two things: one is to never tie your rope to a bollard, whether you're descending or rising, and two: always have a very sharp knife, or even a hatchet, on hand in case you have to quickly cut a rope in an emergency. We had an excellent quality razor-sharp hunting knife which, sometime later, would actually save our boat.

But in the meantime, we had to get through our first lock. The *éclusier*, sitting in his lofty control tower and seeing that we seemed to know what we were doing and had the boat under control, closed the lock gates behind us, and within a few minutes we began sinking (but floating, if you see what I mean) as the water started to exit through the underwater paddles in the gates ahead of us.

We dropped almost four metres in the lock, so sailed out of what felt like a brick warehouse with no roof, and on to – literally – a whole new level of sailing. Yes, with locks you actually can boat downhill (and uphill), which is of course their very purpose.

Just around the corner we found the riverside town of Seurre, so we tied up at an empty pontoon, and had a pleasant lunch on deck in the sun, discussing our so-far-successful voyage and feeling tentatively pleased with ourselves.

Originally our plan was to sail just this far on day one, not knowing how things would go, whether we'd be super-stressed, the boat would explode, or whatever, but so easy had the journey been that we consulted the canal guide book, written in English, French and German (get this… in German it's called a *Kanalführer*) and decided to push onto Verdun sur-le-Doubs, a further twenty kilometres downstream.

This meant tackling one more lock, at Ecuelles, which at just over three metres' drop was no more challenging than Seurre, and once again our radio call over the VHF channel was received and understood.

Verdun-sur-le-Doubs is a small port town just slightly off the Saône on the river Le Doubs which winds its way from almost the Swiss border, though it's not navigable any further upstream than the village of Navilly. That didn't pose an issue for us as we merely wanted to stay at Verdun's port for the night. We arrived just after five, to find the small pontoon almost full, but we backed in next to a Swiss boat that had probably hoped we wouldn't. In turn we hoped nobody would moor in the space next to us, but an hour later a huge hire boat did just that, followed by another which did the same to them, taking the last available mooring space. We were glad we'd arrived when we did, and sat smugly on the fore deck celebrating the end of the real Day One with Champagne. (We do a lot of this celebration thing so you'll just have to get used to it.)

Having covered just over fifty kilometres without any problems we decided to do about the same distance the next day. Given that even this late in the season the mooring was full we wondered if it would be a sort of *Le Mans* start in the morning.

After dinner we took a stroll through the small town and across the river to look back at where we were moored. In the twilight the town, with its 17th century hospital and other lovely old stone buildings looked charming. Slowly, lights came on in the windows, and on the boats on the pontoon, creating a picture-postcard perfect image. It was the sort of experience we had come here for, and we felt well-pleased to have started the voyage at last.

Walking back to the boat we took a look at one of the riverside buildings, on which there was a gauge showing how high the river had risen in the past. It was alarming to see that on one occasion the water level rose actually up to and maybe even over the bridge we were standing on, something we hoped we wouldn't ever have to encounter while on *Liberty*.

CHAPTER TWELVE

We woke to thick fog, so no *Le Mans* start to the morning for the line-up of *bateaux*, but within half an hour 'El Spaniard' (as we'd nicknamed him, due to his flag) had brazenly cast off and disappeared into the mist, like a phantom. We presumed he knew what he was doing, or maybe that he had a deadline that nothing could wait for. Or, perhaps as a matador who'd faced raging bulls for a living, he wasn't scared of anything. *El fog? Pffft!*

The rest of us swabbed decks, cleaned windows, had a leisurely breakfast or went to the *supermarché*, and generally killed time waiting for the *broulliard* to lift. Which it did just after 10am, and then we were on our way.

As we untied the ropes the Swiss next to us on *Rosi* asked, 'Which way are you heading, upstream or downstream?'

We were honest of course and told them we were aiming for Chalon-sur-Saône, down-river, but maybe we should have kept that information to ourselves, as you'll see.

The crew on the hire boat on our port side didn't seem to be in any hurry to depart, but we presumed this late in the season they were probably going back to the hire depot at Saint-Jean-de-Losne, and so were likely on the last day of their holiday cruise.

So, there we were back on the River Saône with a repeat of the previous day; the wide river, not much discernible current, very little or even no wind. The sky retained some of the fog for most of the morning but it was mild enough and visibility was fine at river level so we made good progress and approached pretty Chalon-sur-Saône in sunshine about 1pm.

For the previous hour the Swiss had been slowly but steadily gaining on us from behind, but just before the bridge at Chalon they made a dash for it, overtook and swung left in front of us and into the marina, where we were headed for lunch. Now we knew why they'd been so keen to know which way we'd be going; they were worried we might get the last available mooring!

We trailed them in, only to find them stopped dead in the water at the marina entrance having a gesticulatory conversation on their flybridge about what to do next. Just ahead on their starboard bow we could see the visitor mooring, with enough space for both them and us, so we were mystified as to what they were doing.

In the end they selected a vacant mooring in the marina proper and headed for that, so we figured they planned to stay the night, which was fine by us, as we were able to take the visitors' mooring for ourselves, leaving just enough room behind for another smallish boat.

And sure enough a smaller boat did arrive, within ten minutes, another of the flotilla we'd shared the pontoon with at Verdun the previous night.

Without bow or stern thrusters the elderly Englishman at the helm had some difficulty parking, swinging wildly side-on to the end of the pontoon, but along with one of the marina staff we managed to rope him in, for which he was very grateful. His wife seemed somewhat embarrassed, but we shrugged it off, no big deal. It could happen to anybody, though it made us doubly thankful we had thrusters on *Liberty*.

We shared lunch with a family of swans in the marina, and then set off again. It seems a bit churlish to say that the rest of the day was 'routine,' but truth is it started to feel that way. The weather continued calm and warm, it was bright and became sunnier the further south we went, but the wide river meandered through pretty much the same sort of countryside as the previous day: rural, with trees on the banks, crops of corn and sunflowers, herds of cows and flocks of sheep grazing. (Now you're saying, yeah, but at least you're not having to go to endless boring meetings. And you're right, so I will shut up.)

You might also be wondering why we weren't going into the towns and villages to explore the old churches, discover local treasures, or immerse ourselves in the history. It's not that we weren't interested, but at the time we felt the need to keep going south before winter set in, and anyway, due to the geography of the rivers and canals, we would have to come back this way if we wanted to explore the north, so we decided we could save our investigations for the return journey next summer.

We pressed on, managed another lock at Ormes, the only one of the day, and pulled in at Tournus, mooring on the town's riverside *quai*. Just downstream of us we could see a massive hotel boat, the *Excellence Rhône*. Two-storeys high and 110-metres in length, almost as long as a rugby field, she could accommodate 142 guests in luxury. Unlike ocean-going cruise ships, the river hotel boats look curiously squashed, with flat tops designed specifically to go under bridges. Without funnels or masts they look more like floating shoe boxes.

In the evening we strolled into town (a very short walk since we were moored right beside it) and checked out the location of the town square as next day was market day (another useful piece of information from the *guide fluviale*).

Our walk took in some pretty back alleys with flowers blooming prettily in window boxes, and we stocked up on some supplies at a small supermarket. Tournus seemed a very pleasant place, and we looked forward to mingling with the locals the following day.

As we got back to the boat the *Excellence Rhône* pulled slowly and magnificently away from the quayside and then gunned her engines, throwing up a froth of foam at her stern. She quickly picked up speed and in no time was hurtling up the Saône, streaking past us. On board we could see guests in the dining room sitting down under twinkling lights to white linen tablecloths and silverware, waiters already pouring drinks. It looked cosy, romantic, and for a brief moment I think we were envious. Which of course is silly, as we had our own boat that was also cosy, with a dining room, and its own very efficient wine waiter (me).

We also had twinkling lights, but for the first time since leaving Saint-Jean-de-Losne we were on our own battery power. The previous night at Verdun-sur-le-Doubs we'd plugged into shore power, but now we were independent since there were no electrical outlets on the quayside. We had no idea how long our batteries would last, so erred on the side of caution with Liz reading by just one light and me reading a book on my iPad.

As we were to later discover, *Liberty*'s battery banks had plenty of juice and we would in fact be able to go a full seven days without needing shore power, so our early caution, while sensible at the time, was a bit over the top.

The following morning we strolled back into town expecting to find a small market in the town square, only to discover it actually took up a whole street *plus* the square, offering everything from socks to *saucissons*.

It was, as we'd hoped, colourful, with lovely displays of fruit and vegetables, cheeses, meats, fish, and multiple clothing stalls. The locals thronged, many greeting each other mid-street and stopping for in-depth chats. We eavesdropped and tried to recognise as much French as we could. We snapped photos and bought fresh salmon fillets for that night's dinner.

However, if you think quaint morning markets mean cheap prices, think again. There might be the odd bargain, but it probably *would* be odd; as we discovered, the prices are generally mainstream, and when you see the extent of some of the stalls you can perhaps understand why; some of the butchers' and fishmongers' stalls involved fully-refrigerated display cabinets, almost as though they'd moved their shops into the street.

And here's a tip for those who do want to question the prices: don't ask the stallholder if they have 'something cheaper.' In France, that's not how it's done. The French way is to ask if there is something 'less dear,' *moins cher*.

It's fascinating that an entire nation can base its language, if not its economy, on the premise that everything to begin with is expensive, but some things are 'less dear.'

What if we applied that approach in English, but perhaps in a wider sense, say to emotions: How are you today? Not bad thanks, I'm less grumpy than I was yesterday.

Or kindness: Thanks for the gift, it was so less mean of you.

Or romance. You're in a restaurant – something less expensive perhaps – and stare into his eyes over the flickering candle and whisper, 'I find you hardly disgusting at all.'

If I were to use this as material for stand-up comedy I'd be on a winner. Thank you, you've been a less than appalling audience. Goodnight.

But back to reality. The salmon we bought was fixed-price so no chance of asking for anything *moins cher* in that department. In fact, unlike many other market places around the world, the local French produce markets are generally not places for haggling; you pays your money and you takes your choice.

We continued south on the Saône, stopping at a large and well-equipped marina at Macon for lunch and refuelling. On board we had twin fuel tanks, holding a total of around 600 litres, a decent amount given that most of the time the boat's engine was hardly exceeding 1200 rpm. But although the fuel gauge showed plenty, we thought it prudent to top up while we could, having been warned that waterside fuelling opportunities were few and far between.

It was all very straightforward, the pump even accepting our credit card without question, and so after lunch we cruised out of the marina with full tummies and nearly full tanks.

That night we moored riverside at a small town called Montmerle-sur-Saône, squeezing in to the last available space on the *quai*, ahead of a nice burgundy and cream Dutch barge called *Alicia*, crewed by Phil and Bagusha, from Australia.

We invited them aboard for drinks that evening, our first *en voyage* boating guests, and swapped stories. This sort of thing, we were to discover, is one of the highlights of boating, for two reasons: one is that you get to drill into the wisdom of people who've been boating longer than you have and who might have already been where you're heading, and the other is they have stories of their adventures that help put your own ignorance and mistakes into perspective. Basically, no matter how embarrassing or gut-wrenching your own situation, someone has already 'been there and done that' before. It makes you feel better.

During the evening Liz dropped mention that I'd done stand-up comedy, and of course P&B wanted to hear some. I resisted, because no comedian likes being asked to tell a joke, especially when 'off-duty,' and anyway, I hadn't done any comedy for a year or more.

'Go on,' Liz insisted, 'Do your Billy Connolly!' 'Yes! Let's hear Billy,' Phil and Bagusha insisted. So I gave them a wee taste, y'know? They seemed appreciative and I got a round of applause.

Next morning we waved goodbye to the Aussies as they were headed to Saint-Jean-de-Losne where *Alicia* would be moored for the winter while they returned to Australia. We wished them well and hoped we'd maybe see them again the following year when they returned.

The jaunt to Trevoux was the first we'd done in rain, but it didn't make too much difference. The canvas Bimini top gave good protection, and visibility remained clear, plus it was still warm so we weren't disadvantaged.

At Trevoux we were the only boat on the mooring which was operated by the adjacent campground. The campsite operator told us it was the last day of their season, another reminder that we'd left it very late to begin our adventure.

We used the camp's washing machine (one of the few luxuries we didn't have aboard *Liberty*) but it was an antiquated piece of junk that swallowed our coins and spat out wet and not very clean clothes. Perhaps because it was the last day of business the woman in the camp office was wholly unconcerned, and unhelpful. We made a note to not stop there on the return journey, even if it was full summer and they had plenty of moorings.

Our last day on the Saône saw us go through another big lock, this one at Couzon, but this time we were in the company of two large commercial barges and another boat like ours, a *bateau plaisance*. All the other locks we'd come through we'd had to ourselves, so this was a novel but nerve-wracking experience. We knew that lock etiquette dictated that commercial traffic always has priority, and we were quite happy to let the two giants go in first.

It looked to us that the lock would be completely filled by the two *peniches*, but in fact there was plenty of room for us and the other boat, and in the end it was no more challenging than any of the other locks we'd tackled, just a bit slower going in and out due to the big boats.

Liz and I were starting to feel like we'd got the hang of the locks now, though much *much* bigger ones lay ahead, one of which was a known killer.

CHAPTER THIRTEEN

And so we arrived in Lyon, the third largest of France's main cities, and the southernmost port on the Saône. Just a wee bit further on from the marina entrance the river flows under a couple of large bridges and sweeps into the Rhône, so in reality we'd completed the first part of the voyage and successfully survived the Saône. Or, to paraphrase Kiwi mountaineering icon Sir Edmund Hillary, we'd 'knocked the bastard off.'

Fortune was with us when we arrived. We cruised tentatively into the Confluence Marina, not knowing what to expect other than having heard that the facility was quite new and part of a former industrial area of southern Lyon that had recently been transformed with an enormous shopping centre, trendy new architecturally-fascinating apartments, plus the requisite cafés, bars and restaurants, and of course the marina itself.

As we dithered about where to tie up, one of the *capitainerie* staff shouted and waved to us, pointing to one of the many available spaces on the pontoons. We slid in and he helped us moor. We asked him how much it was for a night. 'It is €13, but this is the last day of the season. Tomorrow the *capitainerie* and marina are closed, but there will be power and water available for free for the next ten days or so, so you can stay as long as you want!'

Feeling exuberant that we'd timed this arrival just right we decided to stay for a few days, unlike the Romans, who in 43BC decided to linger here for a few hundred years, establishing the town of Lugdunum on the hillside west of the Saône.

They must have loved it here because they built a substantial settlement, which became the most important centre this side of Rome itself for a while, and was the headquarters of Roman Gaul and Germany.

As we know from the remains of amphitheatres all over the former Roman Empire, the Romans loved their entertainment, whether throwing Christians to lions or watching more cultural performances, and we found some fantastic evidence of that in Lyon, on the Fourvière hill across the river.

We walked round the Fourvière theatre ruins, agog at the mosaic floor of the orchestra pit. Liz isn't as keen on Roman antiquities as I am as she lived in Italy and France for a while as a child, so she has seen her fair share of amphitheatres, villas, columns and statues. But for me, one of the things I'd missed living in New Zealand was the incredibly rich history of Europe, and the Romans in particular, being able to walk on Roman roads, touch the stonework of their temples, and marvel at their mosaics.

New Zealand is a relatively young country in terms of settlement; even the Māori reputedly arrived there from Polynesia only about a thousand years ago, and European settlement dates back less than two hundred years. Māori constructed their buildings and villages using wood and flax, and while they undoubtedly displayed a flair for clever design and beautiful carvings, there is precious little evidence of their early history. They also didn't have the written word, so the stories of their arrival in the big tribal canoes from Hawaiki have had to be passed down orally through the generations.

The Romans on the other hand engineered their way across Europe in all directions, building roads, bridges, aqueducts, statues, towns and cities, mostly out of permanent materials, and recording their conquests and triumphs in writing and art.

It never ceases to amaze me how advanced the Romans were, seemingly excelling at everything. (Christians and slaves might argue that last point.)

So here we were, walking around the orchestra pit and stage areas of the Fourvière theatre, which could seat around 11,000 in its heyday, and even what's left accommodates up to 4500 people when used for open-air performances today.

The mosaic tile floor of the orchestra area is a geometric feast of inlaid marble pieces that were brought from all over the empire, including Greece and Turkey. That it is exposed to the elements and we are still allowed to walk on such art is remarkable, but to think that toga-wearing theatre goers and performers shared the same stage over 2000 years ago is, well, nothing short of dramatic.

I wanted to stand centre stage, face the tiered rows and in a deep voice proclaim, '*Quam diligenter laboramus!*' ('How diligently we work' – the motto from the front of my school Latin book) but I didn't think the French school kids on their educational visit would have been impressed.

(I was also very tempted to shout 'Release Roger!' in homage to *Monty Python*, but thought better of that too.)

Over the next few days we explored different parts of Lyon on the new bikes, hauling them off the fore deck and pedalling our way through the city's streets, over tramlines, jiggling along cobbled alleys, and weaving through shoppers in the pedestrian areas. It was fun. Neither of us had ridden bikes for years – I gave up cycling when I discovered motorbikes at the age of 15, and although Liz could be seen hurtling through Oxford on two wheels in the 80s, she'd given up cycling when she moved to Wellington and was confronted with its hills – but Lyon (and France in general we were to discover) is particularly cycle-friendly. The bus lanes in Lyon, for example, can be used by cyclists, which is brilliant, and even when you're being followed by a bus and feeling guilty about holding it up, there doesn't seem to be any impatience on the part of the drivers.

As well, cyclists are usually allowed to go the wrong way down one-way streets, and many of the roads have dedicated cycle lanes. And, unlike New Zealand, cycle helmets aren't a legal requirement, though some would argue very necessary, especially in city traffic.

We really liked Lyon, and would cycle through it just for fun, with no particular destination. A couple of times our meanderings took us under some large railway bridges, beneath which were parked a number of white vans. These, we had been told, were basically mobile brothels, the ladies conducting their business in the back of the vehicles.

There was no telling whether business was booming but judging by the sheer number of vehicles there must have been a reasonable market to cater for. We looked in vain for stickers on the vans warning, *Si il est à bascule, ne vous embêtez pas frapper* (If it's rocking don't bother knocking).

On the other hand, if we ever wanted to sell Van Rouge we knew where to come.

Of more interest to us were those buildings in downtown Lyon that featured *tromp l'oeil* artwork. This technique (which literally means 'deceive the eye') dates back at least to Greek and Roman times, and is based on creating the illusion that something exists where it doesn't.

So, there we were on a street in Lyon gazing up at a seven-storey building, the side of which, known as *La Fresque des Lyonnai*, features a massive mural depicting multiple windows, some with 'wrought iron' balconies. At many of the windows and on each balcony there are men, women and children, all dressed in period costume and in different poses. They represent thirty famous figures of Lyon, including pioneers of filmmaking the Lumière brothers, aviator Antoine de Saint-Exupéry, and even the Emperor Claudiu, who was born in Lugdunum.

Down at street level we saw a number of 'shops', and a restaurant called *Le Pot Beaujolais*, at the door of which Lyonnais chef Paul Bocuse stands waiting to welcome his diners.

There are about sixty such murals around Lyon, the genesis of which can be traced back to a core of art students who, in the 1970s, decided that art needed to be more accessible to the local population, and that many of the city's large blank walls provided perfect canvases.

Today the artwork adds an extra dimension to exploring the city, and provided a perfect 'artinerary' for us as we pedalled our way around.

We went back to the Fourvière hill a second time to visit the Musées Gallo-Romains, an absolutely fantastic collection of frescoes, statues, carvings, mosaics… all the sort of Roman stuff that makes me drool. Liz, bless her, endured a whole morning of wandering around the various galleries, spending a lot of time sitting on benches waiting for me to finish gazing at the displays and wiping my drool off the mosaic tile floors.

For all the amazing statuary and frescoes though, the one thing that I loved more than anything else in the museum was a tiny carved silver figure probably no more than five centimetres high. It depicted one of the Roman gods, and was superb in its detail.

I think what I liked about it so much was that it would have been a very personal item, something carried around in a purse, maybe touched for good fortune occasionally by its owner, rather than being a major public work set in a square or other communal area.

Meanwhile, our berth at the marina proved superb, and we made full use of the adjacent Confluence shopping centre with its supermarket and free Wi-Fi. We were already realising that to be in the proximity of Wi-Fi while on board the boat was a thing of luxury; more often than not we had to go in search of it, though frequently found a service available at tourism offices and local bars and cafés. It turned out too that the French McDonalds outlets all have free unlimited Wi-Fi, though we usually restricted ourselves to having a coffee rather than burgers and fries. Otherwise Wi-Fi could become one of those contributors to obesity, and we'd have to do a lot more cycling to counter the calories.

Anyway, the marina was very pleasant, and despite being the end of the season there were other boats coming and going while we were there, which is how we got markled.

We'd woken up to grey skies and a cooler temperature, a bit of a breeze, and looked out the stateroom windows to see men tying striped tape all around the shopping centre, beside the ends of the bridge, and all along the other side of the marina. We'd heard shouting in the night and wondered if there had been a murder, and whether we were being contained inside the Crime Scene. Inspector Clouseau could turn up at any moment, wanting to see our 'lassonce.' Lassonce? 'Oui monsieur, the lassonce for your boot.'

However, far from being interrogated as to our whereabouts the previous night by *les flics*, it turned out the marina was part of a Lyon marathon route, and sure enough, around 10.30 that morning three Ethiopians loped across the bridge to scattered applause from onlookers. About ten minutes later another of their countrymen crossed also, and about an hour later so did everyone else, in their hundreds.

We ducked the tape and went to the supermarket for some pre-departure supplies (to no applause at all) presuming that by now the Ethiopians were all back home, feet up and watching the rest of the race on the telly.

Arriving back at the boat with our shopping bags we made sure to quietly sneak on board so that we wouldn't attract the attention of Cockney Michael (pronounced 'Markle,' as in: 'My name is Markle Caine') because if he spotted us he'd undoubtedly emerge from his boat for a conversation marathon of his own.

Markle had arrived a couple of days earlier in a lovely old launch with beautiful lines, but with a faded elegance and very smoky exhausts. His engine noise had hardly died away before he immediately began to tell us his life story, but luckily we were about to head out on the bikes. No really, we were.

Every other boat that arrived from there on, Markle was on hand to meet and greet, and talk, and talk. You know the sort, well-meaning but incessant. 'D'you know, last time I was 'ere this was all a building site,' he'd say. And, 'What you want to do is this, innit?' and, 'Just the uvver day I was…' and so on. And on. And on.

We decided that to be trapped by someone who wants to tell you their life story is to be 'markled'. We fully expected to be markled again further into the voyage, but we weren't going to let that put us off.

In the meantime we enjoyed our last couple of days in Lyon and continued exploring. To the south of the marina, where the land tapers off at the meeting of the Rhône and Saône, there was more ongoing development of the old industrial area, with some fantastic architecture. Buildings of bright green and orange indented with huge holes bordered the Saône River, and at the southernmost point a huge construction was going up that looked like a spaceship from a *Star Wars* movie. Even our marina's *capitainerie* was a symphony in timber strips, an illusory shape-shifter of a building that fitted in perfectly with the avant-garde nature of the neighbourhood architecture.

On a more romantic note we discovered that the bridge across the marina had attracted the attention of lovers, who – presumably inspired by Paris's bridge of romance the Pont des Arts – had taken to demonstrating their affection by attaching padlocks to the bridge's railings. This was a symbol (presumably) of undying love, the locks often inscribed with the lovers' initials, with the keys then thrown into the water as a gesture of commitment. Love, sealed with a plop.

Or not, since we also saw that some lovers had used combination locks, possibly hedging their bets that if the relationship hit the rocks one or other of them could at least return and rescue the padlock, which perhaps has more meaning than the trend in Hollywood where celebrities now agree to 'a conscious uncoupling.'

Liz and I briefly considered sealing our own love on the span, but we didn't want to do it with some cheap padlock, and decided instead we'd need to find something more robust.

'I reckon we need something more like a car steering lock,' I said to Liz. 'Yes,' she nodded, 'or a wheel clamp. Something that says to the others, "That's not love. *This* is love!"'

Having come with us this far on the voyage you will already by now have picked up varied references to the other nationalities we've met along the way, so for fear of you thinking that we're in some way xenophobic (we're not) maybe it's time now to address the thorny issue of stereotypes, before we continue the journey and tackle the mighty Rhône.

Germans are gruff, French are impolite, young people are nothing but trouble, Belgians don't have a sense of humour, and the Swiss are very precise. Oh, and French food is always fabulous.

These are clichés and stereotypical statements on which many a comedy sketch or series has been founded; *Monty Python*, *Fawlty Towers*, *Not the Nine O'clock News*, *Armstrong and Miller*, *Little Britain*… they've all got mirthly mileage out of cultural stereotypes, rightly or wrongly. So, with living in France and especially amongst a very international boating community, what had we learned? How did the 'stereotypes' stack up?

Starting with the last on the list, French food, in general, we'd found, left a lot to be desired, (and we left a lot of it as it was undesirable). The belief that it's all high-quality *haute cuisine* is just plain wrong. Our experience up to this point in the journey had been that the dishes were mediocre in general, and in many cases just awful, with very little care taken over preparation or presentation.

Admittedly, we weren't dining in Michelin Star restaurants, but the fare in the average café we'd found to be bland, bland, bland. And overpriced. We'd discovered that a simple toasted sandwich, which had all the culinary excitement of cardboard, could cost around £9 (NZ$18), something we also found hard to swallow.

On the other hand, the French as a people in no way disappointed, especially in their politeness, which was incredible. But that might be because we were trying our best to communicate. We'd read in a travel book that when you go into a *boulangerie* or similar, it is imperative you look the proprietor in the eye and say very clearly, '*Bonjour Madame!*' with enthusiasm (always assuming she is in fact a *she*). This establishes you as trustworthy and genuine, which, we learned, is important to the French. It seemed to work, and we cringed when we saw others (English usually!) avoid or ignore any greeting and just point to something, saying loudly, 'Two please' (because, as we all know, the way to make yourself understood in a foreign language is to shout…).

Between themselves the French are inordinately polite. Men shake hands when meeting, no matter how casual the rendezvous, and sometimes even kiss. The women always greet each other with a kiss on each cheek, maybe three or even four kisses – the custom is different in the north and south. As for ourselves as foreigners, we were treated very courteously by strangers, who might just be out walking their dog, but as they passed they'd say 'Bonjour', and often 'Bonjour, Monsieur-dame.' We started to do the same. Captain G at the marina even once shook my hand, something that made me feel almost local. I must buy a beret, I thought at the time.

And kids? Unbelievably, the French youth also seemed polite. We'd had kids as young as ten walk by the boat and wish us a cheery 'Bon soirée' as we sat on deck having a drink after dinner, or bid us 'Bonjour' as they cycled past on the tow-path in the day.

Germans are gruff. Really? Hard to say from our limited experience at this stage – our research could hardly be called exhaustive – but out of all the cultures we'd met at that point in the boating communities, the Germans at Saint-Jean-de-Losne didn't smile, didn't greet us, and didn't even say danke after we helped with their ropes. Perhaps they'd all had bad days' sailing experiences and were grumpy, but by Lyon they were on notice to disprove their reputation, and we looked forward to our next encounter with them. No really, we did.

Similarly, our experience of the Swiss was also fairly limited, though remember those on board Rosi at Verdun-sur-le-Doubs wanting to know which way we were headed as we departed? And then later swiftly overtaking us at the entrance to the next marina in order to get a mooring ahead of us? Rudeness apart, that showed some planning and precision, something the Swiss are noted for. But hardly enough evidence to support cultural stereotypicality, if there is such a word. (There is now!)

Lastly, Belgians don't have a sense of humour. Well, we haven't gone around seeking any Belgians to tell jokes to, but one evening a yacht crewed by two of Brussels' finest moored behind us in the marina at Lyon. The couple spent the whole evening laughing.

Probably they'd heard us complaining loudly about how hard it was to find a decent pint and a nice a meal of fish and chips.

CHAPTER FOURTEEN

The next Sunday morning we finally left Lyon, quietly and without fuss so as not to get markled again.

We suspected he would collar someone later in the day; 'Unbelievable, but those Kiwis slipped their moorings earlier wivvout even sayin' goodbye. D'you know, the last time I left a marina…'

Markle could even be the reason the Ethiopians had run so quickly over the bridge.

And so off we went, out of the marina and left onto the last tiny stretch of the Saône, headed for the Rhône, our highway to the south. No sooner had we left than a giant hotel boat snuck up behind us, so not wanting to get into an argument with the *Swiss Corona,* we let her overtake, which gave us a chance to slow down and view some of Lyon's newest architectural wonders from the river.

Meanwhile, the hotel boat reached the bridge and slowed to a crawl. We could see why… as it gently crept under the span there was barely half a metre to spare between the top of the boat and the underside of the bridge. In fact we saw passengers on the top deck raise their hands to touch the ironwork.

Had the river been flowing even just a tad higher than it was, the *Swiss Corona* wouldn't have been able to get under the bridge at all. We'd heard stories of hotel boats being marooned between bridges during floods, so it did happen.

Knowing that our next challenge was to be the largest lock we had yet encountered we were in fear, nay dread, that we'd have to share it with the gargantuan floating hotel, but phew, after passing beneath the bridge we saw the *Swiss Corona* turn left up the Rhône, while we turned right, and radioed the *éclusier* at the Pierre-Bénite lock that we were on our way.

After feeling quite smug that our VHF radio French had been well-received and seemed to be working well, we were brought down to earth on the Rhône when it turned out that most of the *éclusiers* wanted far more information from us, such as where we had been, where we were headed, how many people there were on board, what our registration number was, and whether we were wearing matching socks. I did my best to respond, and was very glad to have Liz alongside to interpret the barrage of queries.

Anyway, having told the *éclusier* our life stories, twenty minutes later we were admitted to the lock, and found ourselves to be the only boat. As is typical of many of the Rhône locks, this one had a hydro-electric dam off to the side to generate electricity. In fact, the Rhône has a vital role to play in France's energy, supplying cooling to three giant riverside nuclear power stations (more than seventy percent of France's energy is nuclear), and spinning turbines at nineteen hydro dams along the river.

The Pierre-Bénite lock was huge, with a nine-metre drop to the next level. Apart from being our biggest lock to date, it was also the first we'd encountered with floating bollards, basically meaning that instead of having to unhook and re-hook your ropes on inset bollards as you descend, or play them out, you could just wrap them round the bollard on a large float set into a shaft in the side of the lock wall which then floated down with you as the water level dropped. Clever.

Despite our nervousness being novices with this method, it was easy; no rope adjustments, no fuss, and possibly less chance of damage or danger than with fixed bollards, although we were glad not to have to share the space with any floating giants. We didn't know it then, but some months later we'd suffer some real damage, ironically in one of the smallest of locks.

We thanked the invisible *éclusier* over the VHF and exited the giant bathtub to continue south, the only other bit of excitement being that a large commercial *peniche* called *Bonjon* came steaming upstream creating a wake that tossed *Liberty* around like we were in a washing machine, even though I had turned her to confront the wake face-on. Books fell over, glasses tinkled, stuff rearranged itself down below, and we held on for grim death, but nothing serious happened, despite the impressive pitching and waves.

But if we thought that was an issue, we had worse to come that night.

We arrived at Vienne, an ancient Roman provincial capital that dominates a graceful curve in the river. We turned midstream and came gently to rest at a pontoon just south of the main bridge, with our bows pointing into the current as you're supposed to do.

Being boaters of good character, we moored at the very front of the short pontoon in order that any other craft arriving would have enough room to tie up behind us.

Big mistake, because it meant we were adjacent to one of the pontoon's massive piles, and within half an hour a large hotel boat went by at speed, creating such a wake that it slammed *Liberty* into the pile and tossed us around a lot worse than previously. We leapt on to the pontoon and had to physically hold *Liberty* off to reduce the banging, but the wash from the boat continued, unbelievably strong. *Liberty* rocked and bucked, and we held on, trying to calm it like you would a frightened horse.

We think we know what happened: it's like when you drop a pebble in a pond… the ripples go from where the stone drops in to the edge, then rebound, then – if the pond is small enough

– the ripples cross and rebound again off the sides. That's what we figured happened in this case; the wake kept resonating off both sides of the river, which was bordered by solid stone walls, for a good quarter of an hour, during which we made the decision to move the boat back between the two pontoon piles and damn anyone else who arrived after us. Not good boating etiquette perhaps, but this was our lovely (and expensive) *Liberty* we were rescuing.

And it was just as well, because later in the evening a large commercial *peniche* swept upstream destroying all in its path, and once again we were in an Atlantic storm, but thankfully banging off our fenders rather than the piles. It took the shine off the nice couple of hours we had spent in Vienne at a substantial market and fair after riding in on the bikes late afternoon. In fact, we decided the rocking and rolling was a Magnitude Three on the Wineglass Scale.

Anyway, at least moving the boat back and dominating the pontoon reduced the risk of being markled.

But the rock and roll wasn't over. All the books we'd read about boating in France had mentioned it, and now we knew why; it was a dreadful night.

The drama of the previous evening should have warned us, plus in the *Kanalfuhrer* it clearly says that lock operations generally cease by 9pm, except by 'special arrangement' for commercial traffic. Which meant that at least four large commercial barges had specially arranged to bulldoze their way past at staggered intervals through the night, viciously rocking *Liberty*, with the wake legacy continuing after each passing for up to twenty minutes.

We got no sleep, and every time one of the boats passed we lay in the dark, our eyes wide open, wondering whether we should abandon ship, and whether anything was about to fall over or crash to the floor. The irony that the wash from a boat is called 'a wake' didn't escape us.

In the morning two zombies staggered out on deck, vowing that this would be our last day moored on the river at Vienne, and if possible the last time we would moor anywhere on the river at all. From here on it would be sheltered marinas for us, even if we did have to pay mooring fees.

But the walking dead decided to explore more of old Vienne before leaving, so we hopped on the bikes (becoming the pedalling dead) and headed into town.

Vienne has no shortage of quaintness and Roman antiquities. We watched amused as school students ate their lunches (and smoked their cigarettes) among the 2000-year-old ruins of the Roman theatre, and outside the seemingly complete Temple of Augustus and Livia, oblivious to the monumental majesty surrounding them.

We struggled up the steep hill behind the town to the ancient Chapel du Pipet, to find a fantastic panorama of Vienne below, with the Rhône curving its way through the landscape, a toy *Liberty* bobbing at a model mooring in the distance.

On the way back down we noticed how some Roman demolition material had been re-used to build or repair a wall – a piece of slim ochre brick here and there, and even part of a what looked like a frieze. It seems sacrilegious that old Roman buildings should be looted for their materials but it was apparently a common practice, and the fantastic twin amphitheatres in Lyon actually became a recycling quarry after Roman rule ended.

We left Vienne early afternoon and by 3.30pm were at Condrieu, which offered a sheltered marina, hopefully impervious to the wakes of passing commercial boats. It cost twenty Euros for the night, which included power and Wi-

Fi, but the price seemed a bit steep given that we were out of season and other places were closing up for the year. However, we wanted a good night's sleep, so paid up without argument.

Adjacent to us were Brits Richard and Sophie on their boat *Souvenir*. They kindly helped with our ropes on arrival, and Sophie gave us the benefit of her local knowledge (and Richard his about the local wines), having moored here before. We'd seen them briefly at Lyon but not met them (we were trying to avoid being markled), so it was nice to establish contact with people who knew what was what. Like us, they were living full-time on board, and didn't own a house; *Souvenir* was their home. We felt an instant kinship.

Being Monday the town of Condrieu (like so much of France on Mondays) was largely closed but we did manage to get three loads of washing done in the marina's laundry, though not fully dry, so when we set off the next day it was with the aft deck flying flags of shirts, underwear and socks, proclaiming our nationality as water gypsies rather than Kiwis or Brits.

(As with Wi-Fi access, finding laundrettes – *laveries* – in close proximity to moorings was to become an ongoing challenge of boating in France.)

We headed next for the town of Tournon, where we'd hoped to meet up with Liz's parents, Reg and Kate, the next day. Tournon had, apparently, a choice of good restaurants and was only an hour's drive or so from where they lived, plus they'd told us they'd seen pleasure boats moored there before during a visit, so it sounded like a good destination.

However, after four hours' sailing we discovered the mooring there looked dodgy and too susceptible to wakes, so we phoned *les parents* and pushed on for another hour to a place called La Roche-de-Glun, where we found a delightful though small mooring well off the main river in a placid side arm given over to yachting and other *sports nautique*.

Which also, coincidentally, was where Richard and Sophie had been heading, and here they were. We moored behind them, and they later invited us on board *Souvenir* for drinks. Their dog Barney voiced his approval of our arrival, and from them we learned a lot about what we could expect when we reached the south (though Barney didn't have much to say about winter moorings).

Their experiences gave us much to think about. We now knew for example that we should be heading back north in March, whereas we had assumed it would be later, after the spring snow-melt and the high waters in the rivers had dropped. But Richard advised us to go sooner rather than later. 'Go while the snow is still thick on the hills,' he said, saying that we should find the river more benign. 'We made the mistake of leaving in April, and we didn't get to near Paris until July!'

This sort of advice was invaluable, so apart from being lovely people to meet, Richard and Sophie became unintentional spiritual guides. We had them over to *Liberty* next evening and shared more experiences, limited though ours had been to date.

We walked and explored La Roche-de-Glun for a while. The supermarket was hard to find, and not in the town centre. And why do so many French shops look closed when they are actually open? If you look down many a main village street you'd swear aliens had been and abducted everyone, there is so little sign of life, until as you walk past a seemingly closed building you discover lights on inside and that it's actually a *patisserie*, or a *traiteur*, or the hairdresser's. High street promotion isn't one of their strong points.

And whatever it is it will likely be run by an 'artisan,' which seems to be the French way of establishing superiority over any other similar business. Hence you find *Artisan Boulangerie*, *Patisserie Artisan*… we even saw an *artisan* motor mechanic, who presumably hand-crafted his own oil filters.

At one of the markets we saw a stall where the owner specialised in *'Bierres Artisanale,'* which could either be home brew or some sort of alcohol-based colonic irrigation. We're still not sure (having decided not to risk it).

Next day, with our rearranged rendezvous, Liz's parents Reg and Kate arrived to see *Liberty* for the first time. Unfortunately Reg wasn't well, with a bad dose of bronchitis, which reinforced for Liz one of the reasons we'd moved back to Europe; in times of illness or need we'd be on hand. But they'd decided to come anyway and kindly brought a nice bottle of Champagne which we had on board before going to the only open restaurant in town.

They seemed impressed with *Liberty*, possibly even somewhat relieved that we weren't living in squalor.

At lunch we all had the *formule* (set menu), often the best value way of eating in France. At €14pp for three courses we enjoyed Thai soup, beef *bourgignon*, and – as Liz said afterwards – the best chocolate mousse she'd ever tasted, which was presented in individual jars with lids. I agreed about the mousse, but for me the highlight was the wine, a local Crozes-Hermitage which had a surprisingly dominant nose of Turkish Delight. Lovely, and a wine we vowed to try and find again.

And finally, we'd found properly prepared and presented tasty French food!

Reg and Kate left for their home not too far away and we went back to the boat and a blissfully quiet night away from commercial river traffic. But one thing we had learned from Richard and Sophie was that marina opportunities from here down to the Med would be fewer and further between, so we were going to have to plan carefully if we wanted secure and peaceful moorings over the next couple of weeks.

CHAPTER FIFTEEN

And so we continued our journey down the Rhône to Valence, where we met Monsieur Decibel. Sorry, that should be Monsieur DECIBEL. We arrived at the marina, which we'd read was finest in France, and moored at one of the few available spaces, at the end of Pontoon F.

It was very well sheltered from the river and any passing big boats, but we couldn't really see why it qualified for a five-star write-up. Sure the place certainly looked popular, but it was essentially your run-of-the-mill marina, with pontoons and fingers. On the other hand, Richard and Sophie had been right when they'd said that good stopover options were limited, so we weren't about to turn around and leave again.

We threaded our way up to the *capitainerie* office and broke into our best non-fluent French to announce our humble arrival, only to be shouted at by the office manager – the said *Capitain* – who seemed to have turned the tables on us by deciding that the best way to communicate with foreigners was to SHOUT. He told us, in upper case, where to plug in for shore power, the code for the loos and showers, and then bellowed questions, but we weren't sure what about. After asking for him to speak more slowly – *plus lentement* (and in hindsight we should have also requested more quietly) – it turned out he was enquiring about our length and width. Well, not ours, the boat's.

So, details taken care of we retreated to the peace and quiet of *Liberty*, only to find that the on-shore electricity allocated to us didn't work, but, *dommage*, it was too late as the *capitainerie* had closed for the day. Perhaps the boss had left to shout his friends some drinks.

But *Liberty's* bank of batteries was up to the job, since we'd been running the engine for some hours getting here and everything was fully charged, so we didn't suffer. But next morning we went back to Monsieur Decibel (as we'd taken to calling him) and whispered about *le courant* not working. He looked grumpy, checked paperwork and bellowed at us THAT WE NEEDED TO MOVE OUR *BATEAU* TO ANOTHER PONTOON, where we would be able to PLUG IN TO THE CORRECT POWER. He slapped a two Euro coin on the counter by way of COMPENSATION, but only after Liz had requested it.

So we moved pontoons, and all was good. Up to a point. We decided that our first impressions had been correct and the marina at Valence didn't, for us, live up to its reputation as France's finest, and Liz in particular rued the decision to leave La Roche de Glun so soon. We bickered about it for a short while (it *was* my fault) but also decided that M. Decibel didn't deserve any more of our patronage than necessary and that we would move on soonest.

The highlight of being there was that I was able to take a photo of our boat in the Valence Marina, thereby fulfilling my goal of using the caption for the image: 'The Man Who Shot *Liberty*, Valence.'

Liz said to me, 'Anyone under the age of 48 won't get that.'

'That's what the Internet's for,' I replied. 'They can look it up!'

As we prepared to leave Valence and began untying *Liberty*, an English woman from a nearby boat stopped to ask where we were headed.

'South,' we said. 'Carrying on down the Rhône, then the Canal du Midi. '

'Have you booked into a marina?' asked the terribly English woman.

'No, we're just going to see what happens,' we replied jovially.

'Well! *Bonne chance!*' she said haughtily, turned on her heel and left.

And good riddance to you, you toffee-nosed hag, we replied loudly, in our minds. It was the snooty way she said *bonne chance* that got to us. We hope she's reading this book because, as you will see, we did have good luck.

But, you may argue, she had a valid point didn't she? Why hadn't we booked ahead and saved ourselves the worry of whether we'd find moorings? Simple. At the boat-chat-and-book-swap in Saint-Jean-de-Losne, Polish Mike had told us that most of the marinas down south had stopped taking advance bookings, having too often been let down.

'What some people do is book two or three marinas,' said Mike, 'and then choose which one they like best when they arrive, but they don't cancel the others. So now many *capitaineries* refuse bookings until you show up in person.'

That's why.

Anyway, after topping up the fuel tanks again we left, and after an uneventful three hours or so drifting south came in to the tiny marina at Cruas, which had been recommended by Richard and Sophie, along with a warning that the entrance was tricky.

It certainly was, because not only do you have to do a 180-degree turn midstream to head back into the narrow marina entrance against the current, you also have to finely-tune your arrival between two marker posts to avoid grounding horribly on an old submerged wall.

Ordinarily and on a nice day this perhaps wouldn't have been too challenging, but by the time we arrived a howling southerly was blowing, it was cold, and the current at the narrow entrance was formidable. But with much turning of the wheel and gunning of the engine we made it, and were greeted by Monsieur Didier – the *Capitain* of the Cruas Marina, who not only helped us tie up but was ebullient – in a nice quiet way – in welcoming us to his port. He almost danced for joy as he told us that his boat was also an Aquanaut, the same make as *Liberty*, so there we were voluntarily comparing lengths and beams, instead of him shouting at us wanting to know ours.

Monsieur Didier's marina fees were almost half that of Monsieur Decibel's, the electricity worked, there was no code for the toilets or showers, and we were made to feel very welcome. He explained, *malhereusement*, that most of the town would be closed the next day as it was *Dimanche*, Sunday, but that the *boulangerie* would be open. If there's one shop you can usually rely on to be open it's the bakery, and often there's more than one, with some sort of local arrangement between them on which days they will close so that the town is never without a supply of *baguettes* or *croissants*.

(Later we were to see headlines in a village newspaper proclaiming that the local *boulangerie* proprietors had reached agreement over who would open when during the forthcoming holidays!)

All this made up for the fact that we were moored beneath power pylons, just upstream from the formidable Cruas nuclear power station, and within sight of a quarry and cement factory. But Cruas is far from crass, as we were to discover. It actually has something to shout about.

A small hillside town, Cruas is probably better known for what it provides France today than what it preserves from yesterday.

From the river, the first things you see of the place are the four massive cooling towers of the nuclear power station, each chimney belching steam from the controlled nuclear reactions below. Almost five percent of France's power is generated here, and around forty percent of the power used in the Rhône area.

The plant is situated beside the Rhône to take advantage of the river water for cooling, but in 2009 vegetation blocked an intake and caused what the International Atomic Energy Agency calls an 'incident' – relatively low on the Nuclear Event Scale and nothing remotely like Three-Mile Island or Chernobyl. Still, having lived for decades in nuclear-free New Zealand, we looked upon the cooling towers with a modicum of trepidation, though if nothing else the steam from the towers gave a good indication which way the wind was blowing, so if one of the reactors did suddenly go into meltdown, at least we'd know which direction to run.

Following our harrowing arrival through the narrow marina entrance in strong winds and currents, we were generating enough heat ourselves to power a small town, but after a short cooling-off period we ignored the nuclear plant and the overhead power lines and walked into the town, about a kilometre away.

It's not a big place – Cruas's population is under 3000 – and apart from the nuclear plant providing employment the other big local industry appears to be the hillside cement factory, so at first glance it's not a pretty place either. But that's only until you discover the fabulous medieval village and castle on the hillside above the main town. Suddenly, Cruas has something special to offer, something that looks part Minas Tirith, and part magic kingdom, a little bit *Shrek*.

While the 'modern' town is quaint enough, once you leave the main road and begin to walk up the narrow streets you step back in time over five hundred years, and find yourself striding through ancient alleys, up steps worn down by centuries of feet, gazing through slits of windows designed to protect the houses' inhabitants, and exploring cellars and vaulted rooms that once were home to those who lived under the security of the castle above, and who prayed in the eleventh century abbey below.

The state of the buildings ranges from tumble-down to so well-preserved it looks almost as if the original occupants have just nipped out to milk the goat. Two of the old buildings have been converted into *gîtes*, so if the fancy takes you, you can actually book accommodation in the heart of this medieval marvel.

The castle dominating the hillside above the village would, five hundred years ago, have been the ideal place from which to observe the surrounding countryside, and keep an eye out for enemies, but we wondered why the village was built on a very steep slope. Why didn't they build on the more convenient flat land below, where the main town now resides?

Our guess was that the Rhône in those days was prone to flooding on the flats, and that the hill provided both safety and security. Today there are stopbanks to protect the town from the changing moods of the river, and marauders would be few.

We liked Cruas enough to stay for a while in its quiet little marina, and took endless photos of the medieval town, trying to get the perfect shot, the one that showed the old Cruas and nothing else. It took a while to find an outlook without any modernity in it, but we finally got pictures that at first glance seem to show a complete ancient town in original condition, one that you could use for a backdrop in *Game of Thrones*.

It was nothing to do with the nearby nuclear plant, but we left Cruas with a warm glow.

CHAPTER SIXTEEN

And so we reach that part of the journey, just three weeks into the year's voyage, where we almost lost *Liberty*. It was terrifying, a very close call, and not one we will forget in a long while.

After three days at Cruas – one more than planned while we waited for the wind, the *Mistral*, to stop eroding our enthusiasm – we put in a long day and aimed for a small marina at L'Ardoise, up a backwater off the Rhône, recommended to us by Aussies Phil and Bagusha, the couple we'd met a couple of weeks back. They'd jokingly referred to it as 'Lard Arse,' though in fact *L'ardoise* is French for blackboard, or slate.

It turned out to be not such a quiet backwater, as the marina is just past a commercial wharf where barges unload gravel, and a crane operates all day long lifting the shingle by its grabbing bucket out of barges' holds and dumping it noisily into a hopper, from where it gets ground up into various grades of *pierre*, including, disconcertingly, one grade of gravel called *Pierre Ponce*. The mind boggles.

And just further west of the gravel plant there's another industrial complex that generates a continuous hum, so between the two of them Lard Arse was more Loud Arse. Still, having said that, the gravel works stopped at 4.45pm, and the industrial hum quietened soon after, so it wasn't bad in the evenings.

We unloaded the bikes and cycled off in search of a *supermarché*, which required us to go to Laudun about 25 minutes' ride, but it was sunny and warm, with the added

117

bonus that we rode alongside vineyards of the Cote du Rhône *Villages* appellation. In celebration we bought some of the local wine.

Back at the marina a table had been laid for ten on a side annex off the main pontoon, and soon a swag of Germans gathered there for an evening meal. (Not sure what the collective noun for a group of Germans is; an 'invasion' maybe? A 'stein'?)

Most of the boats in the marina seemed to be there for winter, covered over with tarpaulins and fast asleep, but there were five or six vessels showing signs of life. One of them looked permanent, and the owner had even created a little floating house off the back of his boat for a couple of geese, which appeared to be his main friends. Unkindly, Liz was suspicious. 'I wonder if he's keeping them for his own private *fois gras* supply,' she mused.

There was also a charming little floating *capitainerie,* with a tiny bar and outdoor seating, but as with so many such things at this time of year it was closed. Pity. Still, Madam *Capitaine* – when she came round for our mooring fees (they weren't *that* closed!) – was charming and made us very welcome. (In English. It turned out she spoke at least three languages which made us feel totally incompetent.)

As with Cruas we decided to stay a wee bit longer, Liz was keen not to rush onwards too quickly, and anyway the gravel barge had been emptied and had disappeared. In the nice weather we got a cleaning urge and spent a good part of the day scrubbing and cleaning and polishing the outside of the boat, which you see other boat owners doing constantly, but something we hadn't been doing nearly often enough (i.e. at all).

It was the following day that we almost lost the boat, a very scary experience. We left L'Ardoise reasonably early and got back onto the Rhône, with a shortish day planned to get to Avignon to check out its moorings. The waterway bible suggested they weren't great, being a quayside situation rather than pontoons, and subject to the wash of passing boats, but we wanted to check it out and reach our own conclusions.

Avignon's quay is up an arm called the Old Rhône, which means you turn back up against the current to reach it. As soon as we did it was obvious the current was strong, and our speed dropped from around 14kph to just 6kph. But the weather was fine and there was no wind. Which was just as well or we'd have been saying *au revoir* to *Liberty* a few moments later.

After passing the remains of the charming twelfth century bridge of St Bénézet – which spans hundreds of years but no longer the river – we could see the quay ahead off to starboard with a few boats already tied up, but still plenty of room in front for us.

The river flowed powerfully but I gunned the engine and manipulated the bow- and stern-thrusters to bring us alongside. Liz hopped off and looped the mid-rope around a bollard. Seeing we looked secure I hopped onto the quay and suggested, given the current, that maybe the middle rope would be best moved to the front, which Liz started to do while I began tying the stern rope to a ring. While I was concentrating on that I suddenly heard Liz yell, and looked up in horror to see the front of the boat starting to swing wildly away from the quayside and into the current. A *long* way into the current.

'Do not, do NOT, let go of that rope!' I yelled to Liz as she heaved back on it, trying with all her might to hold *Liberty*'s bows from swinging further into the current. She had wrapped it once round a guardrail on the *quai*, but it wasn't enough, and the rope was slipping through her grip.

'I can't hold on, there's not enough rope,' she screamed back. I pulled harder on the stern rope, but could feel it too dragging through my hands as the rear of the boat wanted to follow the bows out into the river. By now the bows were about five metres out from the *quai* and the stern about three. The current was winning. 'We're losing her!' I shouted. '*Pull!*'

But the bow swung out further. And yet somehow the stern seemed to have paused, almost as though it needed to make up its mind what to do. It was the pivot on which the rest of the boat would at any moment completely swing round, the current taking control and pulling the ropes out of our hands.

For the diners at the riverside restaurant opposite it must have been a tug of awe, but we could see *Liberty* crashing into the other craft moored behind us further along the *quai*, then being swept away down the Rhône to collide with one of the giant hotel boats or a bridge support. She would heel over, the green waters of the river surging through her hatches, and within minutes she'd be gone.

Despite heaving with all my might it had hardly any impact. We were, after all, fighting ten tonnes of steel. There was only one thing left to do. I let the rope go, ran to the edge of the quayside, and leapt...

Liz said later that she was agog at my 'athletic' jump and subsequent heroic scramble up off the swim platform and over the rail, seemingly in one fluid motion. I always like to do my own stunts. I guess that's what adrenalin does for you, because I am no athlete, and it had been many a year since I'd done any sort of serious exercise.

But I somehow managed to jump from the *quai* onto the swim platform on the stern, grab a hand-hold and haul myself up and over onto the flybridge.

I dived for the controls, and with much roaring of bow- and stern-thrusters, and revving of the engine, I got the bow of the boat back into the quayside so that Liz finally had enough rope on her side to tie up properly. 'Do NOT get off the boat!' she shouted, as she could see I wanted to properly tie off the stern rope too. 'STAY there!!'

I meekly did what I was told, and tweaked the thrusters, until we were finally secured, snug against the quayside. Liz tied off the stern, came aboard and we fell into a tight embrace, both of us probably suffering a degree of shock, and close to tears. 'Still, that's more exciting than attending meetings!' I said.

A couple of calming glasses of wine later, sitting on deck, our heart rates had returned almost to normal, but we were still feeling very, very lucky that we hadn't lost *Liberty*. It was a close call.

We talked about what had happened. It was all down to inexperience. We hadn't taken into account the fluvial dynamics, which, when you took a moment to look at the curve of the stone quay were so obvious.

The current had been coming towards us and was sweeping past the apex of the curve and past us, which, had we been snugly butted in against the stone and properly made fast wouldn't have been a problem. But once the bow got caught in it, even just over a metre out, off she went. And there was too much rope between *Liberty* and the quay so the more the bow got carried out the harder it was to pull her back in. If the wind had been blowing it would have been a disaster.

And to think that only the day before I was getting a bit complacent, and as a matter of pride had begun trying not to use the thrusters for mooring.

Never again. It was entirely our own fault. Or, as we came to call it, our Rhône fault.

We decided after lunch that Avignon was not the mooring for us, and we knew we'd be back this way again anyway, so we decided to forego exploring the city and instead continued south in search of somewhere easier to stay. We found it just over an hour later; a *Marie Celeste* of a mooring, at Aramon.

We'd been told about a brand new mooring on the Rhône, so new in fact it wasn't yet shown on any maps or in the navigation guide books.

You'll remember that on the rivers and canals you always know exactly where you are thanks to the PK posts, the *point kilométrique* signs that tell you the exact distance you are from the last major port. In our case this was Lyon, and Richard and Sophie the week before had discovered a new mooring at PK 254.5 called Pont du Gard, adjacent to the town of Aramon, a mooring which they'd described as 'smashing.'

We'd already been smashed at Vienne, but assumed in this case they meant the mooring looked good. It was certainly new, gleamingly new, with room for (by our guess) around 25 boats of our size, or almost double that if they were angle-parked. There were power and water supply points, and the design of the pontoons meant that the outer-most arm would afford some protection from passing boat wash. Smaller boats with less *tirant d'eau* could moor further inside that with even more protection.

And yet, for all its convenience and newness, it was deserted. Not a single boat. It was a real phantom of a pontoon. We couldn't believe it, so chose what looked like a safe spot and tied up. There was no *capitainerie,* and we assumed the electricity wouldn't be on so didn't bother plugging in. We also discovered that the gate at the top of the linkspan to the shore was locked, so it appeared the mooring, though new, had been completed just in time to close for winter. Still, that didn't seem to prevent anyone using it, and we unfolded our chairs and put them right on the end of the pontoon, overlooking the absolutely calm and slowly-drifting Rhône, and watched fish jump and bats flit over our heads in the twilight.

Once again we felt grateful to have survived *Liberty*'s dash for freedom earlier in the day, and looked forward to continuing the journey the next day when we would aim for the old Roman town of Arles. (Except it would turn out to be even less welcoming than Avignon.)

The night passed relatively uneventfully, though during the evening two or three hotel boats went by, and some other traffic during the night, but nothing serious, and nothing to bash the boat around or keep us awake.

Next morning we set off for Arles, where the river guide book indicated we could expect to find pontoon mooring on the river as it flowed through the centre of town. Not so. All we saw were high stone quays – admittedly with mooring rings in them – but placed so high on the walls as to be useless for our little *bateau plaisance*.

It looked like whatever pontoon there was had been taken away, and despite searching we couldn't find anywhere safe or convenient to tie up or even stop for a moment, so we reluctantly performed a mid-river U-turn and retraced our steps back to where the Petit Rhône branched off west and followed that.

Instant change. The boating environment went from wide formidable river to narrow ultra-calm tributary, bordered by overhanging trees on both banks, fingering their way into the water as though intent on grabbing our propeller. There was hardly any discernible flow, the sun was out, and there was no wind. The Petit Rhône also meandered a lot more than its big brother, which made it more interesting. We put one of the chairs up the sharp end and took turns sitting in the peace and quiet of 'business class.'

We made good progress, and reached the Saint-Gilles lock – almost a joke of a lock after some of the giants we'd been in. This one had a drop of only a metre or so – tchah – but we had to share it with two of the dreaded hotel boats, their chairs stacked on the tables in the dining rooms, a sure sign their season was over and they were heading for hibernation.

Still, it all worked out fine. We let them go in first and let them exit first, and anyway, they always went faster than we did so it was sensible to let them have priority. We followed them for a short while and then turned right up the Canal du Rhône à Sète, which – finally after all this time – was our first real *canal*, as opposed to a river.

Which was good because there was a lot less chance of being swept away.

CHAPTER SEVENTEEN

The transformation from river to canal was significant, both in terms of the width of the waterway and the depth; neither allowed any room for complacency. We had gone from the Rhône, which was anything up to fifteen metres deep and what felt like a kilometre wide in some parts, via the narrower Petit Rhône, to this canal which was sometimes only just two metres deep and about twenty metres wide, often less. It also meant travelling more slowly, as the maximum allowable speed is around 8kph (about 5mph). But that wasn't so bad; the point of boating like this should be to go slowly and enjoy the environment, not rush through it at speed.

All in all France has around 5,000 miles of navigable waterways, and while many are rivers there are plenty of canals, so we were very pleased to have finally made it to one.

Apart from anything else, a canal offers far more opportunity to just pull over and stop on a whim, plus there are more official marinas and mooring spots than we saw on the Saône or the Rhône. Also, and this is an important point, breaking down on a canal is far less dangerous. There's relatively no current for a start, so your boat's not going to get swept helplessly downstream. You're likely to be no further from either bank than a few metres, so you should be able to drift to safety, and you can tie up alongside the towpath or bank and then walk or cycle for help.

We hoped of course we wouldn't have to do any of that, but I think we both felt a much greater degree of comfort being on a shallow narrow waterway than a mighty river with a mind of its own.

And so in stately fashion we reached the small town of Saint-Gilles, a town of Tijuana Brass, untold cafés and bars, with an almost Wild West nature, and *gendarmes* who had been to the *Starsky and Hutch* School of Driving.

The waterways guide warned us that Saint-Gilles was 'generally rather drab,' so our expectations weren't high.

They weren't helped either by the canalside environment as we approached the town. Until now, our experience of riverside life had been quite nice really. On the Rhône we'd seen the occasional château, ruined tower or castle, hillside villages in the distance, and of course dedicated fishermen who'd set up their own virtual tent villages on the riverside so they could fish in some comfort. Because of the width of the Rhône these sights were nearly always distant, but on the Canal du Rhône à Sète the waterway is narrow, with the vegetation occasionally claustrophobic as it leans into the sluggish water.

Either side of us as we approached Saint-Gilles were spiky ginger-like plants, perhaps a variety of bamboo, along with trees of course, and the odd broad-leafed plants. With these, plus the murky brown water and the heat, there was a definite Amazon feel to it... not that either of us have ever been there, but you get the picture.

This Amazon environment was enhanced further as we got closer to Saint-Gilles as we saw evidence of what, in South America, would likely be natives eking out a subsistence living from clearings in the jungle. Here in deepest southern France, the clearings turned out to be allotments of sorts, some with lush crops of tomatoes or greens, but most with scrappy sheds, and rudimentary fences made from discarded doors or building offcuts. There was the occasional rubbish fire, the smoke drifting lazily through the leaves.

If a dug-out canoe had left the shore to trade with us we would hardly have been surprised. Personally I expected a poison dart to smack me in the back of the neck at any moment.

And so we scraped into Saint Gilles – literally – as our VHF aerial came in contact with the underside of the town bridge, the lowest we had encountered to date; having been on rivers with high bridges for so long we hadn't thought to check.

The small quayside was seemingly full of boats as we idled by hoping to find a space. Surprisingly for a dead-end canal there was even a Le Boat hire place, with all the fibreglass vessels neatly lined up; some even showed signs of life and we could see a group of new hirers being shown the ropes by the staff. We should have taken a photo of this because hire boat instruction, as we were to learn, is a rare thing.

We had almost started on our way out the other side of town when we finally spotted a gap behind a large private *peniche* – a former commercial barge converted for private use – which the owner was working on. Liz asked if it was okay to moor behind, and he indicated it was, so we tied up.

Saint-Gilles surprised us. Yes, as the guide book said, it was somewhat dull – in fact very down-at-heel – but the almost Wild West element just added to the atmosphere. This was augmented in no small part by a Tijuana brass band we could hear somewhere not far away, playing *Guantanamera*. Dogs roamed – not wild, at least we didn't think so, but seemingly just out on their own – and many of the local men had a swarthy, tanned and slightly Mexican look to them. The streets were dull, the houses in need of repair. On many of them the rendering had fallen away exposing the crude stonework underneath.

In the local market, I wasn't surprised to hear a child call out '*Amigo!*' to someone… it just seemed to fit the scene. Had Clint Eastwood sauntered out of a local saloon (of which there seemed more per square kilometre than Dodge City) nobody would have batted an eyelid; they would just have swapped their cheroots from one side of their mouths to the other, scratched their beards and spat in the dirt. And that's just the women.

And yet, for all the Western film-set qualities, Saint-Gilles wasn't lawless. We were on deck, watching three boys aged between 12 and 14 we guessed, emerge from the canal tow path. Two rode bikes, one carried a single bike wheel. The next minute a dark blue car revved down the quayside and skidded to a stop on the gravel. The doors flung open and two *gendarmes* leapt out and made straight for the boys, yelling loudly at them.

We are still not sure what it was all about, but Messrs St Arsky and 'Utch were determined to get these young felons off the streets. Fierce questioning from *les flics* followed, but equally fierce staunch denial and petulance from the kids was returned, and they showed no fear at all. The *gendarmes* took the bikes and lone wheel, left them leaning against a fence, bundled the suspects into their car, then with much revving of engine and wheel-spinning in the gravel, took them away. They were never seen again. Well, not by us.

By the end of the day the two bikes and wheel had also disappeared, possibly stolen (or re-stolen) by some of the town's other dodgy characters.

But on the other hand, nobody murdered us in our sleep or challenged us to a shoot-out at high noon, so we weren't too disappointed. Until the morning, when half an hour before we were due to leave the Sheriff from the *capitainerie* knocked on our hull demanding €21 for staying. For which we had had no electricity or water supply!

We paid up but felt robbed.

After that we were determined to somehow lower our average per-night spend, and we did.

It was only about twenty kilometres (just over twelve miles) to Beaucaire, our next destination, and these days the end of the line for this particular canal. For quite some years now the lock at Beaucaire that gave access to the Rhône has been closed off due to a *barrage* or weir constructed just beyond it. There's talk of reopening it, but it would be a huge and expensive job, so seems unlikely.

For all that Beaucaire seemed popular as a place to winter over, to visit, and to enjoy, and being at 'the end of the line' doesn't seem to have done it much harm. It seemed from the guide book to offer more than Saint-Gilles, and certainly the journey there started off well.

The canal was pretty enough – helped by sunshine and almost no wind – and for once we didn't have to radio ahead to a lock-keeper because it turned out there wasn't one. The sole *écluse* on the way, Nourriguier, was self-operated, but not in the English get-out-your-windlass-and-wind-up-the-paddles kind of way. No, this was automated, though we didn't realise it at first.

Liz took one of the walkie-talkies and hopped off in sight of the lock to investigate, which we could see was showing a red light, meaning it was busy or full. This would also be the first lock where we would be going uphill rather than down.

It has to be said that while we were quite formal in our VHF communications with the *éclusiers* on the rivers, our own personal radio protocol was a lot more casual.

'Darling Two to Darling One,' I said into my walkie-talkie. 'Receiving? Over.'

'Darling One here,' came back Liz's tinny voice through the handset. 'There is no lock-keeper … the lock-keeper is me!'

It turned out that the small shed beside the lock contained push-buttons which filled or emptied the chamber and automatically changed the traffic light system according to which gates would open. Liz had pushed all the right buttons (as she always does, at least for me) and we could see water churning around the bottom of the gates as the lock emptied in preparation for us.

Eventually the gates slowly swung open, the light changed to green and I sailed in, Liz repeating the process to fill the lock and raise us four metres to the next level.

All very sophisticated, but it's another nail in the coffin for the *éclusiers*, the lock-keepers. This dying breed became extinct in Britain many years ago but manage to cling on in France largely due to the existence of commercial barge traffic; the huge locks we'd encountered to date were no place for amateur self-operation, and because many of the smaller canals are hugely busy in the high season from May to September, lock-keepers continue to be needed to maintain a degree of order and control.

But it was interesting to see on the official French waterway website a call for people to adopt old lock-keepers' houses (that's old houses, not houses of old lock-keepers) which gave us something to think about. Did we want to take over an old *éclusier* residence beside a lock? It certainly sounded romantic, but come summer that same bit of water outside our front door would be full of lager-swilling young people (ugh!) on hire boats (ugh! again), getting their ropes tangled and causing mayhem. Hmmm. Maybe not.

Meanwhile, with the lock finally full and the top gates open we gracefully exited and within three hundred metres decided to stop and greenbank for the night. There was no rush to reach Beaucaire.

Greenbanking is basically tying up for free somewhere appropriate but unofficial. The guide books call it 'nature mooring,' but all it really means is finding a place where there's enough depth to park your boat laterally to the canal bank, enough solid ground to hammer in your mooring stakes, and *voila*! Bob *est ton oncle*: free mooring!

Of course there's no power or water, but *Liberty*'s generous on-board supplies meant we didn't have anything to worry about. We sat on the aft deck (I know you're getting tired of this) with a *vin blanc* and enjoyed the peace and quiet of the countryside surrounding us. I think we slept all the better knowing nobody was going to ask us for €21 the next morning.

It was a bit of a mission extricating ourselves – the stern had settled into the mud during the night – but we did it. It did mean however I had to leave Liz behind as she was on the bank pushing the boat off, so she had to walk along the path for a while, until we came to a spot where she could hop on again. (When I say 'hop' it was more a sort of one-legged dance with much huffing and the odd swear word as she tried to swing herself onto the bow. Very entertaining, for one of us.)

And so on to Beaucaire, in more warm sunshine, with a fox who came trotting onto the towpath full of bravado (until he saw us), herons, a flock of elegant white birds of unknown breed (egrets most likely), and dragonflies that seemed to want to fly in formation alongside us.

Idyllic, or it would have been except that the closer we got to Beaucaire the less attractive the canal became, with one particularly ugly factory to the left as we approached, overgrown trees, weeds and a generally dishevelled appearance that made us think we were about to meet Saint-Gilles's uglier sibling. At the approaches to the town there was even a half-submerged boat off to one side, tilted at a steep angle.

Was it coincidence that Beaucaire rhymed with Take Care?

But things improved considerably as we squeezed under the bridge and into the long marina, which stretched out before us like a nautical parade. Boats lined up both sides, those on the left mainly parallel-parked, those on the right largely on pontoons. We grabbed the first available space we saw, right at the end of the first pontoon we came to, though edging in was a bit tricky in the strong wind.

A local boatie came to help us moor, but the woman on the boat we tied up next to gave us a dirty look from inside her salon. Maybe we had spoiled her view. However, being strangers we didn't know if there was a visitors' pontoon, or where the *capitainerie* might be, or anything at all really. The guy who helped secure *Liberty* didn't seem to speak any English, and didn't seem to be French either. We nodded and smiled our thanks, and he returned to his own boat.

Our *voisin* continued to glare at us from inside her boat as though we had just set up camp in the front garden of her house, which in a metaphorical way I suppose we had.

And so we began an extended stay in Beaucaire, which would become our base for the winter, although we didn't know it at the time.

We found the *capitainerie*, and found Monsieur Didier to be very affable (or, as Liz would add: drop-dead gorgeous). He spoke good English, loved rugby, and told us that the All Blacks were to play in Avignon two weeks later. Given that the ABs had beaten France three times that season already we just smiled politely. He didn't seem to hold that against us, and showed us a mooring he had available closer to the centre of the marina, near the *passerelle*, the footbridge across the marina.

The mooring was also, we noticed, almost directly adjacent to a small bar called Le Nautic, so that could be a bonus. (It was!)

We moved *Liberty* slowly down the marina and tied up on the pontoon Didier had suggested, the aim being to stay for about two weeks before continuing. We didn't see if Grumpy Woman watched us go but we assumed she was delighted with our relocation.

CHAPTER EIGHTEEN

A couple of days later Liz left me. Not in any dramatic sense, just to go back to the UK so she could spend some time with daughter Yasmin who was having her first half-term hols. I accompanied her to Avignon's railway station on the bus, Avignon now being the nearest main centre with a good transport hub, including the TGV straight to Paris and a Eurostar connection from there to London.

After almost losing *Liberty* there we had sailed south to Arles, where we'd had to abandon all hope of mooring, and returned back up the Rhône, west along the Petit Rhône, and then onto the Canal du Rhône à Sète, which took us roughly north again to Beaucaire.

What this did was actually bring us back nearer Avignon, which, it turned out, was very convenient, it being only a half-hour bus ride away. In fact, Beaucaire is almost equidistant from Avignon in the north-east and Nîmes to the west, so it turned out a very useful place to be.

And so we found ourselves back in Avignon, but this time in a much less dramatic fashion.

You'll also no doubt remember the French song *Sur le Pont d'Avignon* perhaps. And if you're like me, that first chorus line is all you'll remember about it. So, let's bridge the gap a bit.

Avignon has three bridges to the west of the city, including the one referred to in the song: Pont Saint-Bénézet. Depending on which scholarly works you go to (e.g. Wikipedia, Google…), Bénézet was a child prodigy who, after a vision from God (who arranged angels to take care of his sheep for the duration) designed and oversaw construction of the bridge from the age of twelve. Or not.

Either way, there's no disputing it dates back to the twelfth century, but, as mentioned, today it spans only the centuries and not the river. That's because the very last bit of it that would have reached the other bank has disappeared, so the bridge falls somewhat short of the other shore. Otherwise the song could have been, '*En travers le Pont d'Avignon*', but syllabically that doesn't work. And yes, there *is* such a word as syllabically.

Anyway, the point is that as a result of the Pont d'Avignon failing to reach its destination, you can only ever be *on* the bridge of Avignon and not *crossing* it. This however doesn't stop the tourism people charging you for the privilege of walking on the bridge to nowhere. So much for Liberty, Equality and Fraternity.

While exploring Avignon after Liz caught the train, I therefore avoided being '*sur le pont*' and instead simply took photos '*du pont*' from the old castle tower high above. Call me a cheapskate, but…

In one variation of the song, there are two lines that go:

> *Les jeunes filles font comme ça*
> *Les jeunes gens font comme ça*
> *(The young girls go like this,*
> *The young people go like this)*

What's lacking is instruction in exactly how they 'go,' but given that you have to pay to access the bridge I have a fairly good idea.

Having said all that, the bridge is attractive to look at, lovely to sail around (as we had the previous week) and – if it really is the work of a twelve-year-old – is an awesome piece of engineering and design, for which sainthood is well-deserved.

So there you have it: the story of the Pont d'Avignon – complete, and unabridged.

Beatification should also be considered for Edgar, the bus company that plies between Beaucaire and Avignon, because this reasonably attractive journey cost just €3 *return*, excellent value for what is an approximately 25 kilometre distance.

And Avignon itself is nice, especially the old walled town part of it. In the northern part of the central city is an extensive pedestrian area – though as with other pedestrian city areas in France this is also full of the more expensive shops. Still, the streets were charming, and pleasant to stroll around without fear of being pummelled by a Peugeot.

Up the top of the hill towards the river, from where I got my shots of St Bénézet's bridge, is a gorgeous public garden, with lake, fountains, waterfalls, statues and walkways. Even better, I found a lakeside café where they sold glasses of wine – and I mean generous glasses nine-tenths full – for just €2.50, the best value in any restaurant, bar or café to date.

On the other hand their Quiche Lorraine was awful, but as we'd discovered, this seemed to be the case with much of the general food in French cafés. At least the good-value wine helped erase the taste of the poor-value food.

And so I spent the next ten days or so on my own in Beaucaire. This was late October, early November, but the weather was as we'd hoped it would be in the south: warm and mainly sunny. Some days it reached 27 degrees Celsius, though on others the pesky *Mistral* wind blew, whipping through the cobbled streets and alleys, chopping the water in the marina, blowing the leaves off the trees, and eroding the spirit of the common man.

Autumn had got progressively delayed as we'd sailed south from Saint-Jean-de-Losne, and in Beaucaire the trees were still quite green, although you could see that leaves had started to drop and that soon the plane trees in particular (of which there were many) would become denuded skeletons.

But at that time it felt to me like I was in an extended summer, and all was good with the world. And then I had a close shave with death.

It's OK (I wrote in our blog): *I am still alive. And so I live to tell the tale, of how a football game almost ended my life.*

It had been at least seven weeks since I'd last had a haircut, and it was driving me mad. Not that I was starting to look like a hippy (chance would be a fine thing), but it was the fluff at the back of my neck that was getting to me more than anything else. It was catching on my collar, itching, and as it rubbed it was a daily and annoying reminder that I was OVERDUE for a haircut.

I had been putting it off, I admit, partly because I'd never had a haircut in a non-English speaking country before, and in France the word for hair – *cheveux* – is dangerously similar to *chevaux*. The last thing I wanted was to walk into a salon and ask for my horses to be cut.

But the itchy and scratchy stuff on my neck got the better of me, and I rehearsed instead that 'I have need of a cut,' figuring that if I am in a barbers it will be fairly obvious that it's my hair in question and not some equine quadruped.

I walked the back streets of Beaucaire remembering that I'd previously seen lots of *coiffures* for *hommes*, and it didn't take me long to find one, a pleasant, spotless and bright wee place on the Rue de Mort. (No, just joking about the street name. Read on…)

I walked in, trying not to look anything remotely to do with horses, and sat down to wait my turn. There was one man in the chair just being finished off, and another beside me waiting. The barber looked not-from-these-parts shall we say, and when he spoke to his customers it wasn't in French. Something possibly North African?

My suspicions were confirmed when I saw that the football game on the wide-screen TV was Morocco versus Ivory Coast. It was well into the second half and the score was Côte d'Ivoire 1, Morocco 1. CIV were demonstrating superior possession, no doubt about it, and within minutes of my arrival they scored again, taking the lead 2-1.

The customer in the chair left and the man on my right climbed in. Little was said. The tension was palpable. The only sound for the next few minutes was the clippers as they scoured the head of the latest customer, in a trendy short, back and sides leaving a tuft on top. That was okay; he was only in his twenties and it looked good, but in my head I was rehearsing, '*J'uste une coupe s'il vous plait, mais pas comme le dernier homme.*' (Just a cut please, but not like the last man. Not sure if my French was correct though.)

When it was my turn to take the chair, Omar (no, I don't know if that was his name, but it'll do for now) raised his very dark eyebrows at me. In my best French I told him – somewhat meekly – that I was from New Zealand and didn't speak French well. Before I could explain how I wanted my horses trimmed he shrugged and said, '*Ce n'est pas grave,*' basically that it was okay, he'd cope.

He did this by ensuring I wouldn't utter a single further word whilst there by tying the smock so tightly round my neck I could hardly breathe. No need to worry about answering questions about where I'd been on my holidays then.

The previous customer didn't leave, instead returning to the waiting seats to watch the remainder of the game, which by now had less than ten minutes to go. Côte d'Ivoire were keeping up the pace and Morocco were making lots of mistakes. As Omar started on me with the clippers one of the CIV players was awarded a yellow card and there was a smugness and sureness in my stylist's strokes. I knew now for sure which side he supported.

His clipper use matched the play on the screen; If Morocco gained possession he would pause, if Ivory Coast looked like scoring he would attack my head with a vengeance. I feared that if CIV continued with the upper hand I would lose all that I possessed on my head, which wasn't much.

Then we were into extra time, with the score still at 2-1 to Ivory Coast. The previous customer was on the edge of his seat. Omar was still matching on-field play with his on-head performance, and then as the minutes ticked away it was time to clean up my neck, for which he brought out a *cut-throat razor.*

The phrase 'dying minutes of the game' occurred to me as I tried to watch the screen while he forcibly pushed my head into my chest and scraped at the fluff on my neck. I could only hope he was paying more attention to me than the telly. The soccer was too much for the previous man, he just got up and left, which worried me as my only witness had now gone.

And then it was all over. The final whistle blew. Disappointed Moroccan faces grimaced in the crowd, a jubilant Côte d'Ivoire was through to the semi-finals, and the last strokes of the razor scraped across my neck in slow disconsolate deliberation.

After I was dusted off I looked in the mirror and reflected on the shortest haircut I have had since I was seven. I didn't mind though; at least there was no foul play.

CHAPTER NINETEEN

Death and taxes; the two inevitabilities. Liz and I were successfully avoiding the latter – simply by not earning anything at the time – and trying our best to steer clear of the former.

Had we still been sailing down the Rhône in the first week that Liz was away back in England we may well have been staring death in the face, as the river was in flood and screaming along. There had obviously been some serious rain up north, and sensible boaties wouldn't venture out in such conditions. Luckily for us Beaucaire, at the end of an arm of the Canal du Rhône à Sète, was well away from the turmoil, so we were well protected.

Liberty was, however, now committed to staying in the south for the next few months, as any thoughts of returning north would have been foolhardy, or impossible. Or impossibly foolhardy.

While Liz was away I took one of our bikes and explored Beaucaire, which doesn't take very long as it's not exactly huge. I read books a lot, which seems to be a common thing with boaties, as many *capitaineries* operate a book exchange. The one in Beaucaire was nicely organised into French, English, Dutch, and 'other' nationalities, and was quite substantial.

And don't think for a moment that the books are all nautically-themed; thrillers, mysteries, sci-fi, travel, all the genres and authors – Stephen King, Lee Child, Marian Keyes, and Nelson de Mille to name but a few – are there, and some books so new they were published only a few months earlier. And free!

So I filled my days exploring and browsing, and finding out more about our new environment.

Beaucaire, as I say, turned out to be quite compact – the population is around 16,000 – but it dates back at least to Roman times when it was sited on the first Roman road to pass through Gaul, the Via Domitia.

The boat basin where we were moored was bordered by bars, cafés, restaurants and shops, as well as the local *Office de Tourisme*, which thankfully offered free Wi-Fi, but only one day at a time. I almost got on first-name terms with the women who worked there as I regularly called in asking for access and password. Why they didn't just allow unfettered acces 24/7 I couldn't fathom, since many other tourism offices did, which meant even if they were closed you could at least stand outside or sit on their steps and log on. But not here. They switched their Wi-Fi off at 5pm.

Perhaps they didn't trust me. Maybe I looked *un peu* shifty, in which case you couldn't blame them as Beaucaire has long been stalked by a shape-shifting dragon, *un Drac*. This legend goes back to around the thirteenth century. The *Drac* was apparently invisible to all, and roamed the Beaucaire markets unseen by human eyes, except for one woman who, with one of her eyes only, had the ability to actually perceive him.

This annoyed the *Drac* hugely and he ripped her eye out, so the story goes. I'd seen in the tourism office a picture of an iron sculpture of the local beast in one of the town's squares, and being a fan of dragons I was determined find it. Or at least keep an eye out for it.

On reading the notices in the *capitainerie* I also discovered that the port of Beaucaire, like Saint-Jean-de-Losne, had its own regular VHF radio broadcasts for those of us boat people who were 'resident' or staying a while.

The first one I listened to was very entertaining as the radio operator was a woman with a broad north of England accent, which sounded totally out of place in French Beaucaire, but very welcome from the point of view that it was at least English and I didn't have to translate. It was also nice to know there were other English people in port.

Sandra, for that was her name, went through the regular routine, which was rather like a vocal village noticeboard and included a call for anyone needing help, medical assistance, parts or services, or wanting a ride anywhere. Likewise, anyone offering a ride was invited to speak up.

There was a weather forecast, local news and information, and, delightfully, 'Treasures of the Bilge,' where anyone with anything to buy, sell, exchange or give away had the opportunity to do so. At the end, each person listening signed off with their name and boat's name.

It was charming, and I decided I must go and seek out Sandra and say hello, since we would be staying here for a couple of weeks or more. (More, as it turned out.)

It wasn't hard to find her boat, which was called *Sally Beth*, since she and partner Jim were parked just a bit further up the same side of the basin as us. And what a gorgeous old boat! Not sleek and lavish, not shiny and new, not even in tip-top condition, but she absolutely oozed charm. If the *Sally Beth* had been for sale in Saint-Jean-de-Losne when we were looking to buy she is exactly the sort of vessel we would have fallen for, peeling white paint and all.

An ex-Thames workboat, *Sally Beth* was made of mahogany, with a curving graceful bow and a gorgeous shape. She was moored on a pontoon to which the access was guarded by a locked gate at the top of the gangway, and by a black dog on the other side of it.

This, I was to learn, was Bella, who was more bark than bite, and was delighted that a visitor had arrived. On deck enjoying a glass of afternoon conviviality was Sandra, along with Jim. I introduced myself from the path and they kindly unlocked the gate and invited me aboard. This was the start of a very pleasant friendship which would extend through the winter.

I learned that they'd been living aboard their boat in Beaucaire for the past four or five years. Both spoke fluent French. Jim had even worked in Beaucaire and was involved in local politics. So, as 'locals' they knew everything there was to know about Beaucaire and its sister town across the Rhône, Tarascon.

The bar Le Nautic, adjacent to which we were moored, Jim informed me was a regular meeting place for ex-pat boaties in particular, as well as being a good place to mingle with the indigenous locals. I promised I'd see them there the following Friday evening.

Before then however, I had another date with death.

Keith and Hilary, who we'd last seen in Saint-Jean-de-Losne where they left before us and headed south, had voyaged along the Canal du Midi and onto the Canal Latéral à la Garonne, where they'd reached a place called Castelsarrasin. Here they decided to moor up for the winter. Since Liz was still in England I decided to take the train over to see them.

Their boat *Picton* was tied up in a nice spot at the end of Castelsarrasin's basin, a short walk from the centre of town, and handily placed for a stroll along the canal, which is what we did.

We walked along the old towpath, which passes the local cemetery. Unlike some of the more gloomy grey churchyards and graveyards in the UK or New Zealand, French graveyards are a lot more colourful. The one at Castelsarrasin looked more like the Chelsea Flower Show than memorials to the departed.

People here don't just bring a meagre bunch of flowers to leave by the graveside once a year; instead they surround the graves with potted plants, planters, and flower boxes, as well as more formal tributes on anniversaries.

From the blaze of colour it was obvious the relatives of the deceased regularly tended the plants, ensuring continuing and flourishing growth. This was no place to find faded blooms in old cellophane; this was more of a living memorial, bursting with colour and contrast, and life.

Keith told me how he had called in to a florist to buy some flowers for Hilary, and was taken by a gorgeous display of chrysanthemums. He asked for a bunch, only to be advised by the shocked florist, '*Mais Monsieur, ces fleurs sont pour les morts!*'

So chrysanths are for the dead, apparently. As too are poppies, and fast approaching was one of the most important days in the French calendar: Armistice Day; the 11th day of the 11th month, when in 1918 at 11 o'clock in the morning, the Armistice was signed between the Western Allies and the Germans, heralding the close of one of the bloodiest – and arguably most pointless – wars in history.

The recognition of those who gave their lives during both World Wars in France is huge. Every town has its war memorial, even the tiniest of villages – perhaps especially the tiniest of villages, since the deaths of locals from such small places would have had a bigger, sadder impact than in the larger populated cities.

The names of the fallen are engraved in stone or marble, and in the hearts of the locals. There are often fresh flowers on the memorials, not just on remembrance days. But every year on the eleventh day of the eleventh month the nation comes to a silent standstill, in recognition of the debt owed to the departed.

For me, seeing the graveyard and knowing Armistice Day was just around the corner was poignant, as four days later I would receive word from New Zealand that my step-father had died.

His role in World War Two had been more administrative than aggressive, firing off memos rather than mortars. I sent flowers for the funeral, numbly selecting a random bunch of spring blooms online (as it was late spring in New Zealand) but maybe I should have specified chrysanthemums.

Meanwhile, in Castelsarrasin it was nice to stay on board someone else's boat for a change, and to be looked after royally by my hosts. *Picton* is very comfortable and even has a wood-burning stove, so its salon has more of a cosy cottage feel to it rather than anything afloat. Keith designed and built it from scratch after purchasing the bare hull a few years previously, and it has all the comforts you could want, including a washing machine (jealous!).

While there, Keith and Hilary, who had their car parked conveniently beside the boat, took me on some drives through the local countryside, which was very pretty despite a few showers. Or maybe because of the showers; I always think raindrops bring greenery alive, especially if the sun comes out immediately afterwards. Scientifically it makes sense: millions and millions of raindrops sticking to and hanging off leaves must create an overall prismatic effect, magnifying and transmitting the green of the chlorophyll, and enhancing the depth of colour. Lovely.

Lovely also was a winery we stopped at where Keith wanted to get some more of a favourite tipple. As you know, the French are famous for their wines, but what surprised me was how relaxed they are with the concept of selling wine in bulk, and I bought five litres of their second cheapest *rosé* (yes, I know, big spender…) for a price that worked out the equivalent of around €1.40 for a 750ml bottle. Of course there were plenty of bottled wines available also, including some medal-winners, but none that I would have called prohibitively priced, and I looked forward to many more winery visits with Liz once she was back.

The three of us stopped at the ancient town of Moissac, also on the canal, where we took a stroll along the town's marina, which was run by an Englishman and – perhaps because of this – seemed to attract a large English boating contingent.

Many of the boats were covered over for winter, their owners away, but we could see some activity on an old *peniche* across the other side of the basin. A man was working on the towpath side of his boat, the back of which was covered with a green tarpaulin hanging down almost to the water.

We thought our eyes were playing tricks at first; was that a string of Christmas lights attached along the bottom of the tarpaulin, twinkling away? No, the line of light was slowly creeping up the tarpaulin.

'Is that on fire?' I asked Keith and Hilary, who peered intensely at the boat. 'Looks like lights,' Hilary said. 'No,' Keith remarked, 'that looks like flames. It is! The tarpaulin's alight!'

Being on the other side of the boat the owner hadn't seen the flames and was going about his business blissfully unaware. 'What's French for 'your boat is on fire?' I asked Keith. 'Dunno,' he replied, scratching his beard.

We began calling to him. '*Monsieur! Monsieur!*' The man turned to look at us as if we were mad. '*Votre bateau, er…*'

'*Regardez!*' Keith shouted, pointing at the tarpaulin. The man lazily made his way across the stern to see what all the fuss was about, leaned over and shouted, '*Shit!*'

So he was English then. He beat at the flames with his hands, then found something better to tackle them with, and within a few seconds had extinguished the small but decorative fire. He looked relieved, as we were.

We couldn't understand how the whole bottom edge of his tarpaulin could have caught alight, especially since it had been hanging over the side of the boat and not anywhere near the engine, or any other heat source that we could see. It was *un mystère*.

I made a mental note to check the condition of our fire extinguishers once I got back to *Liberty*.

CHAPTER TWENTY

Liz returned from the half-term hols in England, having spent some quality time at her sister's house with Yasmin who was finding life at her Yorkshire boarding school very different to what she'd been used to in New Zealand, and that her Kiwi accent was (as we'd predicted) regarded as something of a novelty. She wasn't going to let that get in the way of becoming a world leader though, but that's another story altogether.

Meanwhile it was nice to have my Number One back on board, as we planned to set off again soon and explore further south.

However, one thing I'd learned from my visit to Keith and Hilary is that we would have to revise our plans to continue cruising in the south during winter, as certain sections of the canals would close towards Christmas for maintenance and repair. We'd heard rumours of this before, and although a check of the French waterways website didn't reveal anything definite in the way of closures, Keith's local knowledge was likely more reliable. But we were determined to at least get down towards the Mediterranean before any canal stoppages interrupted our plans.

First however we had to wait for the wind to drop.

For three days we'd been in the teeth of a gale. I quite like it that gales have 'teeth,' wind 'whistles,' and that you can be out in a 'biting' northerly. There is something very human and very oral about wind.

Now it has to be said that a bit of wind doesn't faze us. We'd lived in 'Windy Wellington' for decades, so we both qualified as full-blown citizens of New Zealand's capital city. As such, a measly day or so of 100kph (62mph) breezes is nothing, and hardly worth a mention.

But now that we were living on a boat and happened to be in the South of France we were subject to that freshest and Frenchest of breezes, the *Mistral*. And being on a boat you certainly know when the wind's blowing, whistling and biting because the vessel rocks and sways, creaks and groans, and bounces and rebounds on its ropes. Water slaps the hull, canvas flaps, loose things on deck roll around and the world is in constant motion. It feels like an earthquake, but one that lasts for days. And that's just when we were moored.

And so it had continued, for about three days. It didn't pose a problem; it was just annoying.

On the other hand, one of the unoccupied boats parted company with its mooring one night, and we learned that a posse of boaties had set off to rescue it from wherever it got to further down the canal. Unfortunately we missed all the action, as well as the opportunity to help.

Also on the other hand (I really do need three hands) at least the French give their annoying wind a name. It isn't just 'a northerly,' it is *Le Mistral*, originating (according to Wikipedia) from the Occitan (Provençal) word for 'master.' The online font of knowledge says, 'The wind masters the population, knocking people off balance physically and out of their minds emotionally.'

Knowing the name of the wind doesn't make it any more pleasant, but it's a lot more romantic than merely being labelled by its compass origin. So why then has Windy Wellington not taken the opportunity to personalise its own two demons, its northerly and southerly? You could call one The Master and the other The Mistress, though it's not as if there's a shortage of other more personal historical options. 'Crikey, that's some Muldoon we had yesterday eh?!' is more entertaining than, 'How'd you get on in the northerly?' Or, 'Jeepers, that Lomu fair lifted the trampoline over the hedge this morning!'

Or choose from any other of the famous Kiwi names and you could find yourself sheltering from a Meads, a Snell, a Hillary or a Clark. (Although, naming a wind after a politician has its issues. What if you found yourself in the teeth of a Clark that forced you to lean to the right? A meteorological-political dilemma.)

In the UK, if you're looking for a name to epitomise extreme damage caused by winds of unimaginable force, so strong as to perhaps be true winds of change, the sort that uproot three-hundred year-old oak trees, lift slate roofing tiles, bring down power lines and flatten the ambitions of the common man, then you are battening down for a Thatcher. A Thatcher wouldn't just blow; it would *handbag*.

In the meantime we tightened our ropes, battened down our hatches, shook our fists at the *Mistral*, shouted defiantly, '*Vive la résistance!*' and waited patiently for it to pass.

There's a lot about canal boating in France that's photogenic. The canals themselves for one thing, especially those such as the Canal du Midi lined with trees, planted in the 19th century in a forward-thinking move to reduce evaporation and erosion.

Then there are the boats themselves, many of them dating back a hundred years or more, with gorgeous lines, curves, carvings and colours.

Add to these the play of light on water, the horizontal beams of sun at dusk or dawn, the egrets, herons and kingfishers, and you have the makings of a *National Geographic* cover almost daily.

We had one such photo-call day too, as we finally managed to extricate ourselves from Beaucaire after our three-week stay.

And I do mean 'extricate,' because it actually wasn't easy to leave, but not just because we'd bonded with the place. We started the engine and cast off, but got only about a hundred metres before we lost power to the propeller.

This turned out to be a good news-bad news scenario; the bad news was that our propeller shaft had parted company with the gearbox. The good news was it happened almost right outside a boatyard or *chantier*, into which we were waved by Monsieur Gerard the proprietor. I say 'waved,' but in fact hauled was more appropriate since we had no propulsion to actually move, but after throwing some ropes and explaining in our best French that the boat wasn't working because the (gestures of a propeller spinning and stopping here) we were rafted up three boats out into the canal, safe and sound. And stopped.

A quick inspection revealed the issue – the nuts holding the propeller flange to the gearbox flange had undone themselves and fallen off with the result that the prop shaft had slipped clear and backwards. *'Pas problème!'* muttered Gerard, and promptly disappeared for three days.

This wasn't unexpected, since we had broken down mid-Friday afternoon, the *chantier* was closed for the weekend, and Monday was Armistice Day, so we knew nothing was going to happen until Tuesday at the earliest.

In fact it was Wednesday mid-morning before anyone came and fixed us, but we didn't mind since we had no rush to be anywhere, and anyway with the *Mistral* still gusting we were quite happy to stay where we were for a while. I did try and see if I could waggle the prop shaft back up to the gearbox flange myself but I couldn't shift it, and anyway I didn't want to exacerbate the problem.

As it happened, even the guy who M. Gerard had appointed to tackle the problem spent almost an hour trying to get it mended until finally the proprietor himself had to come and show him how to do it.

I observed the whole process closely, in case we ever faced the issue again, and in the end it really was only a matter of undoing some Allen bolts to dismantle the flange, replacing the missing nuts and applying Loctite, and tightening everything up again. And for some reason the mechanic was easily able to move the prop shaft back into position, grrr.

With the work done and dusted the mechanic disappeared. Liz and I had a quick lunch and decided we should be on our way, but first we needed to pay the bill. We were now very familiar with the French lunchtime, where everything closes between 12 noon and 2pm, but come 2.30pm the boatyard was still deserted and locked up, so we left a note taped to the door to say we would be back soon and would settle up then.

We'd told Didier at the *capitainerie* that we planned to sail south for a few days and had asked if there would perhaps be a space for us when we returned. He assured us with a charming smile that there would be, that in any case he 'would find us one,' and we were not to worry. This was nice, and something of a relief since we could see that his marina was pretty full.

We later learned that many *capitaineries* will only accept you to stay if you have the 'right fit' for their marina. It may sound odd, even discriminatory, but we think it's based on their experiences. Whatever, we were pleased to qualify.

So, bill unpaid we decided to continue the journey south, and set off by 3pm on a sunny photogenic ISO 100 f11 kind of day.

The aim for the following three weeks or so was to explore further south down to places such as the alarmingly-named yet apparently very picturesque Aigues-Mortes, as well as Frontignan, Sète, and maybe Marseillan (not to be confused with its bigger sister Marseille further east).

Then around the first week of December we would return to Beaucaire for the remainder of the winter, but spend three weeks or so in the UK for the festive season and New Year. Keith and Hilary had very kindly invited us to their lovely home in Malvern for Christmas.

But we wanted to sail as long as practicable, and after leaving Beaucaire decided to just do a very short stretch back along the Canal du Rhône à Sète in the direction of wild west Saint-Gilles.

In warm sunshine and a relatively gentle breeze we tootled along to the automated lock at the unpronounceable Nourriguier, moored up in advance of it and Liz took a stroll to see if it was still operational. Darling One radioed back that it was. We tied *Liberty* up to the bank and walked on downstream to check the mooring beyond as a potential overnight stopover point, only to find a photographer with tripod at work. I've already mentioned how photogenic the canals can be, but this wasn't sufficient, as this photographer was focusing on a woman lying on the jetty in the sunlight.

Liz pulled me to a halt when she realised the 'model' seemed to be wearing only a towel, and – concerned for my delicate disposition in such matters – suggested we shouldn't investigate any closer. Reluctantly I agreed, and was dragged kicking and screaming back to the boat. I mean, I like art and photography! Nothing could have embarrassed me.

On the way back we discussed whether the photographer might have been shooting a series of canal-themed photos. 'Maybe he uses the same young lady in each shot,' I suggested. 'Or possibly it's a, "I need to try out my new camera" thing.'

'Yeah right,' Liz said cynically.

I pondered further. 'Or he could be shooting a series of twelve such poses on different canals, with a different model in varying state of undress in each location, and we've just stumbled on his Miss November shoot.

'Maybe he'll call it *Canalder Girls.*'

We greenbanked overnight and next day continued the journey. As we idled slowly through the small marina at Bellegarde we heard shouting, and noticed a vehicle keeping pace with us on the left bank. The driver was earnestly trying to attract our attention.

'Oops! It's the mechanic from the *chantier*,' said Liz. I throttled back and we pulled over alongside another boat on the edge of the canal. The mechanic by this time was out of his car and clambering across the moored boat waving a piece of paper and shouting, '*Le facture, le facture!*' which is French for 'the invoice.'

We explained as best we could that because nobody had come back to the boatyard we intended to pay the bill on our return and had left a note to that effect on the door. However, it seemed the *Mistral* might have whipped the note away, as he said he knew nothing about it. We were therefore being chased as debtors. '*Ce n'est pas normal!*' the mechanic said. I felt like telling him that the lengthy duration of French lunchtimes wasn't normal either, but of course in France that wouldn't make sense.

We had enough cash on board and settled the account without fuss, and with a few *désolés* thrown in. He seemed suitably consoled, and headed back to his car, while we untied and carried on down the canal. Sometime later we were to learn that we had become famous among the Beaucaire boating community as the Kiwi couple that ran off without paying the boatyard, and were briefly the talk of the town, or at least the marina.

CHAPTER TWENTY-ONE

And so we finally got within a stone's throw of the Mediterranean. Well, that's assuming you can throw a stone six kilometres, but the thirteenth century town of Aigues-Mortes is as close as we could get by boat at the time.

The canal does continue on to a place called Grau du Roi, a nice fishing port, where theoretically you could carry on out into the Med then turn right or left and head for Spain, Italy or Greece. But apparently you're only allowed to go to Grau du Roi by boat if you are 'going to sea,' since there aren't many places in the port for pleasure boats. And since the Med was quite choppy with strong winds we certainly didn't intend to go *sur la mer* on this visit.

Despite a name that seems to suggest illness and death, Aigues-Mortes is simply old French for 'dead water' and reflects the close proximity of extensive marshes and ponds, a signature of the Camargue (along with wild horses, bulls and cowboys).

We rode past some of these wetlands on the bikes on the way to Grau du Roi, having secured a berth for *Liberty* at the Aigues-Mortes marina. We wanted to see the Med.

Amid the wetlands, up to their ankles in cold briny water, stood a few of the local pink flamingos, the stupid ones who had decided for some reason not to go to Africa for the winter. Silly them. They stood forlornly on one leg with their heads tucked under their wings trying to keep warm in the biting blast of the strong chill wind off the sea. We knew how they felt, but it's tricky tucking your head under your arm while riding a bike.

However, the ride to Grau du Roi ('Pond of the King') was invigorating, as was our very brief visit to the beach, which we felt we had to do so we could take a photo to prove we'd actually reached the Mediterranean. Unfortunately the sea looked like New Zealand's Cook Strait on a bad day. And the beach was deserted; no bronzed bodies, no beach umbrellas, no Germans claiming the loungers… just desolate wind-whipped sand, and fierce white-capped breakers. We quickly snapped off a selfie and decided we must come back in warmer weather.

The fishing port was nice and colourful though, despite most of the shops and businesses being closed for winter, but to escape the chill Liz suggested we find somewhere for lunch. Down a side alley she spotted La Crêperie du Gard du Roi – the Pancakery of the Pond of the King – which looked like it needed our business as there was nobody else there.

It turned out this was to our advantage as we had the tiny cosy place to ourselves for the entire lunch, and the full attention of the two slightly flamboyant owners. We perused the menu of the *crêperie* of the pond of the king, and Liz decided to go for the *galette* – the basis of which we weren't sure since it translates as 'slab,' but, what the heck. 'One of your finest slabs *s'il vous plaît*, and mussels and chips with curry sauce for me, *merci*.' Nom nom.

While we waited, the large widescreen TV high on the wall was playing for our entertainment, but for once it wasn't one showing France being beaten by some other rugby team, or any other sport for that matter. No; instead, something far more useful, and in fact riveting: a home video made by the owners of the *crêperie*.

Crêperie Productions presented a silent yet thoughtful video that started off with nice pictures of Grau du Roi in warm sunshine, fishing boats arriving, the swing bridge swinging, and – somewhat sadly – shots of the exterior tables of the restaurant itself with absolutely no customers.

But then: the money shots. Suddenly, the camera is on a tripod in the kitchen, and we are treated to a step-by-step sequence showing how the chef (we could tell it was the same guy who served us by the tattoos on his arm) prepared a *galette*. Which isn't a slab; it's a savoury *crêpe* mixture spread onto a hotplate, formed into a square, folded over in each corner, with two eggs broken onto it and ham and cheese added (or any combination of all sorts of accompaniments). It cooks on the hotplate (during this the chef/cameraman nipped round the back of the camera and zoomed in once or twice, just so we knew it was ham, eggs and cheese cooking) and, once browned, is plated up.

This was excellent, and when Liz's *galette* arrived it looked more or less the same as the one in the movie. I said to it, 'Hey, haven't I seen you on TV?'

But the best thing of all was we now knew how to make a *galette* ourselves, having had a free cooking lesson.

The *moules et frites* with curry sauce were lovely too, as was the *demi-pichet de rosé*, and during the meal we were able to watch a video of chef cooking a *crêpe*, adorned with Nutella (obvious product-placement), icing sugar, cream and ice cream. Nom, *encore*, nom.

So when he came to ask if we would like dessert I had to tell the waiter in my best broken French that having watched him prepare a Nutella *crêpe* on the screen I would just have to have one.

The only way I could feel good about gorging myself at lunch was knowing that we would have to ride the bikes back to Aigues-Mortes, and therefore burn off a few calories, which is what we did. The flamingos still had their heads tucked in, and it was still blowing and cold, but the power of the Nutella coursed through me and gave me increased strength. Oh, and the wind was behind us, which Liz blamed for almost sending her into the canal at one point. I blamed the *rosé*.

Anyway, over the next few days we explored Aigues-Mortes, in particular the old walled city part of it, which is really charming. Except that, as with nearly all French towns and villages, no matter how narrow the streets are, vehicles are still allowed, which means you're constantly on the watch for cars barrelling towards you, or coming up from behind.

At least with cobbled streets you can hear them coming (all the cars sounding like they're driving on flat tyres), but often the so-called pavements are scarcely more than a foot wide, so there's not much margin for error.

Nevertheless, we could see that old Aigues-Mortes would be a wonderful place to come back to in sunny warm weather, and we put it on our list of Places To Visit On Our Return. This late in the season though there were too many places closed, and the chill wind blowing through the narrow streets and alleys took the shine off what is indisputably a very pretty town.

We needed to stock up at a supermarket so set off on the bikes to find the shopping centre, not far away. At the entrance to the mall was a hairdressers. I didn't need another *coupe* quite yet, but what appealed to me was its name.

Hairdressers have long been known for their love of puns, evident in the various names of their salons, from *HairPort*, *British Hairways* and *A Cut Above*, to *Scissor's Palace*, *The Best Little Hair House*, and the undeniably clever *Crops and Bobbers*.

The other thing hairdressers are famous for is inane chatter. Who hasn't sat in the chair only to have the stylist start off with, 'So, where are you going for your holidays? (Or, 'So, where've you been for your holidays?').

They're not really interested in your answers of course. When I was having my final haircut in New Zealand, the

hairdresser asked, 'So, got anything planned for the weekend?'
'Yes,' I said, 'I'm moving to France.' 'Oh, that's nice,' she replied,
clicking her scissors. 'I'm going to the Gold Coast for a couple
of weeks, doing all the theme parks…'

That was the end of the conversation. I don't think it was
in her repertoire to cope with a customer who was going any
further than Australia, let alone moving to France, so in a panic
she did the only thing she could and quickly put herself in the
picture instead. To no effect, since 'doing' the Gold Coast theme
parks sounded to me like the worst possible sort of holiday. For
once it was a blissfully quiet haircut, the only sound the whirr
of the clippers, the snip of the scissors and the ring of the till.

But it was fascinating to find in Aigues-Mortes a hair salon
with a name that unashamedly addressed its core business; it
was simply called 'Interview Coiffure.' Therefore, I present to
you – in the style of the former great *Punch* columnist Miles
Kington – a *'Let's Parler Franglais!'* lesson:

Lesson quarante-huit: Dans le salon de coiffure

Madame Styliste: 'Bonjour Monsieur. Bienvenue à *Interview Coiffure*. Take a chaise.'

Me: 'Merci Madame.'

Mme Styliste: 'Quel est votre nom?'

Me: 'Mon nom? Er… c'est Michael… porquoi?'

Mme Styliste (shrugs): 'Rien. Now, how voulez-vous vos cheveux?'

Me: 'Plus longer!' *(laughs)*

Mme Styliste (*rolls ses eyes*): 'Oh, nous avons un joker. Un Alec de smart. Fatastique – not. Sérieusement… short derrière et sides? Un cut de crew? Le Mohawk? Quoi?'

Me (chagrined): 'Peut-être un trim… s'il vous plait…'

Mme Styliste: 'Bon.'

    (*Elle utilise le clippers électriques pour a few moments. Elle stops, et holds un brush under ma bouche*)

Mme Styliste: 'So, aujourd'hui nous avons dans le studio Monsieur Michael. Bonjour Michael!'

Me: 'Er, bonjour Madame…'

Mme Styliste: 'Nous will start avec la première question: où allez-vous pour vos holidays?'

Me: 'Ah, during le Noël c'est possible je will stay ici en France.'

Mme Styliste: 'En France? Avec tous le trouble avec les Gypsies, les "Romas"?'

Me: 'Trouble? Avec Gypsies? C'est news to me.'

Mme Styliste: 'Mais oui! Every day, c'est la même thing: Quoi to do about les Romas! Et votre opinion?'

Me: 'Eh bien, je n'ai pas une opinion sur les Gypsies, er, les Romas.'

Mme Styliste (ruffled): 'Pas d'opinion? Mais si vous êtes le ministre de l'immigration, quelle est votre policy?

Me: 'Mais je ne suis pas le ministre de l'immigration. Je suis un customer…'

Mme: 'Just répondez la question Ministre! La policy de Gypsies… c'est quoi?'

Me: 'Er, well, if je were le ministre de l'immigration en Angleterre, où les Gypsies – nous préférons le term "Travellers" – make beaucoup de mess avec leurs encampments, je suggest… bring back hanging.'

Mme Styliste: 'Hanging? Porquoi pas la guillotine?'

Me: 'Ou peut-être la guillotine, oui. Ils sont un blot sur le landscape!'

Mme Styliste: 'Vous et votre party sont trés right-wing Ministre. Vous êtes afraid for your vie peut-être?'

Me: 'Mais non! Je suis as safe as maisons.'

Mme: 'Not quite Minister. Regardez dans le miroir… mon brother and his mates sont arrivés. Ils sont "Gypsies." C'est serieux.'

Me: 'Ah, désolé Madame! Nos policies have changed. J'ai l'intention to double le benefit pour les Romas, provide free maisons, et health care. Et aussi les subsidised haircuts.'

Mme (*speaking into le brush encore*): 'Et c'est all we have time for ce soir, à *Interview Coiffure*. Merci pour joining us, et Merci Ministre.'

Me: 'De rien Madame.'

(For much funnier original Franglais material, search Miles Kington, *Let's Parler Franglais* online)

CHAPTER TWENTY-TWO

The weather had turned decidedly cold, not helped by *Liberty*'s heating system breaking down. We unbolted it from below decks and dismantled it on the table in the Bond Lounge, but couldn't identify the problem and in the end decided to pack it into a box. We'd find somewhere to get it fixed later. Luckily we had a spare electric oil-filled radiator, which worked fine while we were plugged into shore power but would be a big drain on the batteries when we weren't. And of course we had each other to cuddle up to, so no shortage of heating options.

We left Aigues-Mortes, but since it had got so chilly we abandoned any thoughts of heading for Marseille or Sète, and retraced our route back along the Canal du Rhône à Sète, stopping a couple of nights along the way back to Beaucaire.

When we awoke on our second morning it felt particularly chilly, our breath steaming in the air inside the boat, and when we drew the curtains we saw why. 'It's snowing!' Liz screamed in delight. It was true, we were covered in snow, And it definitely was still falling.

Well, not exactly true; it wasn't so much *falling* as being blown horizontally by the wind. It was such a novel sight that we both laughed, put on warm clothes, and went outside to take photos. *Liberty* had a decent coating, as did the towpath and trees around and we decided it would make the perfect picture for our Christmas cards.

We weren't far from Beaucaire, so set off optimistic that the snow, even if it thickened, wouldn't cause us any serious problems. I steered from the indoor position in the salon, but still wrapped up in scarf, jacket, hat and gloves, and supported by steaming hot coffee (with a touch of Irish whiskey) from Liz. What a gal!

The windscreen wipers coped okay with the blizzard, and by early afternoon the snow had stopped. More than that, the clouds cleared, the sky was blue and the sun shone, so by the time we arrived back in the marina at Beaucaire it was, remarkably, a very pleasant afternoon.

Even better, Didier, as good as his word, had saved us a sunny quayside location for the boat, which was at a convenient height for getting on and off – no clambering up or leaping down onto wobbly floating pontoons. It was also even more central than the previous mooring. In a word: *parfait*. Presumably he had laughed off the stories of the couple on *Liberty* who'd sailed off without paying their boatyard bill.

And so, with *Liberty* securely nestled in against the quayside, her engine silent, we settled in to life in Beaucaire.

Like Saint-Gilles, it's a multicultural town, and every day we would see Moroccan men sitting on the public benches along the quayside, either in groups talking earnestly, or just on their own with their own thoughts for company. We rarely saw Moroccan women on the seats though; they always seemed to be on the move, walking, browsing the markets, or minding their children.

Bordering the road that ran the length of the quay were cafés and restaurants, in various states of openness. Some threw their doors open before 10am and stayed open till late, while others were more reserved, opening only during the day. Still others had closed for the winter, their outdoor tables and chairs stacked up and chained together. Beside the footbridge, the *passarelle*, a floating restaurant bobbed idly, waiting for winter to pass by.

The *passarelle* itself had become a local celebrity and point of discussion. Designed to lift up on hydraulics to allow boats to pass under, it had recently broken down in a big way, to the extent that it was going to cost tens of thousands of Euros to repair – money the local council didn't have.

Jim of *Sally Beth* said he'd seen a notice announcing that the *passarelle* was broken and would be operational again once it was fixed. You could almost read the Gallic shrug in the words but you couldn't argue with the logic of it.

In the meantime though, only boats with a *tirant d'air* of three metres or less could pass under it. We were lucky, because Didier had allocated us a position in the northern end of the marina, which meant we'd had to squeeze *Liberty* under the *passarelle* – and we mean squeeze! We had to take the whole Bimini canvas top down, drop the equipment rack, and lower all the flybridge windows, and even then the throttle, which had become the highest point on the boat, almost scraped the underside of the footbridge. Liz and I had to squat down as *Liberty* crawled under, but we made it.

Not all boats could though, and there were a few with superstructures higher than three metres that were stuck in the northern part of the marina for the duration, with little prospect of going anywhere until the bridge was fixed. One of the boat owners, whose vessel was his livelihood, was apparently suing the council for lost earnings and inconvenience.

It was hard to believe that we'd only been cruising for just over two months – it seemed like much longer but it had already been an entertaining, mind-expanding time, and we took the opportunity to blog a few of the observations and conclusions we'd reached about life in *La Belle France* so far:

Village life: we had read in various books that the charming and quaint rural French village is heading for extinction, and sadly

– in our brief experience to date – this appears to be the case. Supermarkets and retail parks on the edges of towns are now common, which means people drive there, do a week or two's shopping in one go and head home. Meanwhile, back in the old high street, the only local businesses still surviving seem to be the boulangerie *and the hairdressers. Oh and of course the* Tabac.

Unfortunately, as with many (most?) retail parks around the world, these edge-of-town offerings are ugly, windswept and dull, even though they might have everything in one place. Sad, but seemingly the way France is heading.

(On the other hand, if you wish to buy a little shop in the centre of a cute French village, help yourself, there are plenty à vendre*)*

Dogs: France breeds the smallest dogs in the world. They are designed to fit in handbags, if not purses. If selective breeding continues they will soon be pocket-sized. You'll be able to wear them on your wrist. Especially for Parisians, Apple will invent the iDog. Unfortunately regardless of size the dogs seem to leave the absolute largest deposits on the pavements, some huge enough to qualify for the Guinness Book of Records (if they had such a category [and if they did would it be a scategory?]). To date the French haven't really caught on to the use of plastic bags for cleaning up after their pooches, and are happy for the poo in pooch to be left on the ground. Someone needs to take official steps to solve this problem, much as we take very careful steps to avoid it when out walking.

McDonald's: yes, Macca's is here, of course. However, there's nothing fast about the food; service is leisurely, if not downright slow. On the other hand, when you order a Combo your drink choice includes beer. Civilised. Plus you get free Wi-Fi at every McDonalds. Very civilised.

Supermarkets: These are pretty much the same as anywhere else in the world, except that in French supermarkets you need to be wary of labelling. Liz found a packet of something the other day that – judging by the label – appeared to be pigeon's feet. Turns out on investigation they were actually pine nuts. On the other hand, you can occasionally find lark and thrush on offer, so pigeon's feet might well be available. Nom-nom.

Dogs II: The French adore their chiens, so much so that most cafés, bars, restaurants and many hotels welcome them, so don't be surprised to find one looking longingly at you beside your table hoping for a morsel. Or a doggie-bag.

Supermarkets II: As with most supermarkets in England or New Zealand there is often a separate checkout for 'ten items or less.' As with all supermarkets this is always closed and you have to queue up behind four people, each of whom is buying approximately €400-worth of groceries, at the normal checkouts. Oh, and in France they pay by cheque, which of course takes 15 minutes to write. Apparently cheques are not only common here, they are still taken very seriously, and to default on one is a criminal offence. Having to wait in a queue while they are written out is also criminal.

Pedestrian crossings: Be afraid. Be very afraid. A strip of black and white lines across the road is an instruction to drivers to speed up. So, if you wish to cross a road safely, wait until approximately 2am, when the traffic is less. Then run. Except in Paris of course where it's probably safer to get a taxi to take you across.

Dangerous words: If you need a tampon, don't ask for one – you will be given a rubber stamp instead. Equally, if you want to know your food is organic, ask if it is 'biologique.' Don't risk guessing and asking if it contains 'les préservatifs.' Hopefully it won't, since they're condoms. Eew.

There are various observations of life that have been made by some clever wits, such as where does your lap go when you stand up, and if you dismantle something can you mantle it again? Deep questions, well worth asking.

So it stands to reason to also ask, what happens to mariners when they're not marinating? What do boaties actually do when they're not cruising? Because, from September through to around April, most boaties in France don't live up to their name; they don't go anywhere in their boats. They don't use the word boat as a verb, they just stay put on their noun and wait until *printemps* to activate the verb again. (Or they cheat, cocoon their boat for winter and scuttle off home or to warmer climes, the scum.)

Those hardy souls that remain continue to live aboard their vessels, like we were doing, using their boats as a base, a home, somewhere to stay. We were therefore not sailors any more, at least not for a while; we decided we were *staylors*.

There were quite a few staylors in the Port de Beaucaire, living on boats ranging in style from the cute and aforementioned *Sally Beth* to *Fiere Magriet*, a pretty converted barge or *peniche* that dated back 107 years. In between were other boats, from extremely up-market models with gleaming hulls, radar and remote-controlled gangplanks, to the more ordinary run-of-the-mill cruisers, like ours.

As with the boats, their occupants ranged widely, in length, beam and overall condition. Some needed complete renovation. As we've already revealed, Jim, Sandra and dog Bella were as full-time live-aboards as you could hope to find. Then there was Scottish Kevin, on his ownsome living on an old yacht and working locally. From Holland we met Willy and Ria, with their immaculate vessel looking like it had just come from the Paris Boat Show. They were spending part of the winter on board then going home for a while, with plans that summer to return and take the boat to Corsica.

Mike and Rachael, from England, who were about to let the side down by migrating south to somewhere warmer for four months, were a hoot, and absolute party animals.

And then there was Harvey, older than any of the boats in the marina and about as entertaining as a cranky old gearbox. He had a serious case of *schadenfreude*, and cackled while telling stories of other boaties' misfortunes, the miserable matelot. But we decided there must have been some good timber under the peeling exterior, if for no other reason than he employed some locals to maintain his boat and keep it in tip-top condition.

We felt somewhat guilty about having written him off when three months later he was found dead on his boat. He'd died in his sleep. But he'd resisted all his family's advice to settle down and lead a 'normal' life, and had chosen to live – and die – on a boat. RIP Harvey.

There were others who we hadn't met yet, though we'd learned all about them from the regulars at the pub. These were the ones who didn't come to the regular Friday night drinks and pizzas at the Nautic, the friendly local establishment operated by the hard-working and very amicable husband and wife team, Fabrice and Cécile.

But by not coming they were missing out. It was here at the end of the waiting week that many of the port's staylors formed a flotilla of friendship, a marina of merriment, or a bucket of bilgewater (depending who you were listening to). Social it was, but it was also a very useful occasion for us as we once again found ourselves surrounded by significant experience (some of it literally 'in-depth') – people who lived and breathed boating, and had done for years, sometimes decades. There seemed to be nothing they didn't know, and certainly in Jim, Sandra and Keith's case they knew it all in French as well. For all I know Bella could have been fluent.

Fabrice's pizzas were good too – the best we'd found in France.

So Friday nights were spent splicing the mainbrace. This motley crew did however get together for other occasions, such as organised walks, lunches, dog walking, and so forth – and there was a Christmas party planned. Interestingly, one thing shone through from the Friday night gatherings – and seemed typical of meeting boating people in general – and that was that nobody asked what you did for a living. Nobody. Everyone seemed to be concerned only with boats, and messing about in them, and were quite happy just to accept you for who you were. This pleased Liz in particular as she was excused from having to admit she'd been a policy analyst. Or worse: explain what one is.

Anyway, it was what you might call a buoyant atmosphere, and one we look forward to marinating in over winter.

CHAPTER TWENTY-THREE

We took three weeks out to go and stay with various friends in England over Christmas and New Year, and to take Van Rouge back also. It transpired that the van and its contents weren't convenient guests at Liz's parents' after all, as they had decided to sell their property, so we reluctantly packed it all up and drove it back to the UK, feeling once again like nomads of no fixed abode.

At our friend Shaun's in Merseyside the bright red van took up position for a week or so outside his house, and the neighbours all around were saying to him, 'I see the gypsies are back again!'

Which was funny for a while, but it was close to the truth in that we didn't have any home other than *Liberty*. In the end we gratefully put our most valued possessions in Shaun's attic and took the rest to a commercial storage facility nearby.

But for three weeks over the Christmas and New Year holidays we were able to enjoy the relative novelty of walking into shops without rehearsing what we were going to say, and have conversations without drying up after the first two sentences. We'd had fun talking French, but still didn't feel like we'd learned much.

That's not to say we weren't enjoying our time in France; we definitely were, and while the south wasn't shaping up to be as balmily warm as we'd hoped, it looked like it was doing a lot better than anywhere further north.

The western coastline of France and the south of England were being hammered by extreme weather. Rainfall was incessant, and flooding, particularly in Somerset, was severe. Each night the news bulletins carried images of flooded homes, residents wading through murky freezing waters – or worse – and livestock huddled on high ground trying to escape the rising torrents.

But let's face it: Britain doesn't enjoy a reputation for endless sunshine and ambient warmth, and although this shouldn't have come as a surprise to us, it did make us think carefully about where we might eventually want to settle again post-*Liberty* adventure.

I'd always harboured a desire to own a property in France, which of course we already did; *Liberty* was it, and she had the added advantage that she could be moved around at will, unlike bricks and mortar.

On the other hand, the prospect of buying a do-up in rural France appealed hugely, at least to me, but Liz was typically more pragmatic.

'What's the point of renovating something in France when we can't live in it? What would we do for jobs?' she quite reasonably asked. I didn't have any reasonable answer, other than to draw on experience, and hope.

'I dunno. Something would occur to us. Things have always had a way of "coming right;" I mean we've run an accommodation business before; we could do it again.'

This didn't persuade Liz. 'And what do we do for income during the six or eight months of the year when it's closed?'

Good point. France certainly seems to close down for two-thirds of the year. Try as we might we really couldn't come to terms with this French business model. It just didn't seem viable to own a business that could only operate for a third of the year or less, and yet, judging by the many hotels, B&Bs, cafés and restaurants that we'd seen shuttered up, that seemed to be exactly the way the nation operated.

But, as you already know dear reader, Liz is the logical thinker and I'm the hare-brained one, and the concept of simply owning something in France really appealed to me for heartfelt reasons that I cannot easily explain. Logic and me have never been easy bed-fellows.

There were many times as we trawled along the canals (not literally; we never got excited about the prospect of eating canal-caught fish) that I'd gaze wistfully at a bankside property and think, 'Hmmm. A few new planks, replace those tiles, lick of paint… good as new.'

But of course Liz was right. 'Maybe in ten years' time,' she would say to me, frequently. 'I'm not ready to retire to France yet.'

Nor, it has to be said, was I. Neither of us was ready to give up work completely. We'd read many books written by people who'd bought properties in France or Italy and done them up, but few if any revealed the nature of their financial situations. The subtext was that they seemed to have endless supplies of money to spend on builders, plasterers, plumbers and painters, and equally endless days to spend drinking Sancerre on their newly-paved terraces. Jobs and income were rarely mentioned.

So, lest we be accused of being 'of independent means,' we can unequivocally say right here and now that no, we weren't. We had strictly limited funds available, and – while living on *Liberty* – no income at all.

But that didn't mean we were skint. We had some funds left over from the sale of the property in New Zealand, and we were still keen to see if we could buy something that might generate some income for us. The failure of the two potential house purchases in Liverpool six months earlier had been a setback yes, but not the end of the world. Maybe all we needed was some knowledgeable help.

During our last few years in New Zealand we had often watched property programmes on the television, particularly the ones that showed couples from Britain who couldn't decide whether to purchase somewhere in the UK or overseas.

We were impressed with what money could buy, particularly in certain parts of Europe, and we'd sigh longingly as we watched prospective home buyers being shown around properties from Cornwall to the Costa del Sol, and many other places besides.

Research online backed up the real possibility of buying a bargain, particularly in rural France, but also in Spain, Portugal and other exotic locations, and we'd made a pact to at least investigate some options once we got to Europe.

Late in December after we'd been blown back from Aigues-Mortes I had a cheeky thought. One of our favourite programmes, *A Place in the Sun: Home or Away* always ended with the presenter saying some thing like, 'If you're looking for a new place in the sun at home or away and would like to take part in the programme, visit our website.' So I did.

I read the application details, filled in the form and sent it off. In fact I did it with two property programmes to hedge my bets, but not really holding out for any positive responses, especially so close to Christmas.

Having worked in television though I knew that our story had some appeal: we'd 'cast off safe harbours,' sold up in New Zealand, returned to Britain, bought a boat in France and were travelling the country potentially looking for a place to buy. But we were unsure whether to purchase in France, or England, or somewhere else entirely. The story had the visual elements of *Liberty* and our life aboard, the dilemma of where to buy, and the tension between Liz and me differing over where to live and what to do. The producer in me thought it had all the ingredients for a good programme.

Because Liz had pretty much talked me out of buying in France I'd done some more research and wondered whether the Canary Islands might not be a good place to invest. The climate is good all year round, it's a major tourist destination, it's open all year, and there seemed to be plenty of apartments for sale.

On the other hand, we'd moved back to England – sort of – and there was no doubt that if we wanted to find work again it would be easier to do so there than in Spain, or anywhere else in Europe. Liz felt that Liverpool (my home town) would be a better place to buy than the Canary Islands, partly because we knew it, knew people there, and Liz actually liked it. It didn't have a Mediterranean climate, but we did at least speak the language. (My Scouse was a bit rusty but I could get by.)

Anyway, the Canary Islands, and Tenerife in particular, appealed to me, even though I'd never been there. My web research showed that English was widely spoken, and there were also quite a few English-run estate agencies there, which might make a purchase easier. The potential to own an apartment in Tenerife, where we could live for six months of the year while spending the other six months cruising in *Liberty* seemed ideal, at least to my illogical mind. Liz wasn't convinced, but when it came to choosing two competing locations for the TV programme, our home or away choices were: Liverpool or Tenerife.

To cut a long story slightly shorter, *A Place in the Sun*'s producer agreed with me and thought our story was a good one. She got in touch early in January after we'd returned to Beaucaire, and said she'd send out a production assistant with a camera to get some shots of us living and cruising on *Liberty*, for inclusion in the programme (and, we figured, to see if we really were who we said we were!).

The other programme I'd applied to also got in touch keen to follow up, but I had to tell them they'd missed the boat. How about that? Being chased by *two* TV programmes!

Meanwhile, with a now-empty Van Rouge parked across the marina, we were back on board *Liberty*, which had survived our absence intact, afloat and undisturbed by icebergs or anything else, except maybe the Sahara Desert. We only mention icebergs because those local boaties who'd lived in Beaucaire for some years had told us that a few winters previously the marina had actually frozen over. Jim said he had photos of him standing on the ice ('But holding onto the boat, just in case!').

And as for the desert? Well, when we returned to the boat we found it covered in a coarse red dust.

'Have they been cutting the concrete cobblestones?' I asked Liz, but looking around we couldn't see any evidence of recent work. 'Don't think so,' she said, rubbing a finger through the grit. 'Feels like sand.'

Which is what it turned out to be. We learned later that this was a relatively common occurrence, the sand carried at high altitude by winds from the south, from the Sahara.

We'd rather have sand than ice anyway, and this winter, to date at least, had proved quite mild; it was comforting to watch the weather on TV – the *météo* – each evening which showed a large yellow sun hovering over our part of France while the rest of the country was being deluged. Even residents on the posh coast around Monaco and Monte Carlo had suffered landslips caused by heavy rain. Poor rich things.

We'd been warned that January and February were the worst winter months in Beaucaire, so we weren't getting complacent, but we were keeping our fingers crossed that winter continued to be mild, in the hope that around the first week of March we could begin cruising again, and set off along the Canal du Midi heading for Bordeaux.

In the interim, and while we waited for the thermometer to climb, I bought a new hat. Okay, that's not news that would likely make headlines, but it was a major in my life, as I'd probably bought no more than maybe five bits of headgear in all my mumbledy-years. I could now hold my head up high in Beaucaire society, or at least keep my thinning locks hidden.

Headgear is common in *le sud de France*, and varied. The favoured hat for young Frenchmen is, sadly, the ubiquitous beanie, usually black and woolly. Not exactly *haute* fashion, but practical when the chilly *Mistral* blows. But anyway, many of the young French *hommes* seemed to eschew headgear in favour of showing off their flowing locks, or, more commonly around Beaucaire parts, their shaven heads. Brrr.

Older French men favour the flat cap, usually of tweed or similar. We saw many on heads 'of a certain age,' but conspicuous by its absence was the traditional beret. We saw maybe two in all our time there, though you could buy them in the markets. (And no, I didn't.)

Due to the large Algerian and Moroccan population, one of the most common pieces of headgear was the traditional North African skull cap or *taqiya*, often white, sometimes coloured, and occasionally woven with geometric patterns. We saw these a lot.

And then there were the wizards. Also to be seen sitting on the marina benches, these men wore full gowns of burgundy or brown, with built-in tall pointed hoods. We believe their garb is traditional also, but we weren't sure who these people actually were. However, they seemed to mingle with the Moroccans, so we presumed they were of their kind, but perhaps a higher order. We referred to them as 'Gandalfs,' maybe not politically correct, but oh how we laughed!

The women? Interestingly, it seemed the local French women avoided headgear almost completely, preferring to show off their *coiffures*, and were content to challenge the *Mistral* head-on, as it were. On the other hand, religious practice dictates that the North African women mainly wear traditional head scarves, which added a rainbow of colour to the streets at times, though many also wore black.

As for me, well, my new *chapeau* was black also. Liz and I were browsing the market at Tarascon across the river, a weekly, fairly extensive but predictable market much like all the others, with a dominance of clothing stalls, household wares, bolts of cloth, tat, rotisserie chickens, cheeses, tat, fruit and veg stalls, tat and – *bien sur* – more tat. And one hat stall.

It was a cold day, and I hadn't worn my New Zealand All Blacks beanie, so I paused at the *chapeau* stall, just to browse. Next thing the vendor was homing in on me with cries of, '*Monsieur! Monsieur!*' and picking up awful examples of flat caps and things with ear muffs and thrusting them at me, presumably out of concern for my naked head.

After explaining we were *de Nouvelle Zélande* he then mimed a rugby pass, laughed, and picked up a tweed cap and said, '*Trés British!*'

I said, '*Non, ce n'est pas pour moi. Je préfère celui-là,*' and pointed to a wide-brimmed black Fedora-style hat. His eyes lit up as he explained it was in fact a Camargue hat, but when I put it on and looked in the mirror it was Harrison Ford who stared back at me. Liz made all the right noises, so I bought it. I wouldn't blend in with the locals, but at least if we got separated at the markets she would easily be able to find me, and I could probably rescue her from a pit of snakes if required.

CHAPTER TWENTY-FOUR

Vincent Van Gogh had something in common with Liz and me; the three of us quite liked the old Langlois bridge over the canal at Arles.

When Van Gogh was there, he was struck by the geometric loveliness of the bridge, and the tranquillity of the scene, and so he sat on a canvas stool and captured it forever in oils, watercolours and sketches. Unfortunately, as we arrived at the famous bridge we discovered we'd just missed him by 126 years. Frustrating.

Still, it was worth the detour. With Van Rouge now back with us in France, we'd driven one day to take a look at Arles, the city that failed to welcome us at its quayside when we arrived there on *Liberty* back in October. Despite a prominent position on the Rhône, Arles has no marina or pontoons on the river for visiting *plaisanciers*, as we boaties in France are called. Both banks of the Rhône in the city are steeply walled, with old iron mooring rings that entice, but which, as we had discovered, are set so high on the walls as to make them impractical to use, since there would be no way to get off the boat unless you were Spiderman.

We learned later that there are moorings up a nearby canal arm, but they required 24-hours' notice out of season, so wouldn't have been any use to us.

Anyway, although we were unable to stop there the previous visit, we nevertheless managed to pay the place a visit by road.

Like so many other old cities in these parts, the Roman influence is very evident, with a Coliseum-like amphitheatre that is still used today for festivals and events, such as bullfights. We were pleased to read that the bulls are not killed; instead the bullfighter has to deftly capture a couple of tokens hanging on the bull's horns, while keeping his own tokens out of harm's way. So the bull lives, the bullfighter gets adored (or gored if unlucky) and the crowd give the performance the thumbs-up, just as they might have done 2000 years ago.

Unfortunately on this particular chilly mid-winter's day there were no performances, and the cold wind swept the sand of the inner ring and whistled strongly through the empty tiered seating. But the place still looked good. There's a Roman theatre too, also still used for performances, and the old centre *ville* has many narrow cobbled streets to explore, which we promised ourselves we would do once the weather warmed up.

Meanwhile, before turning for home we decided to find Van Gogh's famed bridge, partly because his paintings of it elevated it to star status, and partly because bridges over canals are something we were dealing with every day when cruising, so we'd become the bridge equivalent of train-spotters.

In 1888 when Vincent was living in Arles, he probably would have walked or ridden on horseback to the Langlois bridge, or maybe hitched a ride on a wagon. He certainly wouldn't have had to wrestle with multiple roundabouts and a section of motorway; nor would he have consulted a Sat-Nav device that steadfastly refused to acknowledge the existence of the bridge at all. In the end it was Liz's map-reading skills that got us there. So quaint, so… last century.

But at least the sun was shining, even if the trees were devoid of leaves, and the scene carried something of the warmth that VG captured in his renderings. The bridge itself is a lovely little example of engineering; a counter-balanced drawbridge that splits in the middle, each side rising up on hinges to enable tall or masted vessels to pass by. It's not operational any more, and instead is fixed in the open position, its two halves raised skywards as if in salute to the great artist.

The nearby lock house is now painted in 21st century style, unfortunately by taggers. Instead of being a nice little museum, a homage to Vincent who was so taken with the Arles area, the house is seemingly abandoned, and has become a canvas for young French graffiti artists, some of whom had even had the gall (Gaul?) to sign their names to their works.

Still, we could see why Vincent liked the Langlois bridge, and so we captured it digitally, and enhanced it later on the boat so that, as Vincent did, the colours were more vibrant, and we diffused it somewhat as a nod to the impressionist style. I thought maybe we could make it into a poster, or a T-shirt.

And speaking of Vincents, a saint of that name dragged us to church one Sunday in January. This, as God will testify, is a rare event for us, but it was for a good cause. Basically we were there to pray for a healthy vintage later in the year, and heaven knows we all like a good vintage.

So, unusually for us we were up and ready for the off by 9am, at which time we met up with Jim and Sandra who had kindly offered to drive us to the nearby town of Jonquières Saint-Vincent on this fine morning, to take part in the annual wine festival.

This was to invoke the pleasure of the local patron saint, Vincent, to look benignly on the growth of the grapes, the principle being that come September this blessing would yield a bountiful harvest during the *vendange*, which of course would ultimately turn into a damn fine tipple.

The day's ceremony started with the serious stuff: a church service – Mass in fact – in the chapel of St Vincent, at which the *confréries,* or brotherhoods, representing the local regions, attended in their colourful robes, some with ceremonial silver wine tasters or *tastevins* hanging on ribbons around their necks.

Or, in the case of the Order of the Garlic, ceremonial wooden pestles. This coven, whose members were dressed in *aioli*-coloured capes, wore the garlic pestles apparently as a bit of fun, possibly in the hope of meeting members of the Brotherhood of the Mortar so they could consummate their rendezvous with a good grinding. Our French wasn't up to asking, and anyway, we didn't want to spoil the conjecture.

The church service was something of a mystery also, and Liz and I struggled during the liturgies to understand what was being said. We gathered that the sermon was based around how Jesus endorsed wine as way of remembering him, (Cheers Jesus!) plus there may have been something in there about how he turned water into wine. To illustrate this miracle, four bottles of wine stood tantalisingly in front of the priest, ranging in size from an ordinary bottle to a giant six-litre Methuselah. We looked longingly at them, but no miracle of dispensation was forthcoming. God knows we prayed hard enough.

We hummed along with the hymns, tried to work out which was the Lord's Prayer, and wished we'd got there early enough to secure a pew.

When the priest got to the passing round of the communion wine and holy biscuit we and a few others near the door decided to renounce Catholicism and get out into the sunshine. Outside a crowd had gathered, patiently waiting for the start of the formal procession through the vineyard.

They didn't have to wait long – obviously the remaining congregation had downed their wine and munched their crackers with gusto – because in no time the carved wooden effigy of St Vincent was borne aloft from the chapel, on the shoulders of four *confréries,* followed by the Order of the Garlic, the other covens, and finally the parishioners.

The first part of the parade was very short, and wound only around the back of the *Bar Tabac*, through the local winery yard and into the car park, where it stopped, and St Vincent, with carved bunch of grapes in hand, was placed onto the back of a leaf-enshrouded farm trailer attached to an equally verdant ancient tractor. Nearby, Condor – a musical group of diffuse number but which included a guitar player, multiple drummers and flute and pipe players – struck up some tunes that would have been at home as themes to the second *Blackadder* series. Don't get me wrong, they were very good, and we were disappointed not to see CDs on sale.

However, we did buy our tasting glasses, engraved with the St Vincent logo, and carried these with us when the entertainment had finished and the ancient tractor started up, towing St Vinnie at an *escargot*'s pace. The rest of us followed respectfully, the *confréries* immediately behind the tractor with their embroidered banners swaying colourfully in the mild breeze. It was a sight to stop traffic, but the local police did that for us instead, as we crossed the main road and wound our way through the winter vineyard, the gnarled stems pushing through the earth like arthritic fingers reaching for the sun. It was hard to imagine these same vines would be dripping with grapes in seven months.

Various pipe players and drummers tooted and thumped as we proceeded at a dignified sixteenth century pace, until all the *confréries*, others garbed in clothes and costumes of bygone days, and dignitaries, assembled on a little hillock, already prepared with microphone and speakers. Adjacent was a gently sloping hillside with trestle tables on which were many platters of finger food, and multiple bladder-boxes of wine: *vins blanc*, *rosé* and *rouge*. Having already spent an hour in the chapel, and another half hour listening to the music and parading, Liz, me and our boating friends were definitely ready to tuck in to the food and wine, but first of course there were speeches.

The first was by what we supposed was the Grand Master of Everything. His French was very good, in that he spoke very clearly, slowly, to the extent we could understand much of what he was saying. There was much laughter from the crowd, which we think was something to do with Jesus turning water into wine again, and how much we all appreciated that he wasn't tee-total.

The second speaker spoke in the regional Provençal dialect, so that was lost on us, but we did get the last bit, which was that we all had to toast three times '*Vive St Vincent!*' We gave such a desultory performance the first time that we were forced to do it again with more enthusiasm, but our reward was that the tables were declared open, and in we launched. Or lunched. Or lurched if you failed to remember the sloping hill.

The next hour passed very pleasurably as the large crowd munched, filled their glasses, drank, munched some more and mingled, all the while the sun shining on St Vincent as he waited woodenly behind his tractor. Unfortunately his carved expression was one of sadness, or annoyance – hard to tell – but he seemed to disapprove of the jollity going on a few metres away to his right. By way of compensation a small terrier, wearing a traditional *confrérie* coat of its own, was tied to the trailer to keep him company... and cock a leg on the wheels.

And then, tables bare, everyone moved off on some invisible signal, walking once again in procession, to the Château de Vincent, where we assumed we'd be getting back into the cars and heading home. But no! There in the farm courtyard were more trestle tables, more free wine, a number of tasting and sales tents representing local and nearby wineries, and a stage for (alas) more speeches.

However, as any good event organiser should know, there's no point having any speeches once alcohol has been consumed, but somebody forgot to tell this lot, so while various dignitaries stood at the microphone, the rest of us toasted St Vincent again, nibbled on more food and, naturally, bought some bottles of wine to take away with us.

Jim had nominated himself as our sober driver, for which we were very grateful, and we got back to the marina safe and sound and ready for a nap. But we could have stayed, because the morning's festivities were just the start of a day-long programme, though you'd have needed a cast iron liver to survive it.

Still, what a lovely way to start the day! Vive Shaint Vinshent! God blesh him!

CHAPTER TWENTY-FIVE

With having Van Rouge available we decided to explore a bit further afield, and chose one particularly sunny January day to drive back in time twenty centuries or so to the Pont du Gard.

This magnificent 2000-year-old Roman aqueduct is in an awesome state of preservation, and it would have been a crime not to go and see it.

In fact the aqueduct is so well preserved as to look fully functional. Unlike various amphitheatres scattered around Europe, Hadrian's Wall, or the Forum in Rome, where you get a hint of what once was, the Pont du Gard is so complete that you have the whole thing before you, almost as if it had been built yesterday. It needs no imagination, interpretation or renovation. It just *is*.

The aqueduct is a three-tiered structure, with large arches at the base, supporting similar arches above which in turn support around thirty smaller arches on top. These in turn carry the channel on the top for the water. The whole structure spans the Gardon River, and was built in the incredibly short space of five years to supply water to the Roman citizens of Nîmes. It was so well constructed it remained functional for around 500 years. Ha! Show me something built in the 1960s or 70s that is as good now, less than fifty years later. Okay, the Sydney Opera house, I'll give you that. And the Los Angeles Airport iconic theme building, yeah I guess. Oh alright, Auckland Harbour Bridge... but you know what I mean. They won't still be serving their purpose four or five hundred years from now, and almost certainly won't be standing in 2000 years. In general, we don't build things to last any more.

So the Pont du Gard is testimony to a bygone age, when people (well, Romans in particular) built not just with decades in mind, but centuries. But functional engineering apart, it is, well, just awesome. The warm honey-coloured stone glowed in the bright winter sunshine. Backlit from the A-side, the B-side reflected some of the sun from the river below, spreading a warm glow over the structure that made it almost luminous.

(Why A-side and B-side? Because the aqueduct has had a more modern addition at the level of the lower arches on the downstream side that carries a service road, and a means for the general public to cross the Gardon without having to touch the aqueduct. But viewed from upstream you see the aqueduct as the Romans originally built it, so we dubbed that the A-side.)

Our cameras clicked and beeped non-stop, and we scrambled up and down rocky riverside paths looking for the best view, or *belevedere*, as the French charmingly call it. We worked our way to the top tier, curious to know whether the Romans protected the water channel with a lid as it gurgled south, high across the Gardon towards the thirsty throats of Nîmes. They did, and much of the roof over the sluice remains, though today it is gated and off-limits.

We'd brought folding chairs with us, and had a riverside picnic down below the arches in the sun, our eyes inevitably drawn back again and again to the spans. Yes, there were tiers in our eyes.

We were virtually alone, still being winter, but grateful to have the view uninterrupted. In the summer months the area is so popular they even have lifeguards on duty at the river.

We wondered whether, 2000 years ago, the residents of Nîmes ever travelled up to the aqueduct for picnics, to swim in the river, and marvel at the awesome construction that spanned its banks, surely a marvel of the age. Or did they just take for granted the water that flowed to their troughs and fountains, and treat this as some distant public work that was paid for by their hard-earned taxes?

Anyway, thanks Romans. You gave us a great day out, and we got multiple photos to prove it, including The Money Shot: not a picture of the bridge itself, but its reflection in the river, which – due to the lazy current and swirling eddies – looks like a gorgeous impressionist painting, especially when inverted the 'right way up.'

Whichever way you look at it, on reflection, the Pont du Gard is a winner.

We blogged: *There has been chaos in Beaucaire recently; chaos, bad weather, and great excitement.*

The occasion was the 44th *Étoile de Besseges* cycle race, which for a short while had Beaucaire in a state of almost Monaco Grand Prix fever, except much quieter.

The first we knew of the race was notices on the windscreens of all the cars that parked daily on both sides of the marina, and along the one-way traffic circuit which is a key artery through the centre of town. Our own Van Rouge got a notice, which advised of restrictions on parking and driving on the upcoming Tuesday and Wednesday, pending preparations for, and the running of, a cycle race.

Basically there would be no parking in any of the usual places, subject to being towed away, from early Tuesday evening. To reinforce this, bigger signs had been cling-filmed to trees. (Not sure if this is a particularly French thing, but in the Provence/Languedoc-Roussillon area it seems common to advertise various things by placing your notice on a tree then wrapping it firmly to the trunk with cling-film. Nigella would be amused, and the trees probably like it too.)

And then there were the other signs plonked unceremoniously between parking bays, the principle being that you would have to get out of your car while parking to make sure you hadn't crashed into one, at which point the authorities presumably hoped you'd read it.

We took it with due seriousness and shifted Van Rouge to a safe location by the boat yard. Meanwhile, on Tuesday night it started to rain. On Wednesday, race day, the rain redoubled its efforts aided by a gusty wind as we awoke to a ghost-town Beaucaire, the streets devoid of vehicles either parked or mobile, an eerie silence that only enhanced the sound of the rain pelting against *Liberty*'s windows. We looked at each other and wondered why anyone would hold a cycle race in weather like this.

In the main car park, team support vehicles lined up… not just any vehicles either; these were huge pantechnicons, shiny and splendorous and plastered with sponsors' logos. Each would have been worth hundreds of thousands of Euros. The French take cycling very seriously.

Meanwhile, officials in hi-vis safety jackets stood around morosely with their hoods up, hopping from one foot to another to keep their circulation going. It was a miserable sight, made more so by the complete absence of any cyclists. Perhaps flooding had closed the route further up the road and *les cyclistes* were now floating down the Rhône clinging to their Shimanos and heading for the Med.

But then, glory be! A rider sped past our windows, followed by another, and another. We scrutinised these die-hards in Lycra, and discovered they were all terribly young, barely teenagers. It turned out this was a local 'cadet' race around the marina, not the main event. We mentally applauded them for their stamina and sheer guts, silently yelled our support, turned up the radiator and made another cup of coffee.

After the cadets had finished there was a lull, during which – frustratingly for them – it stopped raining and brightened up, to the extent that we ventured out for a stroll. A few tens of kilometres away, unbeknown to us, the real race had already taken in two or three nearby towns and was on its way here.

The first we knew of it was a group of four *gendarmerie* motorcyclists with blue lights flashing riding fast and in loose formation around the marina, along with other official vehicles and motorbikes, and the odd ambulance, which presumably carried bandages, salve cream and spare Lycra patches.

There was an increase of tension in the air, and people began to line the route, especially on the other side of the marina where the finish line was. A commentator started broadcasting over the PA system, even though there were still no cyclists, but he sounded excited. I said to Liz, 'Is a cycling commentator a spokesperson?' but she just shook her head in despair and scanned the crowd for a potential new husband.

And finally, with a surge of applause and yells of support, the race leaders swished into town, dozens and dozens of them in two or three colourful bunches, or whatever the collective noun is for racing cyclists. A Saddle? A Pump? Actually, a 'Blur' sounds about right, because as we tried to capture some of the action with our cameras in sports-mode that's pretty much all we got... a blur. And we were getting multiple shots of race cyclists' backsides, the rest of them already having left shot. If the *gendarmes* had confiscated my camera and checked the images they would probably have locked me up.

We lost count of how many times the two or three Blurs went by – four or five maybe – each time faster and more tightly bunched, except on the second to last lap when all of a sudden they seemed to idle by as though on a Sunday jaunt. We decided this was to conserve energy for the Final Push (but at least we managed to get some decent photos).

As the commentator's babble reached top gear, the lead Blur came into sight, the faces of the front cyclists masks of determination, some with gritted teeth, one guy with his mouth permanently open (too much wind resistance I would have thought) and another with his tongue hanging out like a dog leaning out a car window. Knees pumped, thighs strained, the crowd yelled, my camera went *kitchickitchickitchik*, the commentator orgasmed and the guy in the blue Lycra threw his arms in the air in victory as he swept over the finish line to the delight of the crowd.

But the one we watched for was the poor guy who was last. We'd seen him on his own a few minutes each time behind the main bunch as they'd gone through, valiantly pumping along, his race support car alongside him to protect him from all the other support cars festooned with spare bike parts which were overtaking in pursuit of their more successful riders. He did finish eventually, to some good-spirited support from the crowd, which was nice to see.

We went back to the boat, proposed a toast to the Spirit of Cycling, and deleted all the bum photos for fear of being labelled cycling perverts. Or 'pedalphiles.'

CHAPTER TWENTY-SIX

And so our winter continued in Beaucaire, which turned out to be a nice place to be 'stuck,' and we sort of wished that the haughty English woman at Valence who had cynically wished us *bonne chance* could join us to witness our suffering.

That winter Beaucaire really did seem to be the sunniest place in the country, and although there were plenty of cold crisp days, there were also many when the thermometer climbed into the late teens and even early 20s, if the flashing temperature sign outside the pharmacy could be believed.

It didn't matter anyway what the official figure was; there were plenty of days when we were able to sit outside on deck in comfort and watch the world go by.

So mild was it that the temporary ice rink set up in Tarascon's central plaza across the river had trouble keeping its cool, and the equally temporary Christmas trees in tubs around it were sprayed with fake snow, there being a total shortage of the real thing.

We read lots of books, and sometimes in the evenings watched French television in the hope of improving our grasp of the language. One of our favourite programmes was the French equivalent of Britain's *Come Dine With Me*, which the French called *Un Dîner Presque Parfait* – An Almost Perfect Dinner – where four or five people take turns to put on a meal with a different theme each week, and then score each other's efforts.

The French dinner conversations, being colloquial, were very useful in terms of knowing what's usually said, as opposed to what the books tell you is correct. We discovered, for example, that it's perfectly acceptable to say *'bon app'* in place of the more formal *'bon appetit.'*

At Le Nautic we bonded with Patrick and Marina, who became our first proper French friends. Patrick owned a boat which was moored at the nearby *chantier*, the same place we criminals fled from to escape paying our bills. In fact it was he who had first helped us get *Liberty* out of the main channel when she broke down, valiantly towing us in his dinghy.

He was ex-navy, and then ex-something in the diplomatic service, about which he wasn't very forthcoming. 'He was probably a spy,' Liz whispered to me when he wasn't listening. As long as he hadn't given the order to blow up the *Rainbow Warrior*, we didn't particularly care.

Marina, curly-haired, petite, and 27 years younger than her partner (this *is* France!), was studying computer graphic design and building up to some exams. They both spoke very good English, but we tried our best to converse in French, and Marina was very patient with us, and also not afraid to correct us if we used a word or phrase incorrectly, which was nice.

I was telling her one evening that I had once been *sur la télévision*, to which she smiled and very kindly pointed out that in actual fact I had been *à la television*; otherwise I would have been more like a vase of flowers and physically on top of it.

Another Friday evening at the bar we celebrated our wedding anniversary, and were surprised and delighted when Fabrice and Cécile presented a cake they'd made for us, festooned with candles. They were lovely hosts.

Ivan, one of the locals, who had survived a number of operations for throat cancer and who sounded like Yoda, took

Liz for a celebratory dance and twirled her expertly around the floor. Me and my two left feet remained firmly in place.

We went to the street markets, which were many, and I regularly trawled through the Wednesday morning *brocante* market, held under the bare trees of the Champ de Foire between the old castle walls and the river. Here stallholders set up their trestle tables early in the morning, or spread out carpets or tarpaulins on the ground beside their vehicles, and laid out all manner of antiques and collectables, from postcards to Prussian helmets.

There were some gorgeous items, including a pair of old puppets that looked vaguely Indonesian. I loved also the old bits of decorative stonework from buildings, or pieces of wrought iron, and for a brief moment longed for a home with a garden again.

I talked with Liz about the possibility of using Van Rouge as the basis for setting up an antiques business back in England. 'We could make regular forays into France to markets like this, buy up lovely collectable stuff, then head back to the UK to make a fortune!

'Or buy a property here in France, do exactly the same thing, but set up the business online and invite buyers from around the globe to browse our treasures!' I was enthusiastic.

'And what would I do for a job?' Liz asked. As usual my heart had run off with an idea. 'I'm not ready to give up work yet, and I'm not sure second-hand stuff is going to bring in a decent living wage,' she added. I went off to look for a phone box, somewhere where she could change out of her Logic Woman costume in private. Maybe I'd find one at the brocante market.

So the vision of me as a sort of roguish French *Lovejoy* faded, though I still went every Wednesday and looked longingly at the treasures, but I never bought anything.

We were definitely starting to feel 'local,' and our affection for Beaucaire was growing, as were the new leaf buds on the trees. Spring was coming. It was all rather lovely.

And then life became hectic again; it was time for our close-ups.

We'd heard from the *A Place in the Sun* producer that she would be sending someone out with a camera to get shots of us on board *Liberty*, and do a brief interview with us.

This would be followed by shooting for the programme proper, and we were to be flown back to Liverpool for a three-day shoot, looking at three apartments there, followed by a flight to Tenerife to do the same all over again in that location. Exciting!

Having worked in television in various capacities, including as a producer and director, I had a good idea what was coming, and told Liz what to expect.

'It's unlikely they're just going to take us to see three apartments one after the other; what you see on the telly is three days' worth of shooting condensed into what looks like a quick trip around the properties. Instead you'll find there'll be lots of waiting around between shots, and a little bit of "acting" required too.'

Liz wasn't as keen on the idea of 'doing television' as I was, but she recognised the opportunity this gave us to do some real close-up investigation of properties and opportunities.

They sent Sarah, a young production assistant, who arrived one afternoon with a camera and tripod, and spent a couple of hours shooting us – on the boat, tootling down the marina, berthing, sitting on deck drinking wine (surprise!), and she did a brief interview about why we wanted to look for properties in England and Tenerife, what sort of properties we wanted, and what our budgets were for each place.

Sarah had only a couple of hours available as she was on a same-day return ticket, so there wasn't any time to get lovely shots of *Liberty* gliding along the canal through the countryside, with Camargue horses regarding us as we passed by. But she seemed happy with what she'd got of us cruising up and back through the marina, and the sun shone, which was a bonus.

A short while later we were flown to Liverpool and put up in a hotel. That evening we met the director and the crew, and presenter Jasmin for drinks and pre-shoot chat. We'd be shooting over the following two and a half days – and I was right: where it looks on the programme like they whizz you from property to property in a short space of time, in fact it's a lot less hectic, at least for us as the 'talent.'

Next morning we started with the opening shots which were done at the waterfront, and later we were shown our first property, an apartment in a tower block overlooking the River Mersey.

The director does go to some lengths to capture your first impressions, and we got used to waiting on the street or in corridors while the cameraman shot various bits inside and set up ready for us to walk through the door and capture our astonishment (or not as the case may be).

Liz and I had already agreed that we would *not* say 'Wow!' the moment we walked into any of the properties, even if they blew us away, because it's what everyone seems to say on these programmes. The other thing we'd agreed on was to avoid saying 'bathroom' when looking into the bathroom, or 'kitchen' when viewing that. Given that TV is a visual medium there's no point in stating the bleeding obvious.

The three properties in Liverpool were all nicely central and were all for sale for about the same price, but they varied widely in their appeal. Liz and I scored each on a chart so we'd know we were comparing them against the same criteria. Jasmin liked the chart and it was included in the finished programme, but there was a lot of other stuff that wasn't used, which was a bit disappointing.

For example, I'd asked Jasmin on camera why apartments were called apartments when they were joined onto others, above, below, and maybe to the sides. If anything, I said, they should be called 'togetherments.' She liked this and it became a running gag through all our Liverpool shooting, yet it wasn't used at all in the finished programme.

Also, there were some negatives we highlighted which weren't used either, such as the possibility that the wasteland in front of the tower block might be built on, thereby obscuring our views, or that the alleyway that led to one of the other apartments had iron bars over all the windows at street level and the view from the apartment showed roofs across the alley covered in coils of barbed wire. It was intimidating and ugly, but no mention was made of it, or the fact that we'd noted that this particular apartment still had the feel of a commercial office (we suspect that's exactly what it was but was being marketed for the first time as residential).

However, having worked in television production, I do understand the need for editing, and that the ratio of shooting to finished production is usually about 4:1, so I wasn't too concerned when we finally got to see the programme a year later.

Meanwhile, after Liverpool had put on a nice display for us, with bright sunshine and blue skies, and three apartments that showed there was certainly the potential to find something near the river in our price range, it was now time to go and do the same thing in Tenerife.

We decided to build in some extra time at our own cost to explore this Spanish island for three days before the director and crew arrived, so we booked to stay at a hotel in the north, directly opposite the locations they'd be taking us to in the south of the island.

The Apartamentos Bella Vista in Puerto de la Cruz turned out to be a multi-storey hotel built in a crescent shape. It sat atop cliffs and its convex side looked north directly out over the *Oceano Atlantico*, which was a myriad of blues ranging from deep aquamarine through teal to light blue, according to the swells, the wind and the dance of the sunlight on the water.

The hotel on the other hand was basically white with a bright green trim. The rendering was a stucco-style finish, both inside the rooms, reception, the bar, the restaurant and on the exterior. The vivid green trim had been applied lovingly everywhere, from door jambs, coffee tables and picture frames to handrails, curtain rods and even plant pots.

And when we say 'lovingly,' we mean it; the precision and quality of the green paintwork was superb, and obviously the work of an artisan. As DIY people ourselves, we know how tricky it is to get a straight edge when painting on stucco, or any stippled surface. Your masking tape often doesn't stick very well, and even if it does, the rough surface usually means some paint will dribble in underneath your carefully-applied tape, making your painted edges look like the work of a two-year old.

But not at the Bella Vista. Here the borders where green met white were razor sharp. And where there was an opportunity for highlighting in green, it was taken, and executed professionally. Take the curtain rails for example; someone had gone to the trouble of taking them off the walls, undone the finials at each end, then removed the mounting brackets. They had then painted the rail itself white, and the finials and brackets green, probably with two or even three coats each, and when everything had dried they'd reassembled the lot.

They'd done the same with drawer handles, table legs, hinges and edges, throughout the hotel. No opportunity, no matter how minor, had been missed.

And the quality of the paintwork, as mentioned, was absolutely fantastic… not a single drip or run. The gloss paint gleamed; you could see your face in it.

What a pity then that the trim colour was such an awful, *awful* gut-wrenching shade of the ugliest green known to man. It was not a green you would even find in nature, unless a plant needed to scare away absolutely everything on the planet from pollinating insects to any other life form. It was such a truly revolting hue that any species bearing it would surely die off and exit the evolutionary ladder, since nothing on earth would ever want to help it in its survival. Maybe it was even called Extinction Green.

To support this theory, we went to the *Jardin Botanico* in Puerto de la Cruz one morning, and despite the myriad array of some of the world's lushest foliage, this green wasn't present.

But someone somewhere in the Bella Vista's hierarchy liked green, and this particular shade over all others. Either that or some decades ago there was a paint sale *gigantesco* in which *'El verde de la extinción'* was being sold off very cheaply, if not being given away. Perhaps there's still ten thousand litres of it in the hotel's basement.

On the other hand, we chose the Bella Vista for its location and its reasonable tariff. Sure there were hotels more central, more modern and better decorated. But if the guests staying there knew what we were paying they'd probably have been… well, green with envy.

Anyway, over the three days we took walks and rode buses around the north of Tenerife to familiarise ourselves with the landscape and the sorts of properties that were on offer.

It was windy and cool, not the sort of Canary Islands temperature we'd been expecting, and once again we had to revise our expectations of just how far south you had to go to find guaranteed warmth. Further than here, it seemed.

But we discovered that the north is well known for its wind, so perhaps we shouldn't have been surprised. Also, decent beaches seemed few and far between, and much of the coastline was rocky and uninviting. The other thing we found is that this part of the island is, for some reason, a firm favourite with Germans and Scandiwegians. They were everywhere. All the British, we were to discover, were in the south.

And that's where we headed too, to meet up with the director, crew, and the '*Away*' presenter, Sara.

Our bus journey took us right round the north of the island, including over part of the volcanic inland area, and down the west coast, and we realised just how relatively small Tenerife is.

Staying in a much less gaudy hotel this time, in Costa Adeje in the south west, we met up with the crew and over drinks once again were given some indication how the next three days would play out.

Having heard of the reputations of the more well-known Playa de la Américas and Los Christianos areas as being full of British lager louts, 'Irish' bars, fish and chip shops and endless night clubs, we had asked to be shown places away from there, figuring that it would be more peaceful, and probably more affordable. Hence we were at Costa Adeje, which was much better – and at last, it was warm!

Liz and I took a stroll the evening before the shooting began. Standing overlooking the beaches with the lazy waves of the Atlantic flopping in as though tired after a long journey, we turned and looked back inland, where the land rose gradually towards the volcanic centre. Higher up on this hillside we could see a very large concentration of apartments tiered into the landscape, the highest of the residential buildings at that point. Up beyond that there seemed to be nothing but volcanic scrubland. The cascading apartments were all the same orange colour, and they looked ugly.

'I hope they're not taking us there tomorrow!' Liz said.

They were. In fact, they took us to the top-most row of the apartments, the ones just below the scrubland. This meant that the residences had wide uninterrupted views to the sea, but the zig-zag road to reach them, and the complete absence of any sort of shops or other facilities locally put us off from the start.

Still, we hadn't come all this way to just moan – it was after all part of our research, even if someone else was paying for it, so we played the game and viewed the apartment with our reservations held in check. But then Sara told us the apartment was for sale a bit beyond our budget, so we were able to dismiss it without seeming too mean-spirited.

Shooting with Sara down on one of the beaches the next morning we discovered that television crews must be two-a-penny in Tenerife, and are regarded as part of the landscape. This is presumably why the elderly bare-chested gentleman on his morning stroll chose to walk right through our shot, three times. It also explained why an elderly and completely bare-breasted woman did exactly the same. 'I say Madam, don't you realise there could be children watching this programme?!'

The remaining two apartments were, thankfully, much closer to the coast, and within budget. They were diametrically opposed in their appearances, styles and locations, which we liked because it showed us the variety our money could buy.

We viewed one top floor apartment in a large complex that included its own communal swimming pool and private beach access, but the one we liked the most was a little way out of town.

Despite being more remote it at least had a local shop and bar within walking distance, had good elevation and sunny views of the coast, two tiled terraces (the bottom one of which was beautifully planted in exotic flowers), and even an internal garage. The price was right too. I liked it, even though we still had some reservations.

That evening Liz and I talked about what we might do if we did actually buy a place here, and whether there were any opportunities for work.

'We've seen so many houses and apartments with terraces,' Liz said, 'but so many of them are boring. Hardly any of them have anything other than maybe a barbecue. There's barely a plant pot. I can see myself starting up a terrace garden design business here!' Liz loved gardening, and I could see she would probably make a go of the venture.

I too had had an idea for an enterprise; having long ridden motorcycles I had taken an interest in what sort of two-wheeled tourist and motorcycle-hire ventures there were in Tenerife. My brief online research showed, unsurprisingly, there were already many motorbike hire businesses, and even tours where you could ride pillion behind your guide and be whizzed around the island's hot spots on a big throbbing Harley-Davidson or similar.

But nobody seemed to be running a motorcycle tour business with a *sidecar*. With a sidecar you could take a *couple* on a tour – one on the pillion and one in the sidecar. You could pack a generous picnic in the sidecar's boot, and take picnic blankets, maybe even a sun umbrella.

Over an outdoor evening meal we talked over what we might do, and suddenly the idea of living in Tenerife didn't seem so far-fetched after all.

But the next day was the final day, and also that time of the programme where we had to reveal whether we had chosen home, or away. Sara sat us down on a sunny terrace in the bright hot sun and under the unwavering eye of the camera asked us what we'd decided.

And that was it; the end of the shoot. Next morning, very early, we were driven to the airport, and flown back to France via a transit stopover at Barcelona.

Although there was a brief drama to be played out yet.

CHAPTER TWENTY-SEVEN

It was here, while waiting for our connecting flight to Marseille at *Aeropuerto Barcelona* Terminal One – we saw a moving sight: a luggage trolley handler taking photos of… luggage trolleys, on his phone. We secretly named him Rodriguez, and imagined his situation, as he returned home that evening…

(Rodriguez closes the front door behind him, throws his keys on the sideboard, and sees his wife Consuela as she emerges from the kitchen, wiping her hands on her apron.)

Consuela: Rodriguez *mi querido*! You are home at last! How was your first day at the *aeropuerto, carino*?

Rodriguez (shrugs): Consuela, it was overall a *buen dia*. You know, it had, like most days, its ups and downs. Or, in my case, its pushings and pullings!

(Consuela laughs delightedly at her husband's sense of humour and takes him in her arms.)

Consuela: Oh Rodriguez, you are so funny. You should be on the stage!

Rodriguez: *Si*, and there's one leaving in five minutes! I know that old joke…

Consuela: But seriously my love, how did it go, your first day as a trolley wrangler?

Rodriguez (pulling his phone from inside his jacket): I will show you, *mi carino*. Come, let us sit on the sofa… I have *muchas fotos* to show you.

(They sit, Consuela visibly excited. Rodriguez opens his phone gallery and begins flipping through his album of pictures.)

Rodriguez: See here? This is a solo trolley, the typical model, with one wonky wheel always at the front so it never goes where you want it. This is one of the most challenging aspects of my job.

(Consuela tuts appropriately.)

Rodriguez: And here… this is a line of twenty trolleys pushed together. Very heavy, and *muy* difficult to manoeuvre, or even… womanoeuvre!

(They laugh uproariously and slap their thighs. Their own, not each other's. That comes later.)

Rodriguez (wiping tears of laughter from his eyes): This one though, is more typical… thirty or forty trolleys in haphazard circumstance… in *muchas* disarray, all over the place. People, they just don' care you know? They treat the trolleys like so much rubbish, it's… it's… (his bottom lip trembles).

Consuela (placing her arm around Rodriguez's broad shoulders): Oh there, there, it is not so bad. It is a process of education that is needed. This can be your goal… to teach the filthy careless tourist scum some humanity!

They both mime a synchronised spit into the fireplace.

Rodriguez (looks at her in amazement): You are right, *mi quarida*, you are so right!

(They kiss, briefly, his eyes sparkling. Then he turns his attention back to the phone.) But look here: in the background of this picture of the Trundelez 5000 – the model with the automatic brake for going on the travelators; you can see *dos personas Inglés*, coming out of the *aeropuerto* bar after having a few wines. Now see in this next picture what happens…

Consuela (taking the phone from her husband and swiping to the next image): *Madre de Dios!* They have both tripped over the Trundelez and fallen flat on their faces!

Rodriguez (smiling broadly): *Si…* they were completely *trolleyed!*

(They laugh uproariously, slap each other's thighs, and slowly dance towards the bedroom…)

And so we flew into Marseille from where we caught the train back to Tarascon, and trundled our suitcases across the bridge over the Rhône and back to *Liberty*. Home again.

It was a full year later that our programme finally screened on the UK's Channel 4, by which time we were watching it from the comfort of our apartment in – *spoiler alert!* – Liverpool.

And, overall the programme was an accurate depiction of what we'd seen and where we'd been. Except that in the second half, which featured the three apartments in Tenerife, we felt they missed out some crucial information that would have explained why we didn't choose to buy what appeared to be our ideal winter retreat, the apartment a little way outside of Costa Adeje, the one with two bedrooms, internal access garage, and two terraces – one upstairs, and a lovely garden terrace below. It faced the sunny south and had a sweeping view of the Atlantic. What wasn't to like?

What they didn't show was us expressing concern about the motorway that was being built some way below the apartment – quite distant but still near enough that we could hear the reversing beeps of the bulldozers and trucks. And, at the bottom of the garden terrace was a communal septic tank, a *smelly* septic tank.

But there was something else, perhaps more major; the Spanish government had recently been enforcing legislation prohibiting holiday lets in Tenerife of less than three months' duration, which could effectively destroy the apartment holiday industry.

They'd done this to protect (they claimed) the local hotels, and had even allegedly employed undercover inspectors to check that apartments weren't being let for just a week or two. These inspectors would apparently knock on doors and say they were doing a tourism survey, which, if true, is underhand and sneaky. And costly for those caught; we heard of one property owner who was fined fifteen thousand Euros!

So, although the legislation was at the time being challenged in court, it frightened us off buying in Tenerife, even if we'd compromised on the motorway and septic tank issues. But none of that came out in the story, and some viewers must have been left wondering why on earth we'd choose Liverpool over sunny Spain. Well now you know.

Anyway, overall we enjoyed the experience, and it did prove to be very worthwhile and useful, not just a free holiday. It convinced us that we *did* want an apartment in Liverpool near the river, even though none of those we were shown ticked all our boxes. Later in the year Liz spent nine days viewing a whole lot more apartments in Liverpool and found one which we eventually bought.

Are we sad we didn't buy something in Tenerife? Not really. Having left New Zealand and its earthquakes, Liz reminded me about my fear of seismic shakes and said, 'Why would you want to then go and live on the slopes of a volcano that could erupt any day?!'

Good point. Thank God you're here Logic Woman.

And so having got back to Beaucaire we promptly left it again. Spring was underway, the canal system was open, the weather was looking good and we had miles and miles of waterways yet to explore. It was time to start up *Liberty*'s engine and get going again.

After a last call-in at Le Nautic to say farewell to Fabrice and Cécile, Jim and Sandra, Keith, and Patrick and Marina we did all our below-deck checks and the next morning, a Monday, we set off.

The day was lovely, blue sky, sunshine, and much better than forecast. Not particularly warm, but a nice day – as Billy Idol once said – to start again.

Patrick and Marina hailed us from the shore and bid us farewell again, which was a nice surprise.

We burbled along the now-familiar stretch of canal between Beaucaire and the lock at Nourriguier, our first lock in over four months. Again we were the only ones using it and after dropping the four metres we continued on south, through Bellegarde where just a few weeks earlier we'd enjoyed a picnic lunch after cycling there on a nice spring day. And this time nobody chased us shouting '*Le facture! Le facture!*'

We crept through Saint-Gilles and reached the 'nature moorings' just shy of where the Beaucaire canal meets the Canal du Rhône à Sète, the same place where we stopped in early December and woke up to snow. Of the three simple moorings, one was occupied, so we took the second, and an hour or so later a young Dutch couple on a hire boat arrived and I helped them moor at the third. So, even this early in the season, a full-house.

The weather turned cool and windy, clouds came up, so we hunkered down inside and had dinner with the boat's repaired heater on, cosy. A quiet night.

The cloudy cool weather continued the next day so we stopped at Galician where we went to the *cave* and bought some of the local wines, onions from the tiny shop, and had a coffee and Wi-Fi check at the town's bar-café. By the time we strolled back to the boat the sun had come out and it warmed up considerably, to the extent we sailed in short sleeves for a while.

It turned out to be a long day's sailing of six hours. After passing the canal entrances to Aigues-Mortes we continued heading west, aiming to find another free mooring or at least a greenbanking opportunity. However they were scarce, or occupied, or too shallow.

So we found ourselves passing Carnon and Palavas-les-Flots and finally, just beyond the Quatre Canaux (Four Canals – say that quickly!) we found a reasonable mooring just past the main road bridge.

After another quiet (free!) night we strolled in to the nearest supermarket, also to check out a rumoured *gazole* (diesel) opportunity, but discovered that the hose at the *gazole* pump at the Carrefour supermarket wouldn't reach the tantalisingly close pontoon.

Instead next day, after sailing the boat there, we made numerous short trips back and forth with our jerry cans, but it was worth it to get cheap supermarket-priced fuel, the cheapest we'd found up to that point.

During this period of two days it was nice to see spring growth on the trees, but in general we found the Camargue area to be quite boring. It's definitely big sky territory, but is basically flat, windswept and dull, at least from the canal viewpoint.

Maybe it was because of the cool overcast weather, but the combination of flat landscape and boring straight canal lent a sombre mood. People rave about the Camargue, the romance of its white horses, the wind in the grasses, the bulls... but it can hardly be called pretty. Maybe we missed something.

So come that Wednesday morning we were glad to cast off and begin to get closer to the fabled loveliness of the Canal du Midi, though with still a few miles to go first. But the weather forecast, which said showers and cloud, was wrong, and we set off in warm sunshine, though on a very short half-hour journey to Maguelone. Here we found a nice greenbank mooring, with wetland *étangs* on both sides of the canal and a view of Sète's hill in the distance.

Where we moored the canal was bordered on one side by some colourful fishing cottages, the sort that makes you want to get out an easel, brushes and palette. We had brought artist's pencils with us, with the best of intentions of doing some sketching, but for some reason every time we tried to lay a hand on one we found we'd somehow grabbed a corkscrew instead. So the only things we drew were corks.

We walked to the nearby Maguelone Cathedral which dates back to the fifth century, though much restored and rebuilt since then, lots of times in fact. But it's a lovely cathedral of pale stone, charming proportions, and completely lacks the ornate décor of the bigger Notre Dames and suchlike. This felt somehow more humble, more real. A woman in the gallery upstairs sang solo hymns, her voice pure in the cathedral's vaulted ceilings – an added bonus.

We took another look at the Med just beyond the cathedral, but it was still in an unsettled mood and not keen to receive visitors.

On the stroll back Liz tried in vain to get the definitive flamingo photo, but they always seemed to be just far enough away as to make focusing and composition a challenge, and would stick their heads underwater and turn their bums to the camera just before she pressed the shutter. So, nothing for the cover of *National Geographic* yet; the idea was sound, but our attempts were more *Notional Geographic*.

Once again the cloud came over, the wind got chilly, and by mid-afternoon we ended up back at the boat with the heating on again as a few spots of rain tried their best to evolve into a proper shower. Over towards Montpelier we could see it looked like it was bucketing down. I rhetorically asked Liz why people rave about a Mediterranean climate. I wrote in that night's blog, 'I don't get it. It's *cold*!'

But it was still early spring, so maybe we were being optimistic setting off quite so soon.

Anyway, we decided there was nothing for it but to push on, and so it was that within a day we finally made it to the famous Canal du Midi – that seventeenth century engineering marvel that links the Atlantic with the Mediterranean. You might already have seen it if you've watched chef Rick Stein on the telly travelling on a hotel boat along the waterway, cooking his way through southern France. Or Timothy West and Prunella Scales exploring the same route in a hire boat.

The profile the canal gets is hardly surprising as there are a number of reasons why it's famous, not least of which is that it ranks among those achievements – such as heavier-than-air flight, flying to the moon, and saying 'bum' on the BBC – that once came under the heading, 'It Can't Be Done.'

Monsieur Pierre-Paul Riquet, was one of those who turned his back on the nay-sayers in the late 1600s and persuaded the government of the time that *oui*, indeed the canal could be built because he had solved all the problems in constructing it. The long story short is that he was given the green light, and despite constant criticism from his opponents, went ahead and built it, introducing some of the best working conditions in the world at the same time.

The sad thing is he died just eight months before it opened.

Since then the canal has been used for commerce and tourism, and today is extremely popular with pleasure boaters, winding its way as it does from near Sète on the Med to Toulouse, where it becomes the Canal Latéral à la Garonne, to Bordeaux on France's south west coast. Its meandering course, taking it through some of the nicest locations in the south of France is another reason for its popularity. There are quaint bridges, many *many* locks – including the celebrated staircase lock at Fonserannes – and it passes through numerous historic towns and villages. We were looking forward to it.

CHAPTER TWENTY-EIGHT

F onserannes was something we had anticipated with trepidation. The six-lock staircase climbs up 21 metres, over a distance of three hundred metres and although it's controlled by an *éclusier* with a remote-control box that looks like a video game handset, it is nevertheless quite a challenge, especially for first-timers, and doubly-especially when going up.

Our first view of it from the bottom chamber was frightening; all we could see was cascading water tumbling down from open gates ahead of us. We shared the staircase with another boat, skippered by Swiss man Mark. He was on his own, but very much seemed to know what he was doing. We think this is why he always let us go into each chamber ahead of him; it allowed us to bang and crash around as we tried to moor *Liberty* against the curving edge of the lock.

The locks on the Canal du Midi that we'd encountered to date were different in design to those on the Rhône à Sète. Rather than being straight-sided boxes, these on the Midi were ovoid, which made coming alongside the edge neatly somewhat challenging.

We read later that the staircase at Fonserannes is the third most popular tourist destination in this Languedoc-Roussillon region, (the others being the Pont du Gard and the town of Carcassonne, where we would arrive in due course).

This would explain why, on this bright and warm Sunday afternoon, we were watched by dozens of gongoozlers on the banks and bridges.

(If you think the word gongoozler is one we made up, you're wrong. The Oxford Dictionaries Online defines it as, 'Early 20th century [originally denoting a person who idly watched activity on a canal]; rare before 1970: perhaps from Lincolnshire dialect *gawn* and *gooze* 'stare, gape'.' So there.)

Because we'd been greenbanking and using our on-boat power for a few days, there wasn't much juice in our thruster batteries, so I was having to manoeuvre *Liberty* using the helm and throttle as best I could to position us close enough to the side for Liz to throw the ropes around the bollards. She wasn't having much luck, but drew applause from the onlookers whenever she did manage to lasso one.

A couple of local men on the lockside offered their assistance, but they didn't know anything about ropes or whether they should be tied or not, so it was a hectic and confusing time, but we were grateful for their cheery enthusiasm nevertheless.

Mark meantime wasn't even breaking into a mild sweat as he deftly positioned *Bon Viveur*, on his own, in each chamber. He even declined an offer of help from a man onshore. We were in awe of his skill. (He later told us over a glass of wine that he regarded 'helpers' as more of a liability, and much preferred to do things on his own.)

Our thruster batteries died completely so the bashing around we'd done in the first chamber was repeated all the way up the staircase, until with a big sigh of relief we finally exited out the top. We'd somehow managed to get up the chambers with nothing more than dented egos, though there was some real damage to come just a short time later.

And so, having climbed the stairs, we were able to once again relax, and enjoy the famed Canal du Midi.

Engineering apart, perhaps the Midi's most celebrated aspect is its plane trees, which, for the past two hundred years or so, have lined the edges, gripping the banks and preventing erosion, while at the same time creating a green tunnel of love under which your boat glides in dappled splendour (when the sun shines and there are leaves on the trees that is).

Picture postcard-perfect, the combination of arboreal gorgeousness and engineering excellence have gained the Canal du Midi UNESCO World Heritage status, and have done the French postcard industry no harm either.

It's estimated there are something like 42,000 plane trees lining the banks of the Midi. In summer they are undeniably gorgeous; in autumn they turn golden; in winter their starkness has a beauty all of its own, and in springtime as we cruised along, the new leaves were just beginning to glow in the pale sunshine.

But it was, it seemed, all about to come to an unbelievable, unbearable and incredibly sad end, because they'd started to cut down the whole blooming lot. Every tree was, apparently, for the chainsaw, the result of a deadly fungus that has been attacking the plane trees for the past five years or so.

As we sailed toward Colombiers one afternoon, still celebrating having survived the staircase locks, our good mood was shattered when we came across the waterway equivalent of road cones – floating orange buoys cordoning off a work area. On the banks we could see fresh stumps, where plane trees had been felled, some showing gaping holes where, presumably, the fungal disease had taken its toll. Around these stumps sawdust lay, the blood at the crime scene, except in this case there was no culprit to be caught, no murderer to be hanged.

Later that morning we were in a small town, looking at postcards of places on the canal, and recognised a statue of a water-bearer at Villeneuve les Beziers where we'd stayed the previous night. What we didn't recognise was all the lovely plane trees in the background. They had all gone. Not only that, the stumps had been removed, which is why we saw no evidence of the trees when we were there. I actually felt a lump in my throat, and my eyes stung.

I guess we were lucky in that the cull was still in its early days, and we'd already sailed along some leafy watery avenues, with more to come. But soon it seemed the plane trees of the Midi would be no more, and it will be years before the new saplings mature enough to be postcard material.

As we progressed along the Midi, we found the crosses on the trees, marking them for execution, to be one of the most depressing sights of our journey.

'GOING TOPLESS IN FRANCE' was the heading of our next blog.

Well, it was sure to get our readers' attention, and they wouldn't be disappointed because the blog really was about going topless. Sort-of.

Some people have qualms about removing their tops, perhaps understandably, especially if summer hasn't quite started yet. But here in France it's just another part of life on the canals. And yes, Liz and I both sailed topless.

Curb your enthusiasm; we didn't do it every day of course, but sometimes it was just necessary. Having decided to leave Colombiers and head for a wee town called Argeliers, we checked in the canal guide and discovered we'd be going under some of the lowest bridges on the Canal du Midi. This meant dropping *Liberty*'s top in order to be able to squeeze under.

What? You didn't really think we personally would be topless when the temperature was only 16 degrees, it was windy and cloudy did you? Get real!

As you know, if you were paying attention back when we

were originally looking for a boat to buy, height-wise your boat's *tirant d'air* needs to be lower than the lowest bridge you're likely to encounter. If it's not you can easily demolish your mast, wheelhouse windows and lose all your superstructure equipment such as radio aerials, horn, navigation lights – or worse if you have one – your expensive radar dome. You can also bang your head rather nastily and suffer excruciating embarrassment if gongoozlers are watching. Your credibility would be seriously dented too.

Many boats are designed therefore with droppable tops. *Liberty*, for example, has a stainless steel equipment rack carrying the forward mast light, aerials, horn and two Kiwi flags, but flip a couple of levers and the whole thing drops down on hinges. Likewise, the canvas Bimini top unclips and folds down, and, for the lowest of the low, we can unhinge and remove the flying bridge windows and sneak under the really challenging spans. It means that *Liberty* enjoys 'Access All Areas' status on the French waterways, and all we have to remember is to duck as we go under low bridges.

On the Midi we had to drop everything to squeeze beneath three particularly low arches, which was a bit of a challenge. We knew there were more to come too, but the canal book included the measurements of every bridge so we had plenty of warning. We got through without bruising heads, egos, or anything else.

One of the other joys of that day's four-hour sail was going through the Malpas Tunnel, the oldest canal tunnel in Europe. In itself it isn't particularly challenging; it's short (160m), high enough for us to leave our top up, and wide enough that we could get through without banging the sides of the boat. What is remarkable about it is that canal-builder P. Riquet, on encountering a hill in the way of his canal work in 1679, was ordered to stop tunnelling as the excavation was considered a health and safety risk (this some-400 years before anyone actually knew what H&S meant, and way before hi-vis vests or hard-hats).

But Riquet was on a mission, and the finishing line was – figuratively at least – within sight, so he quietly instructed his chief mason and his crew to continue the tunnel in secret. Eight days later – *eight days!* – the workers were through, and all Riquet's objectors, nay-sayers and government worry-mongers had to shut up and watch him carry on creating what is today regarded as one of the world's engineering marvels.

So we raised a metaphorical glass to Paul-Pierre Riquet as we slid majestically through his anarchic excavation. In 1679 it was another engineering feat that couldn't be topped. It was – in a word – topless.

CHAPTER TWENTY-NINE

A woman *éclusier* had told us the weather forecast for *Dimanche* was very good. We'd been having a brief conversation about how bad the wind had been, both shaking our heads in collective despair. And she wasn't wrong. Sunday morning dawned bright and sunny, warm – and blissfully calm.

We topped up water and power, and dropped *Liberty*'s top again in anticipation both of nice weather and more low bridges (and cross-canal phone and power lines… the lowth of some of these had taken us by surprise).

By 9.30 we were on our way, winding our way along the Midi with the new green of spring growth everywhere and the sun on our backs. It lifted our moods significantly, and we grinned from ear to ear. This finally was the Canal du Midi as it was supposed to be – the Midi that broadcasters and travel writers rave about; the Midi of Romance. It wasn't to last long.

Liz checked the book and decided a good day's cruising would get us to Trèbes, a meandering journey involving quite a few locks, some of them multiples of twos and threes, the usual bridges, and a few villages. It was a perfect day, during which we shared many of the locks with a hire boat crewed by one jolly Frenchman and his crew of six women who scuttled about the quay not knowing how to manage the ropes while he was in charge of not knowing how to steer the boat and banging his way in and out of the lock gates. Heaven knows what the insurance premiums are on those hire boats.

In each case we let him and his matelots enter the lock first – partly for our entertainment and partly for safety – and only when they were tied up did we cruise in and (a matter of pride on my part) use minimal or even no thrusters to moor alongside. Liz and I had honed our rope skills by now and we knew what we were doing, so our tie-ups looked professional by comparison. (Mind you, a two-year-old with a toy boat in the bath would have looked professional by comparison.)

The Frenchman even applauded us as we glided (glid? glad?) alongside, which made up for our own disastrous crashing and banging in the staircase locks at Fonserannes exactly a week previously. We'd come a long way since then, in experience if not distance.

(Having said that, there was one lock where we made a bad mistake. One of our ropes was accidentally wrapped twice round a bollard [my fault], and as the water in the lock dropped the rope got tighter and tighter, and the boat started tilting. A quick slice with our sharp 'emergency knife' and all was well, but if it hadn't been within reach, or worse, not on board at all… well, it doesn't bear thinking about. Luckily no-one was watching!)

Anyway, it was nice to be on the up after a seemingly interminable period of gloom. The things that had affected our mood barometers the most in the previous couple of weeks had been the almost constant grey skies, cool temperatures and wind, ever since we left Beaucaire. We had been lulled into a false sense of spring and security at Beaucaire, where more often than not the sun shone. There, the bars and restaurants were beginning to spruce up their outdoor areas ready for returning *al fresco* business. The restaurant boat near our mooring, which had lain dormant since we'd arrived back in November, suddenly reopened, its tables glaring with crisp white linen. We saw the owner on his knees painting the boat's planters along the quayside, or possibly praying for good business in the coming summer.

So when we sailed out of Beaucaire it was with hope in our hearts, a firm belief that *printemps* had arrived and the canals were emerging from hibernation, that the sun would shine more, it would be warmer, and we could dig out the T-shirts, shorts and sunblock.

Wrong. As we made our way through the Camargue there had been very little sun, and it wasn't warm. The famed Camargue white horses looked as miserable as they had when we'd seen them in wintry December on our way to Aigues-Mortes.

The day we reached the Étang de Thau to cross over to the start of the Canal du Midi we had blue skies and sun – but it must have been a fluke, because once on the Midi we were back to grey, the clouds stretching unbroken from horizon to horizon every day, our moods as gloomy.

On a bright note though, we did manage to sail a full seven days before needing to plug into shore power, or top up with water, but even at foggy Colombiers, a small but busy port on the Midi, the marina was only in the early stages of waking up after winter, the *Office du Tourisme* finally opening but on restricted hours, the *capitainerie* also seeming reluctant to function, rather like many of us feel waking up on a Monday morning after a great weekend, knowing that we have to go to a job we don't like. The fog only added to the somnolent atmosphere.

We'd passed canalside bars and restaurants, their chairs still stacked, their canvas awnings still furled. Blackboards, dirty from winter non-use, promised food, drink, tapas, and tastings… but not yet. It was still too early, still too cold, still too grey for customers.

Liz found it particularly hard.

There were a few boats braving the elements along with us, but not many. As we cruised further west each day, and March became April, we wondered when the weather would begin to pick up, but instead the clouds got heavier, the wind strengthened, and when we reached a little place called Roubia it began raining. All night it teemed down. In the morning it stopped, but the wind picked up even more, as if to say, hah, fooled you.

We took a stroll into the town because the guide book promised a grocery store with Wi-Fi, but found nothing. The local wine *caves* were closed, the whole town seemed deserted, as though invaded by body-snatchers. A lone dog took pity on us and came for a walk, but failed to guide us to any signs of life. He left us when we proved too dull. Later, the sun made a half-hearted effort to pierce the clouds but it was still windy and cold.

Back at the boat we turned the heating on. It failed. Again.

Next morning dawned as moody as we were, and very windy. We did some washing, read books and the newspaper from the previous weekend, and waited for the wind to abate. It didn't, but the day brightened considerably, and since it was less than five kilometres to the next town of Argens-Minervois we decided to risk it.

The two bridges proved easy, the one lock a bit tricky in the wind, but when we got to what we thought was a public marina we found it full of hire boats belonging to the Locaboat company there, with seemingly no room for us, and also the tiniest and trickiest marina entrance to date.

We aborted our one attempt to enter in the wind, which wanted to blow us into the concrete sides of the entrance, and instead moored on the canal further along. At which point Liz declared she'd had enough. Of everything. The lack of good Internet access, limited phone coverage, not being in the UK to help Yasmin at half-terms and other breaks, the wind, worrying about bridges and locks, the endless grey skies…

I knew how she felt. This wasn't what we signed up for, and as the saying goes, when the going gets tough it's time to go home.

So, I gave Liz the option of going back to the UK for a month or so. Maybe she could find us an apartment to buy. Maybe she could fly back out in May, when – please God – the weather would be improved. Or maybe she would decide not to come back at all.

With scarves, coats and hats we went for a walk around Argens-Minervois. Dogs snarled at us from behind fences. One, on the loose, charged up a street and snapped around our heels. Only the local cats seemed pleased we were there.

But again, it was another ghost town. No shops, closed restaurants (three), nothing happening. No obvious way up to the old fourteenth century *château* on the hill either. It didn't help our moods, even though a pale sun was shining.

We decided there was nothing for it but to press on. Liz decided that going back to the UK wasn't really an option for her (I was relieved), but we both knew that if things didn't improve weather-wise soon we would have to think of a Plan B.

As it happened, we woke next day at last to sunshine and blue skies. However, although the wind was less, it was still challenging, requiring use of the thrusters as we came into various locks and tried to manoeuvre daintily. This sort of thing involved me managing the boat's wheel, forward-and-reverse throttle and thrusters while poor Liz would run back and forward on the edge of the lock trying to loop ropes around bollards. I would have happily swapped places but she said she wasn't confident enough yet to manage the boat. To a bystander it must have looked like pure chauvinism, but what could I do?

Luckily for us there was a hire boat ahead which was just far enough in advance that it was entering the locks before we could get there. Darling One, who had walked ahead to make sure the *éclusier* knew we were coming reported back that the hire boaties were all over the show, which made us feel a lot better.

In fact, despite the wind, we did quite well, and we got the impression that the lock-keepers were relieved, a) that we weren't a hire boat and, b) we at least seemed to know what we were doing (even if we didn't!). Their smiles were a tonic.

At our last lock of the day the *éclusier* had a small stall selling local products, from wine and *pot-pourris* to preserves and even captains' hats. We bought some sparkling wine and jam to celebrate the sunshine. Captains' hats, we'd been advised by one of the staylors in Beaucaire, were worn only by hire boat skippers who liked to look the part. No serious boatie would be seen dead in one. As a result mine had remained tucked away below decks.

At the village of La Redorte we encountered the town's banana-shaped (croissant-shaped is probably more appropriate) quay and moored up. It was a nice location, but with very few rings for mooring – not sure why; you would think they'd see the benefit in encouraging boat people stop over.

Take us for example; within an hour of mooring we'd walked along to the local supermarket and bought fifty Euros' worth of groceries, and stopped at a *patisserie orientale* caravan on the way back, where the patron treated us to two glasses of sweet tea while we perused his goods. We settled on two stickily-rich dessert pastries, which he then proceeded to douse in syrup before putting them in a box. In my best Gerard Butler voice I said to Liz, 'Tonight we dine in hell!'

We actually slept in hell, and still don't know if it was the chilli con carne or the syrup-drenched desserts that did it, but all night long I felt like I had two stomachs, one lying heavily on top of the other. Bloated wasn't the word. (Actually, yes it was.) As I said to Liz romantically the next morning, 'I am the wind beneath your sheets.'

But we woke to a nice day, warm, cloudless, and sunny. After a visit to the boat's head I announced to Liz there would be no more wind, from me or France.

She smiled and said, 'Either way is fine with me!'

The journey continued, and we reached one of the highlights of the Midi, Carcassonne.

Highly recommended by tourist books, but more importantly by Francophile friends of ours from New Zealand Tony and Liz, who love it so much they make regular pilgrimages to Carcassonne, we'd been looking forward to reaching this particular milestone.

So once moored in the marina we wasted no time unloading the bikes, and set off to explore.

Our destination was the old city, which we'd seen from the canal in the distance. With its huge walls, battlements, towers and slit windows it looked like every castle you've ever seen in a fairy tale, its distance making it all the more mysterious and enticing.

Unfortunately it was one of those one hundred percent overcast days, the sort of flat light that photographers loathe because there's no relief, no contrast. And so, as we puffed up the hill towards the old city, it still looked formidable, but lacked definition.

On the other hand, we'd chosen a good time to visit, because apart from a couple of parties of disinterested school kids the place was deserted. We entered through the ancient gates, and wound our way through narrow cobbled streets with overhanging buildings, through more open spaces, to the ancient moat and bridge, and up steps to views over the stonework to the countryside beyond.

It was charming. There were plenty of shops selling everything from postcards and pashminas to food and fine wine (including one called Château d'Arse! Wonder what the nose on that one was like?), but this early in the week, and in the season, there were very few customers.

We saw the old city as having a film-set quality, though when you think about it, that's wrong; film sets are usually illusions built of polystyrene, plywood and even *papier mâché*, whereas this was the real thing – a solid, medieval fortified town, complete with castle and Gothic cathedral.

Its apparent completeness can be traced to an inspired restoration campaign by Eugène-Emmanuel Viollet-le-Duc, in the last half of the nineteenth century. As a result of his foresight, dedication and work he is today recognised as one of the founders of the modern science of conservation.

Along with the Canal du Midi, the old city of Carcassonne is recognised as a World Heritage Site by UNESCO, and deservedly so. As we cycled away we looked back across the river Aude towards the ancient walls and towers, marvelling at the sheer enormity and preservation of the city, and cursed the unbroken cloud cover that made it impossible to get a decent photograph.

And then, as seems to happen just when you start to get complacent with a boat, it all turns to custard. Yes, an almost disastrous day, our second major scare since buying *Liberty*, and one that could have seen us literally in deep trouble.

It started beautifully. We had moored in the country on a peaceful stretch of water, on the doorstep of the next lock which we anticipated going through first thing in the morning.

During the night I'd got up for a call of nature and decided to peek outside to see what I could see. In a nutshell: stars, and lots of them. Plus a half moon as a bonus, low in the sky. So I decided to quietly sneak on deck so as to not wake Liz, and admire the heavenly view – the same one I grew up with for the first 15 years of my life: the northern hemisphere night sky.

Now, let's get one thing clear: the southern hemisphere night sky is a lot better than the northern, mainly because it faces more towards the centre of our galaxy, which is what is generally known as the Milky Way. That's because it looks, to the casual naked eye, a bit milky, a bit fuzzily-white, but in reality that fuzziness is made up of millions and millions of stars, so densely packed together as to seem – from this distance – like breath on a bathroom mirror.

From northern latitudes however the night sky is less dense, but not necessarily less interesting. That night for example, I viewed the half-moon's 'seas' and craters through the boat's binoculars, then identified Jupiter and saw three of its moons. Over to the east, glowing a fiery red was Mars, very close to Earth at that point, and therefore particularly bright.

Above me was The Plough – which in America is called The Big Dipper – and off to one side Cassiopeia, the big W. I found the North Pole Star, and identified Castor and Pollux, my birthday Gemini Twins. It was magical, and all of France's southern frogs noisily agreed with me. And then I went back to bed.

In sunny and blissfully calm conditions we were first through the lock when it opened at 9am, being right at its gates, and sailed on through avenues of plane trees not bearing any crosses and therefore perhaps still under stay of execution, shimmering in the morning sun. By now their leaves had formed nicely and we could enjoy the dappled green tunnel effect as we travelled beneath them

By the time we reached the lock at Bram though we had caught up with two hire boats waiting to go into the chamber, so we gallantly let them go first, having realised that it always pays to 'know thine enemy.' They weren't too bad actually, and tied up reasonably well, so we cruised in slowly to take our place behind the one on the right. The phrase Devil Take the Hindmost now springs to mind, because as Liz, on the lockside, was looping our bow rope on a bollard I pushed the throttle forward to make it easier for her, only to find the boat went dramatically, suddenly, definitively and horrifyingly into full reverse, just as the lock gates were closing behind us.

We went from graceful arrivals to panic-stricken no-hopers within a second. The lock-keeper shouted something, I certainly shouted something, and Liz's face was frozen in a mask of horror, not understanding why I would choose such a moment to put *Liberty* into reverse.

The reality of it was that I was giving her all she had forward (Think Scotty in *Star Trek*: 'I'm giving her all I can Cap'n, but I canna hold her much longer!') yet the boat had decided – as though with a mind of her own – that she was going to go backwards. And she did, at an alarming rate of knots.

The starboard davit, which hangs with its port twin off the stern of the boat struck the closing lock gates first, followed by an enormous BANG as the swim platform followed. The noise was horrendous – I thought we had completely crushed the stern and would start sinking, or at least had written-off the lock gates and would close the Canal du Midi for weeks. No matter what I did with the throttle the boat wouldn't respond, which I tried to explain in my limited technical French with frantic arm-waving to the *éclusier*.

He manipulated his remote controls, seemed satisfied that the lock gates weren't damaged and still functioned, and proceeded to finish his task. Meanwhile, Liz was tugging the boat as hard as she could from the side of the lock to inch me away from the gates, and as soon as he could the *éclusier* helped her. They tied up and we waited while the water in the lock rose up to meet the level on the upward side.

The occupants of the two hire boats, while seemingly worried about our plight, looked equally relieved that it wasn't they who had just made complete asses of themselves. When the lock gates in front opened they took off as fast as they could to escape these two wayward Kiwis who obviously knew nothing about boating.

I tentatively tried the throttle forward and backward, but apart from revving the engine it had no effect on motion whatsoever, so I gave a verbal and physical shrug to Liz and the *éclusier*. It was left to her and the lock-keeper to then physically pull the boat (and me) out of the lock and up to some bollards where they tied *Liberty* safely up against the grassy bank. The *éclusier* then went back to his duties to let a lovely one hundred-year-old barge downstream, while Liz and I wondered what on earth had gone wrong with our equally lovely yet less-than-twenty-year-old boat.

It's at this point I need step out of the story for a moment to remind you I'd grown up with motorbikes since the age of 15. Like most teenagers I had started with second-hand older bikes, which of course broke down now and then. My stepfather refused to help, thinking (I believe) that since I'd chosen a motorbiking life I could damn well learn the mechanic's life that inevitably goes with it. The best (and possibly only) thing he ever did to help me was to give me a set of ring spanners for a birthday present. The rest he left up to me.

So when my various motorcycles had problems, I quickly came to realise that what was required was a process of elimination, where you work backwards from the problem, eliminating issues as you go until you're left with what's really wrong. It's the Sherlock Holmes principle: 'After you've eliminated the impossible, whatever remains – no matter how improbable – is the truth' (or in our case the problem/answer/challenge).

And so it was. We lifted the carpet, the flooring and the sound baffles to reveal the engine bay. With the engine stopped I got Liz to operate the throttles from the flybridge and inside the boat – in forward and reverse – and could quickly see that it was having no effect on the gearbox mechanism. Tracing the cables back I discovered that a small plastic clamp that held the combined throttle/gear cable in place had perished. In fact it lay in pathetic pieces on the engine bay floor, a kitset of its former self. Looking at some of the other clamps still in place I could see what it used to look like, and I also knew that we had nothing like it on board. So, *McGyver* time…

We began searching the boat for anything small and clamp-like, opening cupboards, lifting seats, raising the bed, and generally looking absolutely everywhere for something that might do. Within a few minutes we'd found a smallish hose clamp, but not small enough. So, next thing we found was a clip on the fuel line to the diesel-powered heater, which was the perfect size except that its bolt wasn't long enough. It then took us the best part of the next two hours to scour the boat again – every drawer, cupboard, nook and cranny, even down to unscrewing the handles off the pots and pans in the galley – to locate something as simple as a tiny two-centimetre bolt of the correct thread.

In the end we flopped onto the top deck in exhaustion, wondering what we would do. And then Liz pointed to the nut and bolt holding the boat's horn to the equipment rack. 'What about that?' she suggested. It was perfect! Within minutes it was fitted, Liz tried the throttle/gears from above while I watched what happened down below, and it all looked fine. Putting everything back in place we started the engine and tested the throttle and gears… success!

Wine time! The weather continued to be glorious; the sort of perfect day where we should have been cruising and smiling broadly. But sod it; we had made a temporary repair, got ourselves out of a hole (and hadn't had to call out an expensive French mechanic) and we were still afloat and alive, so we had a glass of wine on the aft deck and toasted my motorbike upbringing along with Liz's observational skills.

We also drowned our sorrows at having suffered a bent davit and a dented swim platform… problems we suspected would cost hundreds of Euros to fix – eventually. But at least we hadn't ruined the lock gates and put the whole of the Canal du Midi out of action.

I thought that maybe, like the night before, I should go out on deck again that night, and count my lucky stars.

CHAPTER THIRTY

O ne Friday we reached a peak in our canal-boating adventure, literally, because once you go through a lock called Méditerranée a few kilometres before Toulouse you are on the watershed of the Canal du Midi. This is the part of the canal where the water is introduced, originating from the Black Mountains to the north. Because canals aren't natural waterways, water has to be delivered to them and they constantly need to be topped-up. *Eau* really? Yes.

I'm not sure how, in the 1600s, Paul-Pierre Riquet and other engineer-types could accurately measure the various heights and gradients of a landscape, other than perhaps watching which way streams and rivers flowed, but they did a damn fine job. (Mind you, so too did the Romans sixteen hundred years previously, constructing aqueducts that dropped just a few metres over hundreds of kilometres.)

Anyway, having identified the Black Mountains as the best (and highest) source of water for his ambitious project, Riquet went ahead and solved all the problems of how to get the water from there to where it was needed – a canal that would join the Atlantic to the Med. This included building a preliminary feeder canal, storage dams and a dividing pound... ambitious projects in themselves.

So we felt slightly special having cruised to the point where it all began. Since starting on the Canal du Midi from the east, every lock we'd encountered had taken us 'uphill', raising us a few metres at a time to a higher level. From this day onwards though we would be cruising downhill, since we had reached the peak of the Midi. Yes folks, from here on it would all be downhill to Bordeaux.

After our scare at the Bram lock where the boat jammed in full reverse, we were being extra vigilant in our daily mechanical checks. Apart from the usual coolant level, oil level, filters and battery observations, we now included a check of the throttle/gear mechanism, which was still operating on its makeshift repair. So far, so good, though after Bram I was still a bit nervous using the throttle in the confines of a lock. On this particular Friday though we were blissfully on our own and didn't have to share any of the locks with other boats, or worse, onlookers.

Watching the water cascade into the locks on this watershed day we felt quite humbled, firstly that the French Waterways Network supply lock-keepers to operate many of the gates and paddles that control the water flow, and secondly that these thousands – if not millions – of litres of water were being supplied, drained, and topped-up again just for us.

(Not that you get it for free; the VNF *vignette* licence system is what pays for it. After finding out how much it cost for one month as opposed to a full year, we'd elected to buy a 12-month *vignette*, partly because we didn't know how long we'd be sailing, but mainly because it was much cheaper.)

But despite nervousness in the locks the day passed without any major incident, and as we cruised towards the absolute peak of the canal I joked to Liz that we were approaching a 'Moses Moment,' where we would witness the parting of the waters. Well blow me down if, when we got there, there wasn't a sign that said exactly that: *'Partage des Eaux'* – 'Parting of the Waters.'

And we looked upon the sign and saw that it was good. And we gave thanks. And the people fell to their knees and wondered, wherefore cometh such prescience?

Here endeth the lesson.

So from there on the water level dropped. The supreme irony of the day – perhaps God getting his revenge for my blasphemy – was that the boat's console alarm sounded and a little warning light lit up. It said, 'Check Water Level.' For some reason it indicated it had started to go down.

Spooky.

Our blog the next day announced, *'Liz has taken up pole dancing.'*

Okay, okay… if you've read this far you'll know by now that there's always a catch, and in this case that's literally what it is. But first, *Canal Locks 101: An Introduction…*

As you know, on a canal a lock is that marvel of engineering that enables you to take your boat up or downhill. It allows canal traffic to go from A to B regardless of how much the local landscape rises or falls. And basically it does it by filling and draining according to need. So, if you are travelling 'downhill' on a canal, you will enter a lock full of water, the gates will close behind you, and then 'paddles' underwater in the gates ahead of you will open. Slowly the water in the lock drains out until you reach the same level as the canal ahead, at which point the gates in front magically open and off you sail. The reverse happens when sailing 'uphill.' Easy.

But how the locks do this depends a lot on where they are, or how many of them there are together. When my Number One and I began this watery adventure you'll recall we headed off down the Saône and Rhône rivers. On the Rhône the locks are huge and designed to take commercial barges as well as piddling little boats like ours.

On the Canal du Midi – and as we approached the Garonne – we had encountered much smaller and less-formidable locks, many of which raised or lowered us only two metres or so. These were far more typical of locks on the French canals in general.

The VNF used to provide *éclusiers* for every lock, but these days many of them are automated (the locks, not the lock-keepers). The remaining *éclusiers* probably realise their days are numbered, which is undoubtedly why some of them look a bit sad.

The first *éclusier* I ever saw in France was a revelation; I think I'd expected a moustachioed, beret-wearing overalled man of small stature, whereas in fact she was actually about 19, blonde, wearing shorts and with her shirt tucked up into her bra so that her tummy could catch some UV rays. She was gorgeous. I fell in love, with canal boating, there and then.

Unfortunately, all the other *éclusiers* I'd seen since had paled by comparison, and had been much closer to the stereotype I'd envisaged, though without the berets. Some of the women didn't have moustaches either. Their temperaments ranged from a surly *oh-mon-Dieu-'ere-we-go-again* attitude, to smiling cheery helpfulness. Most would say *Bonjour*, some engaged in conversation. One, seeing our Kiwi flags, shouted '*Go ze All Blacks!*'

At this time of the year, with not much canal traffic, we realised they didn't have a lot to do. And even when a boat is locking through, it's not a quick process, so while the lock was filling or draining the *éclusiers* were either on their mobiles, doing something mysterious inside their cottages, or – quite frequently – pulling weeds out of the ground. We saw this so often we'd taken to calling them constant gardeners. But whatever their demeanour, we'd always say *Bonjour* on arrival and *Merci, au revoir* on leaving. Occasionally we'd even try and chat to them.

I asked one *éclusier*, based at quite a pretty lock on the Midi, whether the plane trees along his stretch of the canal were safe from the fungus, but he shook his head sadly and told us no, they were for the chop. Then he patted the newly-installed remote control panel beside the lock and informed us that when it came online he too would be for the chop. *C'est tragique*, was all we could say, to both sets of circumstances.

Which brings us back to the locks, how they're operated, and pole dancing. The VNF are slowly but surely handing over responsibility for lock management to us the users, and they're doing this in a variety of ways. One is that they supply a lockside control cabin, in which are some buttons and instructions in French, English and German on what to do. For those of other nationalities or who perhaps can't read, there are coloured arrows beside the two main buttons, so as long as you know which direction you're going you'll have no problem.

Then there are the Grey Sentinels. These obelisks stand to attention beside the lock and simply have a big green button, which you push. The mechanism somehow knows whether the lock needs filling or emptying, and acts accordingly. However like the cabin, it doesn't say *Bonjour*. There's another sneakily-clever automated system that operates by way of sensors in the canalside, and when your boat triggers them the lock leaps into action automatically, but at that stage we'd yet to come across one.

Nor had we yet met the remote control locks, where you are given an actual remote control to operate each lock as you approach. At the end of the remote control section you hand the device back to an *éclusier*.

And finally there's the mid-stream pole. This hangs from a cable that stretches across the canal and is attached to a switch at the top. All you have to do is twist it and the lock ahead prepares for your arrival. When I say 'all you have to do,' it was a bit more complicated than that, and involved me guiding the boat slowly and accurately towards the pole so that Liz, standing on the starboard bow, could equally deftly catch it, twist it, and let it go before it pulled her overboard. This is where the entertaining pole dancing came in, and it was fun for all.

Except of course for the rapidly-disappearing human *éclusiers*, who increasingly have to look towards the local job centre. Which in France, ironically, is called the *Pole Emploi*.

CHAPTER THIRTY-ONE

And so we carried on, to the largest city on the Midi in a while, Toulouse.

It was here that old age caught up with me. Liz and I had unloaded the bicycles and had gone in search of coffee and free Wi-Fi at McDonald's, but on the way we'd somehow managed to get on an on-ramp that was obviously about to take us onto a motorway, where bikes aren't permitted, and where we didn't want to go anyway.

I was in the lead, pushing my bike while searching for an alternative and more friendly route when I heard Liz behind me call me a 'little psychopath.'

I stopped and turned. 'What did you call me?'

She stopped too, and looked at me with pity. 'I said, "There's a little cycle path."'

I decided I really must get my hearing checked.

As with most of the other major centres we'd passed on the Midi, we decided to leave exploring Toulouse, and instead resolved that we'd investigate it more on the return journey, when the weather would be further improved, and because once we reached Bordeaux, we would have to turn around and retrace our wake anyway.

The only other option would have been to go on through Bordeaux and out onto the Atlantic, turning right or left, but although *Liberty* was sea-going in her design, we certainly weren't qualified for going offshore, nor were we inclined to want to.

Just beyond Toulouse the Canal du Midi ends, and becomes instead, with a sharp right turn, the Canal Latéral à la Garonne.

The change in canal environment was immediate; the plane trees disappeared, the canal banks became a bit scrappy and less well-kept, and certainly as we left Toulouse there wasn't much you could call 'pretty.'

But that didn't last, and before too long we were back to trees, and a pleasantly leafy waterway. The bankside vegetation was different though, and we definitely knew we'd left the Midi behind.

We reached Castelsarrasin, where Keith and Hilary had tied up their boat *Picton* for winter, and found them still there at the end of a long quiet marina, there being still not much activity at this time of the year.

At last we were able to swap boat stories, tell them all about our adventures and hear what they'd been up to. They said they'd had a very wet winter, with endless days of rain, and that although the basin at Castelsarrasin had been good value as a winter-over point, the weather had been so dreadful they'd got very fed up with it. We tried not to enthuse too much about Beaucaire's sunshine.

Keith examined the damage to *Liberty* incurred during the Bram lock incident, and said he didn't think it was too major, though the dent in the swim platform would have to wait until the boat came out of the water at some stage. Meanwhile, it didn't pose a problem and was more cosmetic than critical.

Keith and Hilary still had their car parked beside the boat, so offered to take us on a bit of a drive, and to go and see the hilltop town of Auvillar, described as one of the prettiest in France.

The sky was deep blue and the sun strong as we set off. I'd volunteered to bring our Sat-Nav, as they didn't have one, but Keith began arguing with it as soon as it gave instructions.

'*At the roundabout, take the first exit,*' it advised. 'No,' argued Keith. 'That's not the right way, dear-oh-dear. I'm not listening!' he replied to the Sat-Nav and went straight through the roundabout.

'*Turn around when possible.*'

He didn't. He told the Sat-Nav he darned well knew his way there and he was going to stick to it. I switched the device off. Meanwhile Hilary, in the back seat with Liz, unfolded her trusty map and went into navigator mode, her usual role when out driving with Keith.

Hilary checked the map. 'Turn around when possible,' she said.

But we got to Auvillar, and it was just as pretty as anticipated. The main square was dominated by a lovely and ancient round grain market, and photographically we were spoilt for choice, with numerous half-timbered houses, stone arches, a clock tower and a very photogenic church. The views from this early Iron Age settlement over the Garonne River were stunning too, but best of all there was hardly anyone there. A great day out.

We left our matelot mates at Castelsarrasin and continued on our way, through locks, under bridges, past weirs, and occasionally over aqueducts.

It was a good time to reflect on the journey so far, what we'd learned, and whether we could reach any philosophical conclusions about what we were doing. We could – with the help of a vandal.

It was while we'd still been idling along the Canal du Midi that we'd seen a poignant piece of graffiti that seemed to perfectly sum up our situation.

Most tagging seemed to be reserved for the more modern concrete bridges, perhaps because they had smoother surfaces than the old brick ones. Some of the creations were worthy of Banksy, and, this being France, many carried some social comment to accompany the illustrations.

But it was just a single simple phrase that caught our attention under one particular concrete bridge. It was unaccompanied by any graphics, and simply said, 'Seuls les poissons morts suivent le courant. Êtes-vous un poisson mort!?'

This translates in essence to: 'Only the dead fish follow the current. Are you a dead fish!?'

We adopted it as our motto, as it perfectly summed up the way we felt about having thrown all caution to the wind, broken ties, and set off on this crazy boating adventure. Most other people we knew were swimmers who went with life's current, not against it, and while it might be unkind to compare them to dead fish, we thought the spray-paint scallywag had made an honest point.

We even considered using 'Only the Dead Fish' as a title for this book, and made a point from there on of looking for fish corpses floating in the water, something we could photograph and perhaps use on the cover.

Over time we decided that a book called 'Only the Dead Fish' was unlikely to attract a Booker Prize, a picture of a bloated carp wouldn't be particularly attractive, nor would the title neatly sum up the nature of our adventure, although it was close. But we got some nice pics of *poissons morts*. And soon were to come across the mother of them all.

As we cruised north-westwards on the Garonne canal, the temperature rose somewhat, and the trees were by now very much in leaf. We realised that in the six months since we'd started we'd seen an excellent array of wildlife while sailing along – kingfishers, herons, egrets, flamingos, a beaver/rat-like creature called a Coypu, foxes and turtles – and here on the Garonne we noticed small ramps at the water's edge every now and again, and figured they were for animals to be able to get out of the water and onto dry land. We hoped we might see something using one of them, but never did.

But nothing made our mouths drop open quite so much as one particular giant fish.

Watching a canalside fisherman one day at a small port on the Garonne we saw him begin wrestling with his rod. The rod was bent almost double, and I was about to say to Liz, 'He's got it caught in weeds,' when we saw the ghostly shape of a large fish come to the surface at the end of his line, then disappear under again.

The fisherman shouted to a small boy who was with him to get a net, which the boy did, scrambling up the stony bank to where the fishing gear was laid out beside their car. But as the fish was slowly played and brought closer in, it was obvious from its size that the boy would be unlikely to be able to lift it out.

From our position on the bridge we could see the fisherman looked tense and worried – obviously he didn't want to let this one get away, but he seemed reluctant to hand the rod to the boy either, perhaps in case the fish got off the hook, or pulled the boy in. And then whose fault would it be?

In the end, a man from a nearby boat, on seeing the struggle, came and helped, and together they managed to land the struggling fish, an absolutely enormous carp.

The prize was half carried, half dragged up the slope. The *pêcheur* then seemed more concerned with re-baiting his hook and getting it back in the water; maybe he knew there was a bigger one to be had, so it was left to the other man, the one who'd come to help, to hold the fish up for us to photograph.

'*Le dîner ce soir?*' we suggested, but he said nothing other than '*carpe.*'

We'd had no idea the fish in the canals could reach such a size; this must have been almost a metre in length. From the boat's flybridge we'd often seen fish jumping, and thought some of them looked quite big, but now we knew. Sadly, this was one fish that wouldn't be going with or against the current any more.

CHAPTER THIRTY-TWO

W e were now sailing to a timetable, and knew we had to achieve a certain number of kilometres per day, as we'd arranged to rendezvous with our Merseyside mate Shaun at a small port towards the end of the canal. He was flying out from Liverpool, would rent a car, and come and meet us to stay on board for a long weekend.

To date we had chosen how far to travel each day based entirely on whimsy; whether there was a nice marina up ahead, or a recommended greenbanking opportunity, or because we could stop close to a *laverie* or Wi-Fi signal, or top up with water. Or, that where we were was really pretty and so we'd stay for a few days. But now we had a deadline, and the pressure was on.

As we cruised along the waterway we'd occasionally pass unattended boats moored either singly or in groups, but one boat in particular caught our attention. It was the *Anna Marie*, the ex-hire boat from Saint-Jean-de-Losne, the one we decided not to make an offer on despite being invited to gazump. Maybe the Frenchman had finally completed the deal. Whoever had bought it, they'd successfully managed to bring it this far, though the boat looked quite dirty and somewhat unloved, which seemed a bit sad.

Anyway, we did okay with our schedule and reached the small *halte nautique* we were aiming for that had been favourably mentioned to us, at Meilhan-sur-Garonne. It was run by an English couple and they were very welcoming, and although the port was tiny, they did have a small shop with tables outside that doubled as the unofficial port bar. Very civilized.

Over glasses of very good value local wine we sat and pored over the canal navigation map, looking at the short thin line that was the last stretch between where we were and Bordeaux. It didn't look very far, but the more we researched the more wary we became about actually doing it.

'The thing is,' Liz said, 'once we leave this canal and get onto the Garonne River and head towards Bordeaux, we're subject to tides, and I'm not sure we're ready for that.'

I reluctantly agreed. 'Yes, I know, but we've come so far. It seems a shame not to be able to get to Bordeaux, moor up and go in search of some fine Premiere Cru *Château*-bottled wines.' I was joking, sort-of.

But Liz was right. We'd almost lost *Liberty* at Avignon, almost sunk her and destroyed the lock gates at Bram, so why would we now want to put her (and us) to a tidal test on the Garonne River? We decided instead we'd at least cruise along what was left of the safe gentle waterway to Castets-en-Dorthe, the last point before the canal finished and the river began, just to have a look.

And we're glad we did; it was a nice overnight journey with no pressure, reasonable weather and we were headed towards our Turnaround Point, another cause for celebration. Maybe we'd even find a nice bottle of Lafite-Rothschild to celebrate with.

And speaking of wine...

In vino veritas... 'In wine lies truth.' Which basically means that if you've had a drop, don't try fibbing because brain and tongue disengage in the presence of alcohol (as some of us know to our eternal shame).

Hence I wrote this next bit in a blog at 9.55 one morning before a drop has passed my lips, so that our blog-followers would know that everything I said was the real truth, the whole truth and nothing but.

Why bring up the subject of wine now in particular after all these months in France? Because we'd sailed up to the doorstep of the Mecca of wine, Bordeaux. This is the south-west of France, that point on the compass towards which wine lovers everywhere orientate themselves for their five-times-daily prayers of thanks and reverence. So it seems a good time to talk about it.

Not that we need to have waited till now; everywhere we've travelled in France there has been wine aplenty, manifesting itself as rows and rows of vines on hillsides, as row upon row of bottles in the supermarché, *or as wine* caves *in the towns and villages we've sailed through. (*Caves *in this case is pronounced* calves... *they're often wineries or wine cooperatives, but also the name is applied to many wine shops.)*

Wine is not, however, a French invention, as many people like to think. Despite its prevalence here, and its prominence in French daily life, the origins of wine go back much further than France – the Greeks and Romans having also done their bit – but one of these days archaeologists are likely to discover cave paintings of a bunch of grapes, a rudimentary amphora, and a group of Neanderthal pissheads bending over and regurgitating after a fantastic Neolithic night out. There might also be a drawing of a kebab.

At which point we will have to revise our thinking.

In the meantime, and despite the rise of New World wines, France retains an undeniable ranking in the world-wine league table.

Now, you can interpret this as meaning it is still the home of the world's most magnificent – and expensive – wines, or that France is the undisputed home of wine etiquette and snobbery. Or that it's here that the acknowledged and hallowed wine traditions were born, for example white wine with fish, red wine with meat. Or all of the above. Doesn't matter; ultimately, France has a history and association with wine growing and drinking that spans hundreds and hundreds of years, and that's not something you can create overnight in the Californias, Hunter Valleys or Marlboroughs of the New World.

What a surprise then to find that on a daily basis France gives a Gallic shrug to wine tradition. To discover, in fact, that while many New Zealand wineries back in the 1970s used to have wine – and even port and sherry – 'on tap' so you could fill your own flagons (but closed all that down because it appeared 'too common'), bulk-buying of wine in France is, well, common.

It's here you can buy wine in the supermarket in five-litre jerry cans, or sometimes even ten-litre containers. It's here you can take your empty plastic jerry can to the local cave and get it filled. We tapped into a fabulous Syrah-Grenache rosé wine the other day at the Saint-Sardos winery near Castelsarrasin: five litres for just over ten Euros.

Another thing: red wine in the fridge. What? Chilled red wine? Yes. Although not unknown in the New World, in France if you order vin rouge at a café or restaurant you will often be asked if you'd like it fraiche, which in this case means chilled. Maybe not all the time, but in summer when the temperature's up towards 30C, it's not a bad idea.

And speaking of cafés and restaurants, you have multiple choices about how you can order your wine. Obviously bottles are available, as is wine by the glass, but so too are pichets and carafes of varying sizes. These aren't always of the finest crystal either; often a pichet will be a simple pottery jug, maybe holding 250mls. And in most cafés, if you choose to order a plain vin blanc, vin rouge or rosé it will be unashamedly dispensed from a tap behind the bar. It is simply table wine with no pretensions or aspirations. And no pretension seems to *be what general everyday wine-drinking here is about. We like that.*

It has to be said that Liz and I haven't made an exhaustive survey of the French wine lifestyle (despite the numerous sessions on the aft deck), our budget being restricted by having no income at present, so our tastes and expenditure have of necessity been plebeian.

But now we are on the doorstep of Bordeaux, the home of famed Châteaux such as Margaux, Lafite-Rothschild and Haut-Brion. These and their peers are the prestigious 'first growths,' the stuff of legend. It's highly unlikely if we nip into Château Margaux we'll be able to fill up with five litres of their '95 though; they're more likely to show us the door.

So the conundrum we face is, now that we're here, how do we at least experience the fame, the history, the tradition and the excellence of one of the best wine-growing regions in the world, when we can't afford to? How do we taste wine that for decades has set the benchmark for all other wines? Wine that sells for thousands of pounds at auction. How do we pop the cork on the crème de la crème?

It's all too much. I need a drink.

In the end, we decided that the whole wine thing in Bordeaux was so big, so important, it would be better to ignore it and come back at some future point and make it the sole focus of a visit.

But from wine back to wildlife. Let's get one thing clear: ducks are stupid.

As we'd cruised along the various rivers and canals since purchasing our *bateau plaisance* we'd seen all manner of wildlife, including, as mentioned, the ubiquitous heron.

Usually these stand on high-alert on the canal bank, watching intently for any sort of fish activity in the water, much the same as the overly-spotted French *pêcheur*, or fisherman. As we approached in the boat, the herons would finally register our presence, lazily decide at the last minute to take flight, fly gracefully about fifty metres ahead and then re-settle on the bank.

They would do this about five times before it finally dawned on them that no matter what they did, we would maintain our course and speed, at which point they realised actually it would have been better in the first place to have gone over or around us, which they would finally do, resettling where they started from.

Liz, whose degree is in zoology, was on the herons' side though. 'They're territorial,' she explained patiently. 'They get to the edge of their space and that's why they turn back. They're not dumb.'

Whatever.

Ducks are worse. They'd sit mid-stream until we almost ran them over, and then flap with great drama and occasional quacking to re-position themselves... safely mid-stream again about fifty metres ahead. They'd obviously been to the Heron School of Strategy, because of course within minutes we were descending upon them again, ten tonnes of boat bearing down with little choice but to carry on cruising. So they'd yet again up-stumps and fly off, and do exactly the same thing, multiple times. Duh, again. It's not like we were the first boat they'd ever seen. When does the evolutionary process actually kick in?

The other day though one particular duck made us smile. We'd reached the end-point of our journey west. Any further and we'd be on the Garonne River, then the Gironde, and all that that entails: tides, 200 wartime sunken wrecks, and – had we continued – the fury of the mighty Atlantic Ocean. It would have been a titanic undertaking, possibly in both senses of the word.

So we settled instead for a nice safe stroll along the canal bank to the last lock before Armageddon. Along the way we passed an example of that species, the Much-Spotted *pêcheur* lying on his back, his beret over his face and seemingly fast asleep while his rods took care of themselves. We took a photo, since it seemed to combine those two particular French passions: fishing and lethargy.

What we hadn't realised was the lovely juxtaposition of a random duck in the picture, because when we uploaded it later back on the boat, we could clearly see what looked to be the duck perched on the sleeping *pêcheur*'s knee.

Pity it wasn't a heron though, since they're the ones also intent on catching fish. Still, it was a nice moment, and one that we canardly have expected.

One of the other bizarre things we'd seen that week was a swimming deer, which took us totally by surprise. We were idly cruising along the canal, when ahead we heard – rather than saw – an almighty splash. This was followed by a smallish object swimming across the canal from right to left, which on closer inspection through the binoculars turned out to be the head of a very young deer.

Liz grabbed the camera while I tried to stop the boat, but trying to zoom in and focus on a smallish swimming object from a rocking platform isn't easy. Meanwhile the deer reached the other side and scrambled out of the water without the aid of a wildlife ramp to reveal itself as Bambi. It was so little! And so cute! Diddums.

Unfortunately, it had crossed from the safe side of the canal to the side with a main road on it, and so proceeded to bound alongside the crash barrier looking for a way to get through to cross the road.

Our hearts were in our mouths as we anticipated a grisly end any moment, especially as it was a fast stretch of road. But ultimately we lost track of the deer, and thankfully didn't witness any carnage. I did however start singing the Sex Pistols' *'Who Killed Bambi?'*

Perhaps, though, the wildlife highlight of the last few days was one we didn't even see.

We had met Shaun after we got back to Meilhan-sur-Garonne from our trip to the end of the canal, and he'd very kindly taken us for day trips to Bordeaux and surrounding area in his rental car. We all liked Bordeaux, especially the 'mist park' beside the river. This large area of soft rubber has water jets secreted in the surface that spout an incredibly fine mist – so fine that you can walk or run through it without getting soaking wet, or hardly damp even. Instead, it drifts up and seems to hang around like a ground mist, distorting distance and lending a surreal quality to the whole scene. People look airbrushed, their legs gently disappearing into white fog, while their torsos are silhouetted against the background. Stunning.

And, having decided Château Haut-Brion and the like were best saved for some future appointment, we instead asked Mike, the Englishman who, along with his wife, ran the port at Meilhan-sur-Garonne whether he could recommend a smaller, less-imposing winery not too far away that we might visit.

He got on the phone to a place he said was called Château Bois Beaulieu and we heard him speaking in French, saying (we think) that he had some guests who were keen on wine and could they come and see the winery. It was a Sunday morning, but he put his hand over the phone and said, 'How about three o'clock this afternoon?'

Sure, we agreed, that would be lovely. So after lunch we found ourselves following the Sat-Nav to the winery, which turned out not to be a *Château,* or even a charming old stone building. Instead, alongside well-tended vines bursting with new spring growth and grass growing between the rows was what can only be described as '21st century industrial' architecture – basically a large modern shed with stainless steel tanks standing to attention in rows inside.

As we parked the car a lanky Frenchman appeared almost shyly from inside. This was Fabien Tarascon, the winemaker, who was expecting us. He seemed somewhat embarrassed, but we tried in our best French to assure him we were genuinely interested in his winery, and that we would not take up too much of his time.

A small family property of only nine hectares, in the AOC Marmandais (*appellation d'origine contrôlée* – a guarantee that where the label says the wine is grown is accurate – in this case the area of Marmandais), this was, we learned, an entirely *biologique* enterprise. The whole vineyard and the wines were organic and every bunch of grapes hand-picked.

A *biologique* listing may strike you as a marketing ploy, but in France, as Fabian explained in French (his English was limited but Liz translated well), a *biologique* designation requires the vineyard to be free of anything artificial for four years before being able to market its products as '*Bio.*'

Fabian took us on a tour of the winery and explained the winemaking process. It helped that I had some background formerly as a wine columnist, and had done some radio and TV broadcasting on the subject (but am really no expert), and he seemed to relax significantly.

At one point Fabian asked us if we knew what *ver de terre* was, but we didn't. He then tried to mime, wriggling his hands along, but we still didn't get it, until Shaun looked it up via his phone. It's French for earthworm, the slimy wriggling creature which, as Fabian explained, played such an important role in his *biologique* vineyard, seemingly replacing all manner of fertilisers.

With our French language thus expanded, we ended up (as you do in these circumstances) in the tasting room, where we tried a Sauvignon-Semillon blend. When I asked why he didn't just make a straight Sauvignon or straight Semillon he said that under the local AOC rules, it was *interdit;* winemakers were not allowed to make varietal wines, and there had to be a minimum of two grape varieties in each. How bizarre we thought, given that varietal wines have such a following.

We thanked Fabian for his hospitality and time, bought a hundred Euros' worth of mixed bottles (and later wished we'd bought more!), and drove away happy that we'd had the opportunity to at least meet a local winemaker.

Having celebrated the westward end of our journey, we cast off and started heading back east, only to meet up with Keith and Hilary again at a small and isolated port called Caumont-sur-Garonne, a lovely tree-lined spot away from noisy roads or railways. To celebrate this unexpected reunion we had a shared dinner on our aft deck, with hurricane lamps glowing, candles, a proper tablecloth with runner... and to make it even more special it was a gorgeously balmy evening, warm with not a breath of wind. Good company, good food, good wine. Perfect.

Just when we thought it couldn't get any better, around the after-dinner port stage about 11pm, a lone bird began singing in a nearby tree. The sun had long since set, and the regular avian population had gone bye-byes, but suddenly this choral songster started up, its crystal clear notes echoing among the branches. It was stunningly beautiful to hear. I quickly nipped below and got my digital recorder to capture it.

We were stunned. And it seemed to be on night shift, as it continued well past our own bedtime. Perhaps it was celebrating its return from Africa after wintering over there. Perhaps it had just enjoyed our witty after-dinner banter. Didn't matter. It was, of course, a nightingale, the first we'd ever heard, and it was tear-jerkingly beautiful.

But the irony of it was, that despite all our attempts at wildlife photography, we'd probably had the most enjoyment from a creature we couldn't see and couldn't photograph.

It was, however, perfect.

Ducks and herons, take note.

CHAPTER THIRTY-THREE

And so, after a relaxing few days with Shaun aboard (at last, someone else to steer the boat while Liz and I sat in folding chairs up in business class!) he headed reluctantly back to England, promising to come and join us again before summer was over.

We meanwhile began retracing our steps, or wake, but the weather remained nice and it was a different Garonne and Midi that we sailed eastwards on – sunnier, greener, warmer.

I was pleased about the increase in temperature in particular, because I had a date with nakedness coming up, and would certainly need the thermometer to rise further before then.

But, before I bared my all, first I had to vent my spleen.

I lost my temper in French for the first time on Friday 9 May. I only mention the specific day because the French love to name streets after dates special in French history, hence *Rue de 14 Juillet*, etc. *Avenue de 9 Mai* is likely to also take its place in history. Read on…

Liz and I had been going well on a long day of sailing, part of our planned schedule to get us close to Agde so she could catch a train to Nîmes for a flight back to the UK.

Unfortunately, all the locks we came to were set against us, so each time we had to wait mid-stream for them to empty and for the gates to open and let us in. It was getting frustrating, because being able to cruise into a lock with the water at your level is a breeze. And quick.

But it was not to be, and it was hugely annoying to have been overtaken by a boat about the same size as ours only to find when we caught up with them at the next lock that they'd gone in and decided to close the gates against us, when they knew full well we were behind them. Lock etiquette dictates that if you have another boat behind you, you wait for them and let them share the lock with you. It saves the following boat time and, perhaps more importantly, helps conserve water on the canal.

But these people seemed to be in a hurry and to have thrown their etiquette overboard. So, we were forced to tie up at a pontoon and wait for the lock cycle to be in our favour again.

I took the opportunity to stride up to the lock and asked the skipper in question if he was French. He said he was, at which point I ranted (in French with much arm-waving) about there being plenty of room in the lock for two boats but that he had chosen to keep the lock to himself. He tried to tell me something about being new to boating and I told him to *learn*, and fumed off. His wife hurled something at me, but since I didn't feel it land I assume it must have been abuse.

I was shaking with anger when I got back to our boat, though with some chagrin wondered whether my tirade in French hadn't actually sounded something like the British undercover *gendarme* in the TV series *'Allo 'Allo*: 'Fast of all, you are pissing by us on the canal, going at spode. Then you enter the lick and close the goats just as we arrive. Monsieur, you are very road! My woof is very upset and so am I! You 'ave no idea how to soil a bat!'

However it came out I must have put the fear of God in them because they sped away once their gates were open and we didn't catch sight of them again (thinkfully)... until after we'd done our last lock of the long day.

It was just after 7pm, closing time for the lock system, and we were aiming to moor on a pontoon beside the next lock, so we could then be first through the following morning. But we were disheartened to find that the errant new boatie and his woof had already moored there, so we greenbanked a kilometre or more back, out of sight.

So twice they had thwarted us. I was fuming, again. I was shaking. Liz was annoyed too. There were waves in our wineglasses.

Next morning we were a bit late leaving, about 0920, so we hoped that the soilers would have already gone through the lock as we weren't looking forward to sharing with them now, even if they offered. However, having slept on it I was feeling *un petit* contrite, so in case we did meet up with them I rehearsed an apology in French.

And yes, bugger it, as we cruised around the bend to the lock, there they were, sitting on their top deck having breakfast. They didn't seem to be in a hurry, so we activated the pole midstream to begin the lock cycle and I dropped Liz off on the bank so she could go and get ready to catch ropes at the lock. I saw her stop and talk to the delinquent French couple, though I couldn't hear what she was saying, but the man didn't seem too angry.

With the lock gates now open I began to cruise past them and as I did they both gave me a cheery *bonjour*, at which point I did my grovel in French and told them that I was sorry and that yesterday I had been The Devil but today I was very calm. They laughed and the man said they were sorry too for not knowing about the etiquette and that they'd only been boating for three days. I felt a bit sick.

On the other hand, they were probably laughing, a) in relief because I wasn't holding an axe and foaming at the mouth, and b) because my apology probably came out sounding like,

'I apple-juice for my behaviour yestoady, but I was like Satin himself, hoover toady I am very clam.'

I asked if they wanted to share the lock with us but they said they were waiting for friends, so we went ahead. When I caught up with Liz she said, 'I told them that you could sometimes be *un homme fache*, an angry man. They both nodded, but the man seemed quite embarrassed that they'd broken a major rule of canal boating and seemed genuinely contrite. He was quite nice really.'

Hmph. But at least I know I can yell in French… up to a pint.

Remember the film *Jaws*? *Dah-dum… dah-dum…* (pause while girl swimming looks around with a sense of fear)… *dum-dum-dum-dum, dum-dum-dum-dum…* (scream, splash).

One of the best things about the movie, and what made it genuinely scary, was that you didn't get to see the shark much – instead you mainly saw the fear it generated, and occasionally its leftovers. Eew.

The scariest thing about the Canal du Midi *(dah-dum…)* is not an invisible water-dwelling creature, but something much, much more terrifying: *The Hire Boat* (loud scream!).

The Midi is festooned – perhaps 'infected' is a better word – with hire boat operators, who offer you the chance to experience life on the canals *'sans permis,'* which basically means you pay them money and they give you a boat for a week, or however long you want it, and you don't need a licence, permit or any sort of experience. Here are the keys, *au revoir*.

But from our experience – along with the warnings we'd been given by other more experienced boaters – the Hire Boat is to be feared, and avoided if at all possible. It is the shark of the canals.

And like the baddie in *Jaws*, hire boats attack at the most unexpected times, and can wreak as much damage. They tend to appear just as you're rounding a sharp bend, aiming straight for you, but with multiple people up on the flybridge wrestling for control of the craft. Alas yes, it seems that most hire boats are steered by committees, and as we all know, an elephant is a mouse designed by a committee. Therefore, committees on boats don't work, simple as that.

The term 'Captain,' or 'Skipper,' is a *singular* noun, applying specifically to the one person who's in charge of a vessel. The word 'Bungle' is a collective noun, and applies to the group of people up top who believe that they are *all* in charge of a hire boat's speed and direction. When you see a Bungle driving a hire boat, be afraid.

So one day on our return journey we were approaching a bend in the canal and, knowing it was blind, tooted our horn, a lovely stainless steel trumpet of a thing that belts out a 130 decibel parp that says without doubt: We. Are. Here.

But it had no effect whatsoever on the long sleek hire craft that hurtled round the corner in our direction, and as we throttled off and turned our wheel in evasive action, the Bungle on this boat all reached for anything resembling a lever or wheel and successfully steered their craft straight into the bank. Their bow rose up momentarily, and we thought they were about to take a short cut through a vineyard, but in fact the boat just ground to a halt with its pointy end aimed skywards.

As we slid by, they slid slowly back off the bank, with no obvious damage to anything other than egos. Possibly their gin and tonic bottles had fallen over below, but that would be about the extent of it.

That's just one example of hire boat madness. Most of the others we'd witnessed had taken place at locks, where boats have to squeeze through the gap between the lock gates to enter and exit. This gap gives you about a metre on either side of your boat (depending on your beam), and providing you take it slowly – and account for the wind if it's blowing – it's relatively quite straightforward.

But not so for hire boats, on which the Bungle, just before entering the lock, activates their bow and/or stern thrusters to get themselves straightened up, only to slew sideways into the lock and bang and bounce their way in. This is where the verb 'barge' comes from.

The other lighter side of hirers is watching them trying to moor their boat to the lock's bollards. It's at this point the main Bungle splits into individual *bunglers* and *bunglettes*, some of whom stand on deck and throw ropes to others standing at the edge of the lock – ropes that inevitably fall in the water. Meanwhile, the sole bungler left in charge has managed to get his boat sideways across the lock. There is much shouting and yelling between all concerned, often in Dutch, German or even Russian. The sea battles in *Master and Commander* pale by comparison.

We, of course, did all this in the early stages of owning *Liberty*, so we couldn't be too smug, but the hire boats' efforts made us look like experts. One large Russian bear of a guy on a hire craft in front of us called me *Indiana Jones* after he watched me throw our stern rope round a bollard first time. Phnar, phnar.

So why are hire boaties so hopeless? Why do they go too fast on the straight bits, and take the corners dangerously? Why can't they steer their boats neatly into locks, or throw ropes, or even generally know what to do? I blame education, or in this case a lack of it.

We'd decided that, where appropriate, we'd talk to people on hire boats and ask them what sort of training they'd been given by the company they'd got their boat from. In a space of a couple of weeks we'd spoken to three or four hire boat couples and they all told us that they had received little or almost no instruction whatsoever.

Steph and Michael for example told us their hire company representative hardly spoke any English and seemed to just want to tick the boxes on his checklist. 'I'd give them three out of ten,' said Steph grumpily. She and her partner were waiting for someone from the company to come and fix their boat's toilet. Eew, again.

Brian and Jean of England agreed about the lack of education. 'He showed us the gas stove,' grumbled Brian, 'but never showed us where to turn it on! Turns out there was a hidden switch, which, luckily, we found.' (On the other hand, Jean blamed it all on celebrity TV chef Rick Stein, whose Canal du Midi hotel boat series had given them the idea of a boating holiday. Unfortunately they had brought no warm clothing or wet weather gear, and had got wet, cold and miserable. 'If I see Rick Stein I'll kill him!' said Jean. She sounded like she meant it.)

Few had any instruction on how to manage a lock, which, of all the aspects of canal boating, is probably the most risky, and little or no mention was made of speed restrictions, which explains why so many hire boats swept past moored boats causing rocking and rolling. (Mind you, I have to confess I did exactly the same the first time I went out in one of Keith's narrowboats in England many years ago. As I passed a guy working on his boat he called out, 'Oi, he's fallen off!' 'Who has?' I asked, alarmed. 'The water skier!' the bloke replied. I laughed, and then humbly realised it was his way of telling me to slow down…)

John and Veronica of Australia said much the same thing of their hire boat introduction, as did an American guy we spoke to in a lock. 'What instructions?' he asked rhetorically, shaking his head and chuckling at the absurdity of the concept.

In the end though, there really can only be one skipper in charge on a boat, and it's this lack of understanding that causes the most problems.

We arrived back at the neat little port of Colombiers, and stayed a couple of nights, enjoying the fact that now that spring was well underway the place had come out of hibernation; the shops and cafés were open, the port office and *Office de Tourisme* operated full hours, and the supermarket just near our boat was busy with boaters and locals stocking up.

We were enjoying a leisurely start to the morning on deck when we witnessed a sequel to *Attack of the Hire Boat*, as a Bungle of Dutch men collectively tried to steer their vessel out of the marina. Despite six or seven people all being in charge they managed to swipe the stern of their boat into the bows of two moored craft, scratching the paintwork on one and denting the railings on the other.

After breakfast, as we (slowly and carefully) left Colombiers, we saw two of the crew sheepishly walking back on the quayside with the boat's insurance documents in hand.

Cue music: *Dah dumb... dah dumb... Dumb, dumb, dumb, dumb...*

CHAPTER THIRTY-FOUR

The return journey along the Canal du Midi was much more pleasant than our westward foray in early spring, but there was one point where it looked in danger of coming to a grinding halt.

As we tootled our way towards Carcassonne again, we thought it might be nice to stop there once more, but we'd been hearing rumours of a possible *éclusiers'* strike. Nothing official – there was no mention on the marina noticeboards, it was just a rumour circulating among boaties, and seemed to suggest that the lock-keepers would down-tools and walk off the job any moment. In protest against what we weren't sure.

'I think we should skip Carcassonne,' Liz suggested. 'We've stopped here before, let's keep going and try and get ahead of the closure.'

We'd heard that the strike would affect the canal only along a certain stretch, from somewhere further east up to and including the lock at Trèbes. We calculated we could make Trèbes with half an hour to spare before the lock officially closed at 7pm, and so quickly descended at Carcassonne and went as fast as we could.

When we reached the Trèbes lock there was another boat waiting ahead of us, and, we knew, there was one not far behind us, so we joined the queue. Liz went to investigate what was happening, as this was a three-lock staircase but the lights were red.

She came back looking annoyed. 'The *éclusier* says he's got a boat coming up in the middle chamber, but says that once it's through he will be closing!'

'But it's only just gone 6.30pm,' I moaned. 'He's not supposed to finish till seven o'clock.'

'I know.' Liz looked back at the lock. The *éclusier* avoided her gaze. 'I'll go and talk to him again.' And off she went. That's my gal.

After an animated conversation, which I watched from the safety of the flybridge, she returned, this time smiling. 'He's going to let us through!' she said delightedly. 'But our bunch will definitely be the last.'

I ducked below and grabbed a bottle of wine and, leaving Liz with the boat, went and took it to the *éclusier*, with a handshake and multiple *mercis*. He looked embarrassed and said it wasn't necessary, but didn't take too much persuading to accept it.

With the two other boats we descended the three chambers and exited, to tie up on the downhill side against the bank, and open a bottle of our own. We now knew at least that we'd be able to cruise a decent distance, even if we reached another closed lock before too long.

When we woke in the morning, boats had arrived hoping to head up the locks only to find them closed due to the strike. It turned out Trèbes was actually the start of the closure, which encompassed a lengthy stretch *westwards*, not eastwards, so we had only just scraped through.

Hotel boats arrived, cruisers, and hire boats, all queued up at the firmly shut lock gates, as we started *Liberty*'s engine and sailed westwards.

And then I found myself alone again on *Liberty* for 12 days.

Not adrift, with no sign of land; I wasn't reduced to drinking my own urine or anything like that. It's just that Liz had gone back to England again, for half-term, to lend some moral support to

Yasmin who was half-way through her A-levels and finding it all a bit stressful.

Meanwhile, we had returned uneventfully all the way along the Latéral à la Garonne and the Canal du Midi, and *Liberty* was moored on the stone quayside in the pleasant port of Marseillan, on the south coast of France. If I stood on the top deck on tip-toe I could almost see the Mediterranean on the other side of the coastal lake, the Étang de Thau.

We had crossed the Étang the first time back in late March when we were heading west to begin the Canal du Midi. Then it was a blue-sky day with a slight breeze, plenty of sun, and we thoroughly enjoyed the approximately hour-and-a-half crossing, opening *Liberty*'s throttle more than we could on the canals, and revelling in how distant the land seemed on all sides. It was like being at sea, but without the risks of fierce swells or huge storms or being offshore.

But the previous week, when we'd finally come off the Midi and back onto the Étang for the relatively short twenty-minute journey to Marseillan, a town with a marina and port on the inland side of the lake, it was after a thunderstorm; the sky was still leaden grey, and the wind was fierce. In fact, it was probably blowing to the point where we shouldn't have entered the Étang, and was whipping up waves and whitecaps, and coming straight off the Med. Again, what's with this hallowed 'Mediterranean Climate' thing everyone talks about? We still didn't get it.

Anyway, *Liberty* corkscrewed her way across, being side-on to the waves. I hummed the theme to *Gilligan's Island*. I know the respected technique is always to cruise into the oncoming waves, and then choose your moment to turn about and have them behind you, as required (at least I think that's how it works), but Marseillan was within easy reach and we decided to suffer the swell and get the journey over with as quickly as possible in case the weather got worse, so we stuck with the corkscrewing. (Not the sort we are used to either!)

Liz was scared, definitely. I was worried a bit too, but only because the boat was moving around more than she'd ever done since we bought her, though I never felt like she would capsize or that we were in any real danger. That's the beauty of naïvety.

The fact that we're writing this now tells you we made it alive, but it was a great relief to arrive in the small port, and find our boating friends Richard and Sophie waving madly from the quayside to indicate where we could moor.

We executed an elegant turn mid-harbour, which belied our previous twenty minutes of terror, and with Richard and Sophie's help moored conveniently right outside a café, into which we all repaired for a celebratory tot.

Originally our plan had been to stay here just a day or so, and then go across the Étang to Sète where we'd moor *Liberty* while Liz was in the UK. I would then have the whole of Sète at my disposal, which could be useful especially since I had some work to do on the boat. But Richard and Sophie wouldn't hear of it. 'No! Stay here! You don't need to go to Sète. We'll look after you!'

I wanted to stick to Plan A, but while I was having a nap, unbeknown to me Liz went to the *capitainerie* and booked us in.

'There,' she announced when she got back. 'You're here for two weeks.'

Actually I was relieved; it took some pressure off, and Marseillan did look nice, plus it was a real bonus having Richard and Sophie around. It was great to see them again.

Two days later and Liz was off to Nîmes to catch her flight to the north of England, leaving me to do the chores on the boat. We both had long lists of things to do. Top of her list was: Buy an Apartment, while mine began with: 'Fix the loose nuts on propeller shaft flange.' I think I got the easier of the tasks.

Marseillan proved to be a great stopover, confirming what Richard and Sophie had told us earlier. They'd spent the winter here on their boat *Souvenir*, along with their dog Barney, and were looking very relaxed and at home.

I could see even from just a short walk around that Marseillan was a well-off town, full of restaurants and cafés all specialising in seafood. The marina was clean and well-kept, and the brackish water crystal clear, just as it was in the Étang. The water quality was no accident though – the Étang de Thau is protected, and boats are not allowed to discharge any waste overboard due to the commercial oyster farms that are a mainstay of the local economy.

The population seemed cosmopolitan, and with lots of English. As I sat on the boat – sorry, as I slaved away trying to fix the flange nuts down behind the engine – the voices I could hear going by ranged from, 'I say, look at that absolutely spiffing old yacht,' to 'Blimey, fink wot that'd cost yer! An arm and a leg!'

Though a bin man did stop one morning and told me in French that he thought *Liberty* was a nice boat, so not everyone was a Brit.

But wait – you're almost certainly wondering why I was down in the engine bay wrestling with the prop flange nuts when they'd been replaced and fixed months ago in Beaucaire. Simple: they'd started to come undone again. Despite having been 'fixed' by the boatyard's mechanic, our regular checks had revealed that they were indeed working their way loose once more.

If nothing else this endorsed the importance of making regular checks, and we'd been pleased to discover them loose rather than have the prop shaft part company with the gearbox half way across the Étang in a howling wind.

After buying some proper spring washers from a local hardware store I was able to make the repair, and from there on the nuts stayed put. The difference between my repair and the one in Beaucaire? Mine cost about €3, whereas the *facture* we were chased with back in December had been for almost €140. I just wish I'd been able to fix them the first time!

There were a few other things that needed seeing to on board, and while Liz was away I busied myself with those, and in between chores went to the local market and *brocante* market, and enjoyed the hospitality of Richard and Sophie on *Souvenir*.

Richard was passing our boat one morning, walking Barney. I was on deck cleaning, and making sure that our hanging baskets of flowers were well-watered, and feeling proud that they would be looking particularly lovely for when Liz returned. I slung my bucket over the side and liberally doused the plants with clear water.

Then a Frenchman on the boat behind said something to Richard, who chuckled and they both looked at me. 'What did he say? I asked.

'He said you might want to start using fresh water on your plants.'

I'd completely forgotten the water in the marina was partly salty. No wonder the plants had been looking a bit sad.

CHAPTER THIRTY-FIVE

Wrinkly bottoms, floppy bosoms, wobbly tummies, and nether regions that should really be no-go regions – there they all were for me to observe without embarrassment. Yes, I did it: I finally went starkers in front of naked strangers.

Have you ever had one of those dreams where you're stark naked, yet nobody else is, and it slowly dawns on you that maybe you shouldn't be, but there's nothing you can do about it? No? Maybe it's just me then, but I often wondered what it would be like, except in this case everyone would be *sans* clothes.

Cap D'Agde, with its famed naturist village, wasn't far from the eastern entry to the Canal du Midi, from where we'd recently emerged. I told Liz I thought I might go and pay a visit while she was in England. 'Fine,' she said. 'I'm quite happy *not* to go!'

So I'd been keeping an eye on the weather for the right day to go and experience Cap D'Agde for myself, and finally that day arrived.

The forecast was for 27 degrees, sunshine, blue skies… perfect for getting your kit off. I had been working on my tan in between working on the boat over the week, but of course there were bits of me that hadn't seen the sun, so I was conscious that I would stand out, as it were, as a newbie.

Still, nothing ventured, etc., so I set off on the bike, with the usual beachy things in a bag: towel, sunblock, hat, bottle of water. The only thing I didn't have with me, as I wouldn't be needing them, were bathers/swimsuit/togs/or cozzie (depending on where you're from).

It took me two sweltering hours to finally track down the location (Liz had taken the Sat-Nav with her), and gaining entry was slowed further by a queue of others all wanting access. This line included five really tall young Dutch men, fit, healthy, full of the joys, etc. I hate being surrounded by tall people, it always makes me feel claustrophobic. And extra short.

I looked at the others in the queue and tried to imagine them naked. I wondered if I would recognise any of them later without their clothes on, and decided probably not, except for the Dutch men who would undoubtedly stay *en groupe*. I also assumed they would be parading around without inhibitions and put the rest of us mere males to shame. I would find out within the hour…

Finally I paid my eight Euros and gained access to the undercover world of naturism. Or rather the uncovered world. I entered the gate. Gate? Entered? Actually I found it difficult to tell I was in, because the scruffy entrance – really more of a hole in a concrete wall – just led into a car park, bordered by a row of downmarket shops, salons and real estate agents. (As opposed to fake estate agents?)

I'd read that there was nowhere to get undressed, no changing rooms, not even a designated area off to one side where you might be able to pack your clothes into your bag, and it was true; it really was nothing more than a car park, and it didn't make me feel like shedding anything, other than maybe a tear. Eight Euros for this?

Other people had entered, and as they walked confidently and fully-clothed further into the complex I followed, slowly, on my bike. I saw more people, all also clothed, and then finally I spotted a naked man. Aged about 75, he was starkers, tanned, lean, and totally unashamed.

Then I noticed the erection. It was a building that was past its use-by date, which expired around 1980, but used to be the centrepiece for the naturist village – a semi-circular tiered escarpment of apartments. To say it was reminiscent of a Roman coliseum would be too kind; it looked more like something out of *Thunderbirds*, and if the garden in front slid back and revealed a launching pad I wouldn't have been surprised. But it was faded and dowdy, and – although I didn't know it at that point – was to set the scene for the rest of the village.

I rode on, my wheels bumping over potholes in the roads. Everywhere there were parked cars, and car parks. Vehicles constantly moved around, some of them commercial vans, interspersed with the odd golf buggy. Drivers and passengers all seemed to be fully-clothed, and I was beginning to wonder if the sole naked man I'd seen was just that: maybe he was the only one. Or maybe he just had Alzheimer's and had forgotten to get dressed. I certainly wasn't ready to strip off yet… I wanted to know I'd be in company. I rode on some more, negotiating the narrow roads looking for nudity, wondering whether those who were clothed could perversely be charged with 'decent exposure.'

Slowly, I did eventually see more flesh as I got deeper into the village… couples, individuals, some starkers, others partly clothed. It seemed common that where a couple walked together the man would be naked while the woman would more often than not wear something, even if only a sarong around her waist. The man just wore a smile.

But this was hardly a nudist paradise. As well, the general air of the village was one of dowdiness. Apart from the potholed roads, many of the buildings housing clubs and bars looked like they had been transplanted from the worst of England's suburban commercial areas. Even the establishments' names seemed drab. Why wasn't there a club called Willy's?

And many were still closed and boarded up, presumably because, despite the sunshine and 27 degrees, the season hadn't properly started. July and August are peak season – or perhaps, in a naughty nudist sense – peek season.

Now I was hot. I had ridden two hours to get here and was still in shorts and shirt, so I decided to head for the beach where I felt sure I could finally shed my clothes. Sure enough, the closer I got to the sea the more naked flesh came my way, all shapes and sizes. And suddenly there it was… the Med, and a long white sandy beach, peppered with bronzed and not-so bronzed bodies. I parked my bike, dropped my shorts, ditched my shirt, and removed my underwear as elegantly as I could, praying I wouldn't get a foot caught in my undies and topple face-down in the sand. I didn't, and next thing I was naked. Just like that, no fuss, no bother, and no need for *Mr Bean*-style undressing where you hope nobody is looking. Because I got the impression nobody *was* looking, but maybe they just hid it well.

And so I strode my manly way onto the beach, looking for a spot that wouldn't crowd anyone else, which I found, since the beach wasn't exactly cheek-to-cheek. I laid out my towel, lay down and contemplated the scene.

To my left was a couple in their sixties I'd guess, lying on sunbeds. They were nude, and brown. They didn't stir, and might have been dead. Almost straight ahead was another couple, this time in their 20s and lying on towels. He was quite tanned, but she was peaches-and-cream, which made me feel better.

In the distance towards the waves, a group of seriously brown people, male and female, stood around talking animatedly. But further to my left was a couple who epitomised everyone's vision of nudism: thirty-somethings, he tall and genuinely handsome, she slim and with fine features, and both of them a deep, deep brown; not a stripe, not a strap mark.

The sun had Access All Areas. If a paint company wanted to trademark their colour it would be called Black Walnut.

Suddenly I felt pink and underdone, whereas until then I'd been doing okay. This was a couple who seriously practised *Faire du Bronzage Integrale*, as nude sunbathing is known in French. I was just... fair.

Seeing these two woke me up to the importance of sunblock, especially as I was now displaying bits of me that don't usually get to see the sun, and so I liberally began applying some SPF. But picture this, there I am, starkers, rubbing sun cream on – well, use your imagination – trying not to arouse attention. I managed it, and spread sunblock liberally on my bum too, but not being double-jointed I couldn't do my back, at least not the centre of it. However, I wasn't about to ask a stranger in my halting French to rub sunscreen on my *'dos.'*

I didn't recognise any of those who had lined up with me to pay the entry fee, except for the high Hollanders, who came strolling as a group along the water's edge, wearing... shorts. All of them. Hah! Come on guys, I thought, what are you ashamed of? And it actually did seem a bit unfair, because they had presumably come to do a bit of perving while depriving everyone else of the opportunity. For a brief moment I considered complaining to the village's Pubic Relations manager.

I walked through the waves a bit and felt very comfortable as those who strolled by were all starkers too, though there were some sights. Such as the woman of ample chest who had so many nipple piercings – including completely covered areolas – that she looked like she was wearing two bouncing medallions. I can only imagine the pain of having such industrial work done. And I can only imagine her explanations every time she walked through airport security and set the alarms off.

There were families, and like the adults, the kids seemed very much at home, and all just getting along fine.

Having increased my comfort level I decided to retrieve my bike and ride back through the village to where I'd seen some cafés and bars to find some lunch. It didn't seem worth getting dressed, so, for the first time in my life, I rode a bike naked. Far from being liberating, I can reveal that you stick to the seat and the pedals are rough on bare feet, but the breeze was nice.

I had noticed earlier that naked diners seemed to be restricted to those bars by the beach. At the establishments further in the village, people generally wore something, though there were plenty of topless women. So, in case it was protocol, I donned my shorts and sat in the welcome shade of an awning for a lunch of pan-fried scallops and a glass of *rosé*.

Fulfilled, I got back on the bike and pedalled off wearing nothing but a contented smile and headed to a different part of the beach for a last lie in the sun before trying to find my way back home. The weather was still glorious, the sky still blue, with clouds so perfect and fluffy they seemed straight out of a child's painting.

And so once again there I was in my birthday suit – the one I now have trouble getting the wrinkles out of. As the afternoon wore on, and I wore nothing, I considered some of the anomalies of nudism. For example, how do you streak through a nudist camp? And if there was a naturist village life-drawing class, would all the art students be naked while the model wore clothes? And if a nudist couple had an argument, could it be said they were just airing their differences? Serious questions.

I really wanted to talk to someone, someone who was a veteran here, to ask how it really is, what happens, what it's like in the busy summer season, what the protocols are, and so on. But I was reluctant to strike up conversation with another naked person.

And then it was time to go. Having spent two tortuous hours getting here I was determined to find a shorter route back, so retrieved the bike and cycled naked again through the village towards the exit.

Photography was 'discouraged' in the naturist village, but as I pedalled towards the exit I saw the most perfect photo opportunity: a genuinely elderly man, stark naked, shuffling along with a Zimmer frame. Wonderful. It was probably the most poignant image of the afternoon, and I wished I'd had a camera; I'd have taken the picture whether the authorities wished to discourage me or not.

I reached the exit, reluctantly donned some clothes and headed off. I found a nice cycle track that took me mainly through countryside, even alongside the Canal du Midi for a while, and an hour and a half later I was back at the boat, tired, sunburned in places that had never been sunburned before, and happy that I'd fulfilled one of my naked ambitions.

As I drifted off to sleep that night, I wondered if during the off-season the Cap D'Agde Naturist Village hangs up a sign saying Clothed for Winter.

CHAPTER THIRTY-SIX

I continued pottering about on the boat in Marseillan, but sometimes just sat on the deck watching the world go by. The boat was moored in the perfect place for this, directly outside a couple of restaurants with tables and chairs under canvas awnings, and the quay was also popular with walkers.

Many people stopped to chat about the boat, while others would stroll by with barely a nod. And then there was Claude, a tousle-haired man of about mid-forties who drove a drop-top car. (I nicknamed him that because he looked like a Claude to me). He wore jeans, T-shirt and brown loafers, and each morning he'd arrive on the quay, park his car, and have a coffee in the brasserie near our boat. Then he would drive round to the other side of the marina, park his car, and have a pot of tea at one of the cafés on that side. After which he'd move himself and his car a few metres down towards the sea and have yet another tea or coffee at a different establishment. If he had a job he was certainly in no hurry to get to work. But he was always alone. And presumably had a bladder of steel because after all that refreshment I never saw him head for a *toilette*.

Then there was Lei-Lei the ginger cat. She, I think, lived in one of the houses on the quayside in between the many cafés and restaurants. She was very vocal, and would meow her story of woe (well, it always sounded sad… 'I've never been fed,' 'Nobody loves me,' etc.) to anyone who would listen and give her ears a scratch. I was one such, and was delighted to arrive back to the boat one day to find her curled up asleep on the 'Welcome Aboard' mat.

She did this a couple of times, and frequently came to say hello while Liz was away, though she'd still hit upon any stranger within range, so it's not like I was her best mate. Some obviously knew her, which is how I came to learn her name was Lei-Lei. Unless it's just French for 'puss.'

There were others I met too, such as English Jenny – a woman of a certain age – who now lived locally. She repeated everything three times. 'There's a storm coming. A storm. A storm's coming.' And she asked me, 'Why do you have a beard? A beard? Why a beard?'

Well Jenny, I like it. I like it, and I like it.

With Liz having booked me into the port for two weeks I was going to be one of the longer-serving tenants on the quay, as most of the other boats stayed for only a day or two. And most of them were hire boats, which meant I was never short of entertainment. Why watch *Die Hard 4* when you can watch a hire boat crew in *Try Hard 1*?

Having witnessed many examples of mooring by committee on the Canal du Midi, none of this came as a surprise. Sophie and Richard said they always went to help hire boats because the crews didn't usually know what they were doing, which was very Christian of them, whereas mean old me was happy to sit back with a glass of wine and enjoy the spectacle.

Well, not entirely true because I actually did often go and help, though I found that the crews sometimes didn't know what help I could give and so didn't know how to use me. Just throw me the rope, I would mime, but they'd be too busy running backwards and forwards, reversing and turning, screaming and yelling at each other and generally doing everything except mooring.

It was during one of these circus displays that I was given

a poignant reminder that it's never too soon in life to go on an adventure.

A hire boat crew chaotically arrived in front of *Liberty*, but one of them, an older man – possibly mid-70s – found it all too much and had to sit down on the quayside, resting against a bollard while the remainder of the bungle moored the boat. Within half an hour it was obvious he wasn't well because an ambulance arrived, followed by a doctor, and the man was eventually taken off to hospital with drip and oxygen mask in place.

I never saw him return. Which is not to say he didn't make it, but it helped reinforce for me that if you have a dream there's no time like the present. Just do it.

Liz came back from England having had a successful trip. She'd viewed many apartments, but only one ticked enough boxes to make us consider making an offer. However, one was all we needed.

She showed me photos of what she'd seen and explained her spreadsheet. The one that scored the highest and appealed the most overlooked Liverpool's marina, and would give us a view of boats, something we'd grown to like.

In the meantime along with Liz, June had arrived (the month, that is) and with it my birthday. Yay!

A few days before the event itself Liz said, 'Do you want to wait till your actual birthday for your present, or do you want it earlier?'

I didn't really know what she was getting at – it seemed a loaded question. 'Why?' I asked. 'Is there some reason I'd want it sooner rather than later?'

'Well,' she said, 'I asked Shaun whether he thought you'd like it now, and he said you would.'

This was the giveaway; I suddenly knew what she'd bought me, and why getting it sooner than later would be brilliant.

'Now please!' I beamed.

She disappeared into the stateroom and came back with a square box, neatly wrapped. This confirmed what it was and I tore into it, genuinely excited.

A couple of hours later we were watching fish swimming underneath *Liberty*'s hull. We examined our propeller, and the condition of the hull. We saw our bow thruster for the first time. Off in the underwater distance we saw seaweed, stones, and more fish, as the sun lazily shafted down through the water.

'This is brilliant!' I said, as I brought the GoPro camera up out of the water on the end of the boathook.

Knowing that I enjoy photography and video, Liz had bought me the latest miniature adventure camera, a GoPro. It's about the size of a cigarette packet, yet has many of the functionalities of professional broadcast quality cameras six times its size. It also comes with a waterproof housing, and it was this I strapped to the boathook so that we could record an underwater view of *Liberty*'s hull.

The quality of the footage was fantastic, and I was like a six-year-old in my excitement, rather than the almost-ten-times that age that I was approaching.

An added bonus was that our hull looked to be sound, and we couldn't see any foreign objects tangled in the propeller or rudder.

I hoped that when we left Marseillan and headed back out onto the sparklingly clear waters of the Étang de Thau that we might be able to anchor somewhere shallow (the average depth is ten metres but there are plenty areas of the lake much less than that); then I could go over the side with my new toy and shoot some more extensive underwater footage.

But, sod's law, it was not to be; after a lovely long spell of sunny, settled weather, the day we departed it was cloudy and gusty – and a bit cool, so I didn't get to play Jaques Cousteau.

Liz and I waved farewell to Marseillan, and to Richard, Sophie and Barney who were staying on – and had in fact put an offer on a house – and crossed the Étang de Thau, but this time head-on to the wind and waves. It was actually a very pleasant voyage; on our left we passed the oyster farms – which looked like rows and rows of semi-submerged soccer goals. Bobbing up and down in their red boat we could see three local fishermen checking on their bivalves.

Two hours later we re-entered the Rhône à Sète Canal, by which time the sun had come out and it was warming up considerably.

I looked back longingly at the now deep blue Étang and regretted the lost snorkelling opportunity. But this was countered by my looking forward to my actual birthday, when I would become what in some circles is known as 'A Gentleman of a Certain Age.'

CHAPTER THIRTY-SEVEN

I have however always been of a certain age. I knew for certain, for example, when I turned thirty, and later forty. I was certain also that I'd turned fifty when I turned fifty. So certain in fact that I remember it as though it were ten years ago. Oops.

And so I was certain, yet completely baffled by, turning – could I really bring myself to say it out loud? – s… sixty. (Except that I called it *sexty*.)

Not that it's without its compensations. For example, as of my birthday I would qualify for free travel on Merseyside Transport's buses, trains and ferries. Yes, as a sixty-something I qualified for a Bus Pass! Unbelievable! Who knew?

This incensed one of our Merseyside friends, who felt that since I'd spent something like eighty percent of my life outside the UK I shouldn't be eligible for free travel when I hadn't contributed any tax in the UK in all that time. However, his issue is really with the *policy* that enables me to qualify, and not with me personally, I hope. Blame the system Stan.

The French rail authority also acknowledged my advancing age by offering me all sorts of discounts, including concessions in First Class on the TGV. *Merci beaucoup SNCF!* There have to be some good sides to this growing older business.

We carried on to Maguelone and greenbanked there again for the night, a nice evening. This time Liz was desperate to get the definitive seagull photo and had been clicking away, plus she still also wanted flamingos, preferably flying in formation, but they'd still always been too distant. Flamingos seem to have a knack of staying just out of reach, unless you're a professional wildlife photographer with a huge lens and all the time in the world, neither of which we had.

Well, we had the time, up to a point, but nothing like the equipment needed to shoot something as distant as a flamingo formation. Liz did finally shoot a seagull, and managed to get a distant flamingo stretching its incredibly pink wings, but the formation fly-past tick-box remained empty. She tried, but it was always a case of... flamingone.

We set off next morning, a Saturday, quickly remembering why we'd disliked the R à S Canal so much the first time... it was still dull even though the weather was much better; a flat landscape, no trees, big sky, exposed. Dull.

Still, we had something to distract us; we'd decided to celebrate my birthday in some style and had booked in to a canalside hotel, appropriately called the Canal Hotel, on the outskirts of the pretty walled-town of Aigues-Mortes. We'd been here for a chilly few days back in December you'll recall, but now six months later it was a different place – leafy avenues and squares under warm, blue skies, the ancient town bustling with people all out enjoying the sun.

We picked the Canal Hotel because it had its own mooring right outside, which they had reserved for us. The woman on reception was excellent, and for the first time in France I understood almost everything that was said. We even joked. She recommended a local restaurant that served, she assured us, regional dishes, and thinking of the Camargue's famous white horses, I said, '*Quoi?* Cheval?'

Horrified, she switched quickly to English. 'Oh Monsieur, you weel be keeled if you say zat out loud in Aigues-Mortes!'

We resolved to hold our horses, and went to inspect our room, which was small but modern and clean, and included a small terrace with a view of *Liberty*. The hotel's *piscine* was also a welcome bonus, because with the temperature up around 30 degrees a swim was definitely in order.

Then, a treat for both of us: a return visit to the local military surplus store, which we'd discovered during our first visit. A huge emporium, with everything from *M★A★S★H* tents and camouflage netting to parachutes and folding shovels. There was even a selection of porn DVDs, which, for some bizarre reason, were lumped in with the nautical hardware. We assumed the titles would therefore be nautically-themed... *Avast Behinds, First Mate (Vol III), Docking Manoeuvres of Deutschland,* or maybe *Stern Thrusters of Belgium.* Disappointingly the movies were just what you'd expect, and there was nothing in the selection to expand our knowledge, either of boats or boat-rocking.

Not finding a parachute in my colour, we instead walked into the old walled town for a lazy beer at an outdoor café in the hot sun, before going to Banares, one of the few Indian restaurants we'd seen anywhere in France. The owner spoke excellent English, and we told him that Indian cuisine was very popular in New Zealand. He said, 'It is popular here too. For example, apart from Banares, there is another Indian restaurant 25 kilometres away, and another one fifty kilometres from here...'

Right. He was joking. The next nearest was probably 100kms distant. Anyway, his food was superb, and what a treat to have curry again.

Next day, my actual birthday – and the first one I'd had in the northern hemisphere (and in summer) for over 40 years – started with Liz and I sharing a bottle of Moët & Chandon... which doubled as breakfast as we were too lazy to go downstairs for the hotel's brekky and there wasn't any room service. No matter; Champagne trumps croissants any day. And even though there was no fridge in the room, we'd left the champers chilling in *Liberty*'s fridge. Liz kindly went and fetched it, plus our ice bucket and flutes. Perfect. Except neither of us can play the flute.

We then caught the train to Grau du Roi, a huge journey of seven minutes, costing just one Euro each. It was gloriously sunny and warm, unlike that day last December when we'd cycled here in the teeth of an onshore wind. This was much easier!

And, unlike six months previously, the Mediterranean fishing port was now alive and kicking – with lots of people and activity, and all the cafés and restaurants open for business. We decided to forego a return visit to the *créperie* and instead chose a waterside restaurant, where I tucked into a local fish dish while Liz had a seafood salad, both delish.

The harbour was busy, with fishing boats, jet skis, and hire boats tootling by, and seagulls hanging around just outside the window where we were dining, hoping for a morsel. It was so nice to be back and see the place alive. After lunch we strolled down to the beach and took a photo in the same spot as we had last December, except this time we were wearing shorts and T-shirts rather than hats and scarves... much better.

We lay on the sand, I went for a couple of swims, Liz paddled, we people-watched, and generally lazed away the afternoon. We saw a Muslim woman formally dressed top-to-toe in the searing sun, while her husband paraded around in his shorts.

We caught the train back late afternoon and later – sorry, this is turning into a culinary-fest! – went out for my birthday dinner to Boem, a restaurant with buckets of ambience, only a few steps from the hotel. ('*Garçon!* Another bucket of ambience, *s'il vous plaît!*')

With no horse on the menu we both had *boeuf*, cooked à *point*, and it was absolutely lovely. A gorgeously balmy evening, and the restaurant had a major indoor-outdoor flow thing going on, with a nice variety of seating, from comfy couches to more formal dining tables. Candles glowed, a water fountain played, a cat wearing a bandana slept curled up on a couch. Perfect. But the celebration, it turned out, wasn't over yet.

Next morning we set off on *Liberty* at a leisurely pace, slightly lower in the water due to the weight we'd put on, looking forward to reaching the end of the Rhône à Sète Canal. We reached Gallician and moored up, with the aim of going to fill up our five-litre plastic jerry cans with wine at the local *Cave Cooperative* (€1.20 per litre!) only to find that it was a public holiday and everything was shut. That's the thing about cruising without a care – you tend not to worry about the calendar or what date it is, so of course we had no idea it was (yet another) French national holiday. Oh well.

After a lunch break we set off again towards the Saint-Gilles lock where we aimed to stop for the night, only to discover the lovely lines of the *Sally Beth* moored alongside the canal with Jim and Sandra having a barbecue with Patrick and Marina and others. It was a serendipitous reunion with these valued friends from Beaucaire with whom we'd spent the winter, as we'd been looking out for them along the way, knowing Jim and Sandra had planned on getting their boat taken out of the water for painting at Grau du Roi.

However, their plans had been thwarted due to there being no space available at the port, and here they were, waiting until it was opportune to find some other boat yard. It was another glorious day and we joined the throng under sun umbrellas on the canal bank for the rest of the afternoon and evening, swapping stories, catching up, strangling the French language and drinking far too much wine. *Magnifique.*

And then the Maritime Police boarded us with guns on hips.

281

CHAPTER THIRTY-EIGHT

L iz and I had returned early to Gallician next morning to fill up with the lovely local *rosé*, then we'd said farewell to Jim and Sandra, and headed to the Saint-Gilles lock which would be our exit onto the Petit Rhône and the start of our long journey back north.

The lock is a pinch-point for the French waterways authority because any boats coming from the west from the canals Garonne, Midi or the Rhône à Sète have to pass through here if they want to get to the Rhône, and vice versa. So it's a good place for the VNF to monitor and record details of boats, and inspect them as they pass through, and sure enough this time they had us trapped.

As we cruised into the lock on another gorgeously hot morning we could see the *éclusier* waiting for us, along with two armed Maritime Police officers.

They took great interest in us as soon as we roped up in the lock, and after ascertaining with visible glee that our boat was French-registered one of them came aboard to inspect our safety gear and fire extinguishers, and documentation.

If we'd stayed with *Liberty*'s original British registration and been flying the Red Duster, the police would have had no authority to board, so we'd been told. However, the ensign was now rolled up in a drawer. We were French-registered, and fair game.

The police officer sat on the aft deck, flipped open his laptop, and began entering *Liberty*'s and our own details into a database. Every now and then he would ask a question in heavily accented English, or sometimes just in French, such as whether we ever had paying guests on board (meaning were we supposed to be registered as a hotel boat), where we had been and where we were going.

He then asked in French about our boating qualifications, which was the very question we were hoping he wouldn't ask. Because we didn't have any.

Why? Well, as with so many other aspects of boating in France, we'd received hugely conflicting opinions and advice as to what was required. The boat brokerage where we'd bought *Liberty* advised us that no particular qualifications were necessary. Others had said that we absolutely *must* have an internationally-recognised skipper qualification that showed we'd had the required training in boat-handling. Still others had said you only needed that if your boat was British-registered, not if it's French. And so on. Even the websites were inconclusive, so we'd sailed from Saint-Jean-de-Losne with nothing but hope.

The sweat poured in rivulets from under my arms, and I could see that Liz was also worried, though trying not to show it. We both knew very well what the police officer was asking, but I feigned not to understand his French. I turned to Liz and asked her, sure that my eyes must have given away my terror that at any moment our boat would be confiscated and we'd be catching the TGV back home.

'*Permis?*' I queried Liz. 'Do you know what that is?'

Liz played dumb, her eyes locking onto mine in fear. The officer, whose laptop had, by now, succumbed to the heat and stopped working, looked up at me and tried in English: 'You 'ave been to ze boat school?'

'Ahhh!' I said with relief, finally (apparently) understanding him. '*Oui, bien sur,*' I confirmed. '*En Nouvelle Zélande.*' I waved my hand in the general direction of the southern hemisphere.

He nodded, shook his head exasperatedly at his dead laptop, and then said he would like to inspect our life jackets and fire extinguishers.

We dug out the only two life jackets we had, the second one thankfully donated to us by Richard and Sophie because until we'd met them we'd had only the one that Liz had bought, and on the Rhône it was compulsory to wear them in the big locks; however we'd bluffed our way through the first few using an ordinary hi-vis jacket until we got the second life jacket from R&S at Roche-de-Glun.

As for our fire extinguishers, well they too were given the big tick, which was very lucky for us.

Because the extinguishers didn't have an actual expiry date on them, or any test certificates, the officer technically couldn't fail them (which was a relief, as they were probably five years old or more).

So we were waved on and passed through the lock without incident. We were, I quipped to Liz with a sense of relief, an unqualified success.

But we couldn't help wondering why the officers were armed. I mean, how can you run from the Maritime Police when your boat probably can't go any faster than 14kph? They'd be able to jog alongside on the towpath, and could certainly overtake you in their high-powered rubber inflatable (which actually had the standard cop car red and blue light bar on too). They would even have time to send a postcard to the next police station so the local officers there could stop you further down the canal. No, they may have believed it, but really these guys were never going to be *Hawaii Five-Eau*.

And so, finally, we were shot of the Canal Rhône à Sète, its wetland dullness, its shy blurred flamingos and its overly-armed marine *gendarmes*. We exited the Saint-Gilles lock, turned onto the Petit Rhône in hot sunshine and began our journey back up-river, knowing it would likely be a long time before we sailed the Midi or Garonne again, and hopefully never the Rhône à Sète.

Ahead of us lay the challenge of tackling the backbone river of France – the Rhône, this time against the current, as we headed for the unexplored (at least for us) canals of central France. As we cruised the first few kilometres of the Petit Rhône, we listened for the sirens of pursuing maritime police – who might have managed to get their laptop going and discovered our bluff – and prepared to duck the hail of bullets…

But there were none of course, and we enjoyed a peaceful journey along the tree-lined Petit Rhône, reached its big brother the Rhône itself, turned left and headed north.

It was strange to be back on the big, broad river after the narrow confines of the canals, but we had timed it right, even though it might have been against the original advice of Richard and Sophie. Any post-winter snowmelt from up north had either already happened, or was yet to happen, and as we forged our path northwards it was on a gently-flowing river in lovely weather.

Nothing had changed about the locks or the routines involved, other than this time we were *montant*, going up rather than down, and we had the sun behind us all the way.

But now, a word about gender.

The French language, as you know, uses gender. Things are either male – *le* – or female – *la*. We didn't always get this right when we tried our mangled French on the poor unsuspecting locals, but nobody seemed to mind, and besides, I'd become an expert in the art of slurring to the point where (I believed) I could be saying either. As long as I got away with it, *porquoi pas?*

Anyway, in the period of around two weeks following our encounter with the *flics* at Saint-Gilles lock, we cruised up the male Rhône, the female Saône, along the male Canal du Centre, and found ourselves on the Canal Latéral alongside the ladylike Loire River.

The rivers at least lived up to their genders. Le Rhône, is broad-shouldered, strong and, if you get him in the wrong mood, can be a bit of a bully. We saw him like this in January from the safety of Beaucaire's shore and it wasn't a pretty sight. We stood there with our mouths open in awe at the immense power of the water as it roared past us, an unstoppable force, the sheer power coming across like a living, evil thing. You can see why there are so many hydro stations on the river.

We were glad to have waited until *Le Bully* became more of a pussycat.

We don't know whose job it was to define the genders of the waterways, but with the Rhône and Saône they got it right.

Locks on the other hand are all female, and here – at least on the Rhône and Saône – we think they got it wrong, because they are huge brutes. Or maybe just butch. Either way, they are formidable, even more so going up. Coming down last year, we were cruising *avalant* – meaning descending, going downstream – so it meant that each lock we came to we just cruised in at the top level, then were lowered gently down. They're all controlled by lock-keepers in their control towers, unseen entities who are just voices on the VHF channel, both male and female. (Not hermaphrodite; I mean they're *either* male or female, if you see what I mean. Why am I even explaining this?!)

This time though because we were *montant*, ascending, it meant that each time we came to one of these giant females she would lift up her iron petticoat and we would slide beneath. You can read whatever symbolism you like into this scenario, but I can tell you that there is nothing feminine about it.

Imagine walking into a massive narrow warehouse without a roof, so steep-sided that you feel claustrophobic, the stone walls so high that the sky is reduced to a blue strip high above, and all around you the dripping of water, the echoes of every sound. Set in the dank walls are floating bollards, to which you secure your ropes. Then, behind you, the massive steel door closes, descending on unseen hydraulics, its rows of rivets slowly lowering and finally submerging in the murky waters with a prison-like finality.

Then the real noises begin – clanks, groans, rumblings – as the underwater gates in the upstream doors open and let in the river water. The water boils with eddies and turbulence, the bollards slowly begin to rise, some of them grinding and protesting against their rails, and the downstream door settles, groaning against its door jamb, the grinding of steel on steel.

Some of the noises sound like whales crooning, others are surely what those who stayed on board the Titanic must have heard – reminiscent of the implosion of the boilers, the creaking and collapse of bulkheads as the enormous pressures of the Atlantic waters sought a way in, the dying groans of a ship in her death throes. There's a Gothic drama to the whole process, an almost-steampunk experience, and if you were to choose an accompanying theme it would have to be Bach's Toccata and Fugue in D.

And then, slowly, you rise higher and higher, emerging eventually from the dank shadows of Mordor into the sunlight, and the Lady Lock finally reveals her feminine self as she delivers you safely from the ordeal. Madame *Écluse* has protected you. She lowers her upstream barrier, silently this time as the lock is full and there are no echoes, and out you drift, back onto the manly Rhône.

CHAPTER THIRTY-NINE

As it was now well into June, with the promise of greatly increased boating activity, we applied the rule we'd been told about back in Saint-Jean-de-Losne, Mike's one about departing early and finishing early in order to ensure a mooring, so when we swerved in to the small marina at Viviers at about 1pm it was to find almost-empty pontoons, and we could take our pick of moorings.

But, sure enough, from around 4pm onwards boats started arriving in numbers, jostling for position. They too swerved into port, not because of anything wrong with their boats but, like us, they were avoiding an old submerged wall or breakwater just outside the entrance – something you definitely didn't want to bump into.

Around 5pm, one of the last boats to arrive was an older and slightly battered cruiser, well-used, with two German lads on board. We, by this time, were sitting in our usual spot on deck with glasses of wine in hand, and we watched incredulously as the Germans, having (only just) successfully avoided the submerged hazard at the last minute, swept into the marina, executed a pirouette and then headed at quite some speed for the rocks of a nearby breakwater.

There was much yelling and gesticulating on the boat, and a definite hint of panic. At the last moment the boat's engine ceased to rev and the skipper managed to coax the vessel away from danger.

Once they'd regained their composure they managed to

slowly nose their way into one of the last remaining pontoons, next to us. We helped catch and tie their ropes, and learned that they had just experienced something similar to our shock-horror situation in the Bram lock, when *Liberty*'s gearbox had stuck in reverse. Only in their case it had briefly jammed in the forward position.

Within half an hour one of the lads had come over to ask if he could borrow a hammer, and to ask if we happened to have a little clamp and bolt. As a result of the Bram Incident we now had enough spare parts to fix a battleship, and were happy to hand them over.

Back with our wines we watched as the other crew member dropped over the stern with snorkel and mask, and disappeared underwater to – so we were informed – hammer a bent propeller blade back into shape.

'We had come up one of the river's deviations,' the taller of the two Teutonics explained in very good English, 'and we were trying to stay close to the edge where the current was less, but we hit something.'

Considering they had actually sailed the boat all the way from Spain after buying it there, they were very lucky if that was the worst that had happened to them along the way!

Anyway, their repairs both underwater and below decks seemed to go well enough. Next day, after we got back from exploring Viviers, they had gone, but left our hammer along with a bag of potatoes and onions, with a note to say thank you and to apologise that this was all they had as an offering. *Danke*.

Viviers was lovely, and we were very glad we'd made the effort to stop there.

It's one of those old towns, like Cruas, where, if you look in a certain direction, with your eyes closed off to peripheral vision, you can see what looks like an original medieval town, as though you'd been transported back in time hundreds of years.

Seen from below, from down by the marina where we were moored, Viviers sits atop a rocky outcrop, an ideal position for a fortified town.

Its walls blend in with the natural rock below, and it holds a commanding position over the surrounding landscape.

We panted our way up to reach it, and entered a wonderful medieval world of stone walls, buildings, tiled roofs and towers. It was beautifully kept, with well-tended lawn areas, and lots of trees.

From its walls we looked out over the remainder of the town, over terracotta roofs glowing in the bright sunlight. To our left a gorge sliced through the hills towards the south, as though a giant had sliced the hillside with a huge cleaver.

Our cameras worked overtime. Back in the shade of the old town itself we were rewarded with cool cobbled alleyways, and steps bordered by pretty flowers. There were blissfully few vehicles, and we lost ourselves in a world of yesterday, the sort of historic stonewalled splendour that a corporation like Disney would spend millions recreating and charge the earth to enter.

Much as we'd liked to have stayed, it was time to push on. We now had another rendezvous with Shaun, this time in July in central France, when he would return, to spend eight days with us instead of the fleeting three near Bordeaux.

We were looking forward to a less hectic visit, but it meant we had to get onto the canal system, and make a certain amount of progress each day.

But then the wind got up, the Rhône got choppy, it got cool, and we decided we'd have to pull into Valence again whether we liked it or not because the forecast was for it to get worse.

This time though Monsieur Decibel was absent, and the silence was golden. In fact the man in charge at the *capitainerie* was all sweetness and light. And the haughty English woman who had snottily wished us *bonne chance* in finding somewhere to stay down south some months earlier was nowhere to be seen. Which was a pity because again we'd have liked to tell her just how *bonne* our *chance* had actually turned out.

Another bonus was that we got a free lesson in rope wrangling from the boatie who helped us tie up. He was somewhat aghast at our knots, and demonstrated how we should make fast without using knots at all, a technique we adopted from there on. After all these months it was slightly embarrassing that we still had some basics to learn.

Liz was feeling under the weather (blame *Le Mistral*, it does that) so while she blobbed on board I cycled into Valence itself for a bit of exercise and a look around. The only object of note that I found was a bronze life-sized statue of a young Napoleon, aged I would guess about 12 or 13, sitting, with a book open on his lap.

I presumed it was *The Boys' Book of Conquering the World*. He seemed engrossed in it.

But that's not to say Valence was dull – it certainly wasn't, and I found plenty of wide open plazas, parks and other public spaces that were both inviting and, blissfully, somewhat sheltered from the wind. People promenaded, sat at outdoor cafés, and enjoyed the warm sunshine.

Liz perked up again, just in time to welcome back Reg and Kate who had decided to come to Valence and take advantage of our passing through to catch up. It was also Father's Day, so after polishing off the very welcome bottle of Champagne they'd brought we went to the restaurant conveniently next to the *capitainerie* and enjoyed a pleasant set-menu lunch. We couldn't fault the quality of the food; maybe the French society of restaurateurs had been reading our blogs and had upped their game. We celebrated not only Father's Day, but also that Reg had fully recovered from his bronchitis, and no longer looked or sounded like he wouldn't see the week out.

There was also no interrogation of how we were going to survive or what our plans for employment were. We figured the parents had decided maybe we knew what we were doing after all (even if we didn't!).

The wind finally blew itself out and allowed us to set off for Lyon.

This time our favourite city proved to be a real pain – for me at least. Our last few days on the Rhône had been relatively plain sailing apart from an increasingly painful toothache, and I'd spent most of the time dosed up on painkillers, flipping through our French language books looking for how to say, 'I am in complete agony and wish either to have the offending tooth out or to be put down.'

What I really wanted to convey was that I have an innate fear of dentists, which since my youth has led me to avoid them as much as possible, only going when the need arose (i.e. when I was in agony). This totally reactive approach meant I was denied a strong dental care regime, and failed to look after my teeth properly. I'm paying for that now; paying through the teeth in fact.

Once we'd moored again at the Confluence Marina I got online and discovered there were a few English-speaking dentists in town, but also discovered that to get a short-notice appointment wasn't easy.

We visited a nearby pharmacy to stock up on more painkillers. The pharmacist, a kindly woman, older – mature shall we say – with gold-rimmed glasses, asked what I needed the painkillers for, and in the ensuing conversation (much gesticulating on our part as our French lexicon didn't include medical descriptions) she told us there was a dentist just around the corner and that she would ring to see if we could visit.

She did, and – thank you Saint Apollonia (the patron saint of dentists, believe it or not) – the dentist said for us to pop round.

One X-ray later and it was confirmed I had an infection beneath one of my (remaining) teeth. The dentist's English was quite good, but she said there was no need to do an extraction, and instead prescribed antibiotics.

We went back to our lovely pharmacist who filled the prescription and gave me stern warnings about how to use the medication, then filled in all sorts of paperwork so that we could claim against insurance if we wished. (Actually, the whole thing, X-ray included, was so cheap we decided not to bother.)

The tooth incident reminded us that one of the issues boaties have to seriously consider when deciding on a life afloat in France is health.

As a couple afloat with no fixed abode, it seemed we weren't eligible to register with a doctor, though as EU citizens we were entitled to health cover under the EHIC scheme – the European Health Insurance Card. This meant we could access state-provided healthcare in the European Economic Area countries at a reduced cost, or where applicable, for free.

It's not the same as travel insurance, and there are, as always, terms and conditions, but we felt it would probably do for us. Anyway, we'd heard great things about the French health system and Liz's parents couldn't speak more highly of it, so we felt a degree of comfort knowing we were in a country that cared, and not one that would leave you lying on the pavement because you didn't have a credit card or cheque book.

In fact, the French are fanatical about health, with a pharmacist every few metres in every town. Those boating communities we encountered were also useful sources for healthcare, and all knew of at least one English-speaking doctor or surgery. But luckily for us we didn't suffer any major illnesses or ailments, and in fact the antibiotics began working in a very short time, and within 48 hours I had forgotten I'd ever had toothache.

So we were able to enjoy exploring Lyon a bit more, and once again hurtled through its streets on the bikes, dodging pedestrians, racing buses and trying not to get caught in tramlines.

Leaving Lyon we exited the marina and turned right onto the Saône, and enjoyed the closer confines of its river banks.

River traffic had increased since we were here last and we met many other *bateaux plaisances* as we threaded our way slowly north. We'd always wave to the crews, and most would wave to us as well, but every now and then we'd find a boat whose crew either ignored us, or stared at us with completely neutral expressions, and no hint of camaraderie or kinship.

Maybe our New Zealand flag confused them, or maybe they just thought we were Australian. The two flags are easily confused (unless you're a Kiwi or an Aussie).

Flags on boats, we'd learned, were vital, and not just because of their extensive historical role defining the nationality of the vessel. For example it was important, apparently, that we displayed the French flag, preferably on the bows, since it was their country we were sailing in. This was a matter of courtesy, and we were happy to comply. In fact we'd been flying the French *tricolor* from when we first set off, having found a variety of flags in a drawer on board, kindly left behind by the previous owners.

We were later to meet boating couple Bruce and Yerda,

whose boat was a lovely ninety-year-old barge, built in Holland. Because they were proud of the boat's heritage, they flew a Dutch flag from the stern, but had actually received abuse from some other boaties for doing so, because they weren't Dutch.

'But why?' questioned Bruce. 'We think it's the boat that has the nationality, not us. It's even registered in Holland, but it's made some people very grumpy!' he chuckled.

On the other hand, it was the norm for a stern flag to represent the nationality of a boat's crew (tricky if you're all from different countries), and we certainly found it helpful, if for no other reason than it allowed us to shout a loud 'G'day!' to other New Zealanders or Australians, or to give a hearty 'Hello there!' to Brits flying the Red Duster (as the Red Ensign is known informally).

It took us a while to work out the nationality of some of the flags, especially the German and Belgian standards, both of which carry black, red and – at first glance – yellow, though the stripes go in different directions.

(The 'yellow' on the German flag is actually gold, but at a distance often looks yellow.)

The Belgian stripes are vertical, and the German stripes horizontal. We eventually remembered this by adopting the mnemonic, 'Germans are always *cross*.'

(Here's another useful *aide-mémoire* if you can never remember your port from your starboard, or which light is red and which is green: just ask yourself, is there any port left? Port [the drink] is *red* [usually], and if there's any *left* it tells you which side it's on. Easy!)

We made good progress and finally reached Chalon-sur-Saône where we could finally leave the rivers and enter the canal system again, this time going onto the Canal du Centre.

CHAPTER FORTY

The introduction was not pleasant, as the very first lock is quite deep, industrial, dark and uninviting. It was much smaller than those on the Rhône or Saône, but all the more claustrophobic for that, and we were glad to finally exit after we'd risen up to match the level of the canal.

From here on the locks treated us with more human interaction, with visible *éclusiers*, real people who did real things in plain sight to get you and your boat from one level to the next.

And if we thought the large locks of the Rhône and Saône were few and far between, the Canal du Centre certainly made up for that, and in one day alone we went through 24 of them, many with only a few minutes' cruising between them, hardly enough time to make a cup of tea.

In some cases itinerant lock-keepers would oversee three or four locks, and would drive ahead in their VNF van to prepare the locks for us – good service, but also perhaps emphasising the importance of their jobs. It was nice to be fussed over though, on a more personal level, instead of being a toy in a giant bath, swirled by invisible fingers.

Liz was starting to get annoyed with the number of locks, and blamed me partly for our need to push on because I'd agreed we'd meet Shaun somewhere he could easily get to without having to travel halfway across France since this time he was coming in his own car.

'We should never have committed to being in a certain place at a certain time,' she grumbled. 'We agreed we'd never do that sort of thing.'

And I had to admit she was right. When we set off we'd decided our motto would be, 'Take us as you find us, but first of all find us,' and it had seemed like a good maxim at the time. I'd even considered getting it translated into Latin.

But of course we didn't want friends *not* to find us, and sitting with a drink looking at the waterways map and deciding, yeah, we can be there okay by then, was easy.

The harder part was actually getting to where we said we'd be, because the canals are definitely not like autoroutes, where your Sat-Nav tells you you'll be at your destination in 45 minutes, and three-quarters of an hour later there you are.

No, the canals are festooned with obstacles to slow you down, such as twists and turns, bridges, and in this case the sheer number of locks. Plus, let's not forget that not only are there speed limits on the waterways, we never wanted to be hurtling along canals in a hurry anyway; that's not what we signed up for.

So I knew where Liz was coming from and regretted having committed to a specific destination for a specific date.

We looked at the map once again and devised Plans B and C, in case we just couldn't make it to where we said we'd be, and having done that (and texted Shaun) we felt a bit better.

We left the Canal du Centre and turned onto the Canal Latéral à la Loire, a very pretty waterway that meanders through what looks like prime English Constable countryside, dotted with white Charolais cattle.

The weather became sunny and warm again after a few blustery grey days, and the farmers were making hay as they should, so we cruised past mown fields that gave the landscape a park-like feel. The canal itself was also well-kept and trim.

And once again the locks couldn't have been more different to their river behemoth cousins. Here, they were small and charming, often with flower borders and boxes, neat gardens beside the lock cottages, veg gardens with crops of carrots and lettuces, and – perhaps best of all – lock-keepers who actually *manually* wound open the gates and paddles. There was nothing electronic about their operation, no grey sentinels, sensors or remote-control boxes.

Here it was *messieurs* and *madames* – and occasionally *mademoiselles* – who looked after us, but as we knew from our experiences of the self-help automated locks on the Canal du Midi, it's probably only a matter of time. If there had been a petition to sign to preserve their roles we would have had a pen in our hands before you could say *s'il vous plaît*.

But anyway, while the *éclusiers* were begging to keep their jobs, others in France were just begging.

We saw them in almost every town we stopped at, and certainly in all the major cities. We're talking street people here: beggars, and pickpockets.

It's unfortunate that beggars are on the increase in New Zealand, when just a few years ago there were none, but in France they've been around for centuries.

Usually we'd see them sitting alone outside a popular store, such as Monoprix or Carrefour, with a hat or piece of cloth on the ground in front of them to catch your loose change. Some of them politely bid you a *bonne journée,* even if you walked on by without donating.

In railway stations they were less passive and a lot less polite, trawling the coffee bars asking – sometimes aggressively – for money. We saw a customer in one coffee shop reluctantly give a beggar some cash, telling him that it was for '*manger*' and '*pas d'alcool.*' The beggar nodded agreement and understanding, and seemed to acknowledge that he would indeed spend it wisely on food and not drink, but we suspected once out of sight he headed for the nearest bar. Maybe that was unfair of us, I don't know.

Another common sight we witnessed many times were beggars accompanied by a dog, or two, or three. We were discussing this with one of our more experienced boating friends who said that the French government provides a hand-out if you're unemployed and have a hungry mouth – or jaws – to feed, which perhaps explained it. And, by and large, the dogs did all look well-fed, though we did see one homeless character on the canal towpath who we thought was pushing his luck, with 12 canines in tow. 'Look at him,' I said to Liz as we cruised by. 'He's probably a millionaire!'

Sneakier than that were the pickpockets. Our understanding was that in Paris in particular, pickpockets operated in abundance, especially at the main stations but basically anywhere there were dense crowds, though luckily at this point we'd had no first-hand experience of it. We would be given a stern lesson though in the months to come.

We'd read of all manner of clever scams that thieves use in France, and, for all we know, throughout Europe. Many are like mini theatrical set pieces. In one of them, a person will ask you to take their photograph and hand you a camera. As you hand it back they deliberately let it fall to the ground, and then demand that you pay for the damage because it was you who dropped it. Of course the camera was already broken and worthless, but suddenly you owe compensation.

Another ruse is where someone comes up to you and quickly wraps a braided string bracelet or similar around your wrist, then asks for an exorbitant amount of money for the 'souvenir.' If you argue or try to return the bracelet you suddenly find yourself surrounded by a very intimidating group, associates of the 'souvenir seller,' who aggressively force you to pay up.

And still another is the 'gold ring' con. Someone bends down and pretends to find a gold ring on the ground, then gives it to you saying that you deserve it more than they do. As soon as you hold it and examine it they will ask you for a few Euros. When you refuse and try and give it back they become aggressive, and again their friends arrive to surround you.

Some years ago I was in France, and, because I was dressed casually I was not an obvious tourist; I was just someone walking along minding my own business. I saw this guy in his twenties coming towards me when he suddenly handed me a piece of paper. It said, 'I am English and I have lost my passport and wallet. Can you help?' I felt sorry for him, thinking, poor bloke, and said, 'How can I help?'

In a heavy French accent he replied, 'Well, you know, per'aps some money?' He'd assumed I was French and that I would fall for his note and his rudimentary command of English. Needless to say he didn't get anything from me other than disdain.

There are many more cons, and if you're heading for one of the main centres it's well worth doing some research online first to catch up on what the latest ruses and scams are.

Increased vigilance is essential, especially in the cities, though of course this applies all over the world, not just France. I think one of the nicest things about our waterways itinerary was that it rarely took us to large cities, and in the towns and villages that we stopped at the beggars we saw were entirely passive and non-threatening.

We just hope that we never see beggars beside the locks, holding signs saying, 'Former *éclusier*. Please give generously.'

CHAPTER FORTY-ONE

Our sojourn on the Canal du Centre, actually heading south, had been relatively short, and after reaching the town of Digoin, we'd turned north-west again, and now here we were on the Canal Latéral à la Loire, which, as the name suggests, runs for much of its way alongside the Loire River.

You might think the early boat traffic could have used the Loire itself, but the fact is it was prone to extremes: flooding in winter and droughts in summer. Its unreliability affected the commercial potential, and as any business person knows, if you can't guarantee delivery, your customers will go somewhere else.

So, the canal was built to provide reliable passage, but with a deadline to meet that didn't mean we were guaranteed to make it.

It was now July, supposedly almost mid-summer in France, and to be fair it was mostly warm and sunny, the countryside either side of the canal green and lush.

Thanks to the detail in the canal guides we knew exactly how many kilometres we'd need to average each day in order to reach the port of Saint-Satur where we were to meet Shaun. The distances weren't particularly long, but the fact that the lock-keepers closed each day for an hour at lunchtime, and that there were quite a few of them (locks, not lunchtimes. Although…) meant we still had to keep going and Carry On Up the Canal, but without the laughs.

Having said that, there was one incident that made us smile. We were on a reasonably long stretch between locks, I was steering and Liz was down below, when suddenly the boat rose up, then down again, almost as though it had just gone over a speed bump, which is of course impossible.

Liz popped her head out of the hatch. 'What was that?'

'Dunno,' I said, slowing the boat. 'I think we might have just hit something.' And yet it had been gentle, with no noise, no thump, no grinding noise like maybe we'd just gone over the roof of a Citroen 2CV dumped in the canal.

Liz came up on deck and we both looked back, only to see what looked for all the world like a wave, continuing its way down the canal, like the Severn Bore, the tidal surge that occurs on the River Severn at the highest of tides, which has surfers and wakeboarders out in droves. But a wave here on a *canal*? Hardly tidal.

We looked at each other bemused, and decided that somewhere ahead there must have been a hefty dumping of water into the system.

'Maybe the next lock gates just broke and the water behind spilled out in a rush,' I mused. 'Guess we'll see when we get there.'

But we didn't. The lock gates were fine, and there was no indication of what caused the wave so we relegated the incident to our own personal X-Files: spooky, but fun.

Anyway, we reached Saint-Satur on schedule, met Shaun, and instantly the weather turned from glorious to glum. On the plus side, we were in the Sauvignon Blanc capital of France.

In our blog we wrote:

Dear folks

Let us introduce you to the Loire Valley. It may sound familiar, in the same way that Burgundy or Bordeaux does, or maybe Meursault. And if you're thinking it likely has something to do with wine, you'd be right.

We recently meandered ('steered' doesn't seem quite right) our boat Liberty *into the heart of Sancerre country – Sauvignon Blanc territory – in central France. The weather had been glorious, with most days in the high 20s or early 30s, and the rural farmland worthy of an oil painting by an old master. (Where were all the old mistresses in the art world? Why isn't there a famous painting by Whistler's Mother?)*

Anyway, as had happened when we were in Bordeaux, our attention turned once again to wine. How could it not? This is France!

Sauvignon Blanc has long been New Zealand's premier grape, its intense juicy flavours putting Kiwi winemaking firmly on the international wine map. Except, except… in our wine guide book, Master of Wine Hugh Johnson said that the country's flagship variety had become 'somewhat predictable.' He suggested limiting cropping, and adding a touch of oak barrel ageing.

Which is interesting, because back in the late 70s there was a flare for making Kiwi fumé, which all but disappeared once Sav. Blanc became all the rage. The grape itself was sturdy and popular enough not to need any augmentation; people wanted its gooseberry-asparagus essence in buckets, and they got it. Suddenly, the region of Marlborough lost its pole position in the New Zealand Savvy stakes as more and more winemakers all over the country started growing and making Sauvignon Blanc.

Meanwhile, the French continued to make their own Sauvignon Blanc in their own traditional ways, and, especially in the Loire valley, Pouilly Fumé. (The fumé refers to a grey bloom apparent on the grapes at harvesting, though confusingly it can also refer to barrel fermentation, where the wine ages a while in oak barrels that have been toasted, literally set on fire inside for a while before use.)

That's the thing about wine: the more you know the more confusing it gets. No wait, that should be the more you drink the more confusing it gets...

But by and large the French rarely call their Sauvignon Blanc by its varietal name. As with Champagne, Burgundy, Bordeaux, et al, it's usually referred to by regional origin rather than the variety, in this case Sancerre.

In New Zealand this would be the equivalent of asking for a glass of Marlborough, except the Kiwi wine-drinking public has been brought up on varietal rather than regional names. It might well be that Otago Pinot Noir growers would relish the thought of people ordering a bottle of Otago in restaurants, but it's not likely to happen any time soon.

Meanwhile, the French avidly protect their appellations, and woe-betide anyone else who tries to market their wines as Champagne, Bordeaux, Burgundy, Chablis or Sancerre. New Zealand's former Montana Wines learned the hard way when they first brought out Lindauer 'Champagne' in the 1980s, which is why it's now referred to as méthode traditionnelle (and the French are even a bit twitchy about that!).

So, we are in the heart of France's Sauvignon Blanc country, but despite Sancerre having many wine shops, we couldn't find a convenient winery for tastings. The one we did drive into was closed, and the two women in the tourism office blew their chance to snare us since they lacked Sancerre-ity, and seemed to not care that we were visitors from half a world away despite us putting on our best confused looks.

Instead we sat at a café in the town square and shared a local Savvy with Shaun. The wine was lovely, fresh, minerally, clean and (this according to Liz) astringent. We decided we didn't need to scour the countryside for a winery, and so bought

*a box of the stuff from a local supermarket – and by box I don't
mean a dozen bottles; I mean a three-litre BIB (Bag-in-Box,
another of those dreadful English phrases the French have now
adopted, along with 'sandwich,' 'weekend,' and 'burger'). We
figured that it had probably been made down the road at a local
wine cooperative anyway, and it tasted fine.*

    Yours Sancerre-ly

    Mike and Liz (and Shaun)

We were gutted that Shaun's visit coincided with the weather
turning nasty, especially when we discovered that the whole
eight days he was with us, England was basking in very warm
temperatures and everyone there was knotting handkerchiefs to
put on their heads.

So, it turned out, was the rest of France, and we were doubly
dismayed to discover that this particularly cool and cloudy patch
of weather was only in central France, directly over us.

In the days before Shaun arrived we'd been cruising along
in weather so hot I was wearing nothing but my Speedos; now
here we were bundled up in pullovers, jackets and hats. But we
weren't going to let that stop us enjoying ourselves, especially
as the most important day on France's calendar had arrived: 14
Juillet, Bastille Day. We'd been tipped-off by an English boating
couple that the Bastille Day celebrations were more likely to
be held on Sunday the 13th than the Monday, even though
it was a national holiday. 'The Monday,' they informed us, 'is
reserved for recovering from the hangovers.' Sounds sensible,
we thought. We liked the French way of thinking.

But we felt sorry for the French too because it looked like
it literally was going to rain on their parade. In Montargis, on
the Canal de Briare where we'd moored, there were notices

outlining the proposed Bastille festivities, which included a parade through town, a dance (outdoors), and fireworks. Oh dear.

All the merriments were scheduled for the evening, starting at 8.30 so we wiled away the afternoon, dozing, reading, counting raindrops on the windows, and generally willing the weather to clear up. We were *Les Miserables*, but then decided to decorate the boat with red, white and blue balloons, silver fern bunting, and an array of different flags we found in a drawer, along with a couple of sets of string lights for after dark. It cheered us up somewhat.

Amazingly the weather changed almost on the dot of 8.30. The rain stopped, possibly because there was no more moisture left in the clouds, but the sky remained leaden and threatening.

Nevertheless we donned jackets and headed into town, by which time we'd missed the parade, which must have been short as it was all over by 9pm. It looked to us like it was all organised around the *pompiers* – the fire brigade – who took the opportunity to show off their extensive range of rescue vehicles, and to recruit more volunteers. There were junior *pompiers* wearing black uniforms and shiny chrome fire-fighting helmets, and more senior personnel posing for selfies with the Sweet Young Things of Montargis. Despite the skies everyone seemed in a good mood.

We found a tent set up in a small park off to one side with an eclectic mix of people milling around holding wineglasses. Always on the lookout for a free drink we veered in, since there was nobody asking for tickets or an entrance fee, and were rewarded with glasses of plonk, one of which was a fizzy red. Around us there were older men in burgundy berets, many wearing medals. There were some contemporary *pompiers*, some more of the juniors in their uniforms and helmets, and a range of other people of indeterminate origin, like ourselves.

Maybe they were gate-crashers too, but in our defence Shaun is an ex-Merseyside Fire Officer and even has a medal awarded him by the Queen, so we felt a kinship to some degree, and refilled with more wine.

Catering staff came round with nibbles – seemed rude to refuse – and we enjoyed the atmosphere for forty minutes or so before slipping away. Unfortunately we never found out what event we'd gate-crashed, but nobody questioned us or seemed to mind. Maybe in the spirit of Liberty, Equality and Fraternity it didn't matter. I'll drink to that.

The rain held off, it got dark so we couldn't see the clouds (which lifted our spirits), it remained mild and we walked around the closed-off streets along with the rest of the Montargis locals avoiding puddles. We ended up in the main square and decided to risk eating out, so chose a sidewalk table at a café, and spent an excellent and convivial couple of hours, much of it talking to Australian couple John and Faye, who seemed desperate to speak English to someone.

After Shaun and John had realised they had a shared interest in motorcycles, in typical antipodean fashion John invited him to come and visit 'next time you're down our way,' and promptly drew a map of Australia and Tasmania, with an 'X' on Tasmania saying, 'that's where you'll find us.'

(We could just envisage Shaun coming out of the airport at Hobart and asking the nearest bloke, 'Excuse me, d'you know where John lives?', and being told, 'Sure mate. Go down that road there, hang a left, then…')

It turned out we couldn't have chosen a better spot to eat because at 11.30 the fireworks started at the *Château* directly opposite the square, and we had ringside seats. Ex-Fire Officer Shaun ordered his own pyrotechnic dessert, a *Crêpe Suzette*, which the waitress obligingly set fire to at the table. She looked a bit nervous doing it so I told her he was an ex-*pompier* and there was no need for worry. Not so much a distinguished guest as an extinguished one.

After the fireworks, the dance started, and again we were in the right place as the dance floor had been positioned in the square. Locals streamed onto it as the live band played cover versions of hits, including the Village People's 'YMCA,' but sung in English. We wondered how it would have sounded in French... '*Ygrec Em Say Aah, c'est bon de rester au Ygrec Em Say Aah-aah...*'

Hmm. Maybe that's why they sang in English.

We eschewed the dance floor – Shaun says he only does 'Dad Dancing' and always gets laughed at – and retired to the boat for nightcaps of port, whiskey, and cigars. *Liberty* looked very festive with her decorations and lights, but we were the only boat on the moorings to make an effort.

Next day Shaun left to drive back to the UK. The clouds disappeared, the sun came out, and the temperature soared. *C'est la* bloomin' *vie.*

If you look at a map of the French inland waterways, south-east of Paris you'll see a spider web of canals and rivers, comprising the Haute Seine, the Petite Seine, the Yonne, the Canal du Loing, Canal de Briare, Canal de Bourgogne, Canal du Nivernais and the Canal Latéral à la Loire. I know, your eyes are glazing over, but the point is we were spoilt for choice in this part of France.

Earlier, down south on the Midi and the Garonne canals – which join end-to-end – we were forced to travel along following our noses; the opportunities for diversions were few. Here though we could turn left or right, north or south, and if we wanted to we could head off to conquer Germany, Belgium or Holland. The more adventurous could even reach the Black Sea.

However, our plans weren't that ambitious, at least not this year, and we were resolved to continue in France until at least the end of this cruising season, after which we'd consider our options. But because the waterway network is so concentrated here, we had, in just a few weeks, been on multiple canals and rivers and had finally turned onto the Haute Seine which flows towards Paris and becomes the famous Seine that pierces the heart of the world's most romantic city.

We decided however to leave Paris for later, and instead headed south again down the Yonne River, and stopped for a day at Sens, which is dominated by its cathedral, an imposing structure right in the centre of town. Unlike Paris's Notre Dame, Sens Cathedral is closely surrounded by shops and other buildings, to the point where you can't stand back far enough to get it all in shot when trying to take a photograph. It is one of those neck-craning things – you can look up, but not at.

The interior was cavernous, as you'd expect. Liz and I were still a bit cathedraled-out though; there are just so many in France, and so many dating back to the eleventh century or earlier, that (sorry to say) we were somewhat overdosed, or perhaps more kindly, spoilt for choice, and so mostly we chose to ignore rather than explore. We will probably burn in hell for this indifference.

But in its defence, Sens Cathedral's claim to fame is that it was the first to use flying buttresses in its design, which makes us think it might also have been part of the inspiration for Ken Follet's novel *Pillars of the Earth*. Liz's claim to fame is that she once had dinner at Mr Follet's London home and stayed over, having been at Oxford with his step-daughter. Okay, end of name-dropping. Whatever, the huge vaulted ceilings and vast cool interior space were welcome on a 30+ degree day. Cheers God.

Sens also offered the usual collection of shops – hairdressers, tobacconists, pharmacies and banks – but also some charming narrow old streets with very nice examples of sixteenth century half-timbered houses. We took photos and bought ice creams.

There was a convenient service station opposite our moorings so we once again topped up with *gazole*, carrying the fuel in jerry cans across the road to the boat. By far and away the cheapest fuel option is to find moorings near a supermarket with a service station attached. The difference in price was as much as forty cents a litre. The service station by our boat wasn't as cheap as a supermarket chain, but it was still preferable to a marina pump.

We needed fuel for ourselves too, and with a supermarket a short bike ride away, we bought some trout, two for just over four Euros. Nom nom. (Especially nom because despite New Zealand being famous for its trout fishing it is still impossible – in fact – illegal – to buy trout there. Unlike salmon, trout isn't commercially farmed, so we took full advantage of France's more liberal approach.)

Back on deck we watched a man in a bright pink polo shirt meet up with a Muslim woman in a basically-black burqa but accessorised with pink sleeves, pink headscarf, pink shoes and matching pink handbag. Her daughter was in a pink and white dress with pink shoes. All the pinks were of the same horribly-bright hue – a truly shocking pink. In fact, a pink so shocking as to require a censor's rating, and R18 wouldn't be high enough. We wondered if today was some sort of religious festival, or National Pink Day or similar.

Unfortunately the world is so on-edge these days that I can't comment further on the garb for fear of attracting a *fatwa*. But I will say that, beliefs aside, it was a fashion crime of the highest order, and surely transgressed a religious dress-code of some sort. We nicknamed her Burqa Barbie, though only between ourselves.

On the hire boat next to us were two youngish parents and three kids, two aged about three and five, the other a new mewling baby. They were Cycling Parents, and had the obligatory bike trailer for the two youngest. It looked like an oxygen tent on wheels. We observed their activities – as you do when moored – with casual interest. The parents didn't smile much. Come to think of it, we'd rarely seen families on boats smile much at all. A few days earlier we had watched as a hire boat moored in front of us, the two teenage girls on board looking as angry as you could without exploding as they reluctantly and petulantly helped tie the ropes. Steam was almost visibly rising from their heads, but their dad seemed blissfully unaware, an ability of most dads when faced with teenage fury. These girls were more bored than on board, but were sweetness and light when we got chatting to them as we later shared a lock. Maybe I'd misread their moods.

Up to this point in Sens we'd been operating on our battery power because the other boats already there prevented us mooring alongside any power or water; the facilities were sparse. However, next day once one of the boats had left we repositioned to be within reach of the shore power outlet, which was free. This wasn't just us being stingy; having shore power meant we could use 220 volts to run our boiler, microwave, kettle, toaster, sandwich-maker and fan without draining our batteries. It also recharged the boat's batteries, so if power was available we'd take it *merci beaucoup*. It's one of those things that becomes a regular aspect of boating in France, finding where can you plug into power. Everyone faces the same challenge, so we had no qualms about shifting *Liberty* to a better position.

Taking water on board at Sens proved a bit trickier than the power; there was just one *robinet* (tap) sunk into the ground, with a thread gauge too big for our hose. However, the nice couple on the boat behind us lent us a dinky little rubber adaptor while they went off shopping. I fitted it, turned it on, and watched in awe as it popped off the upward-facing outlet and created an unofficial yet spectacular riverside fountain. Problem was the tap to turn it off was right next to the outlet, so I had my second shower of the morning as I wrestled with it. Liz stood on the deck holding the other useless end of the hose and laughed. I am so lucky to have such love and support, I thought, as I dripped my way back to the boat.

We flagged the water away, I changed shirts, and put the adaptor back on the couple's boat.

Batteries charged we said *au revoir* to Sens and its fountains next morning, and moved a short distance along the river to Villeneuve-sur-Yonne where we again met the couple who'd lent us the adaptor.

They were Bob and Maureen, he 62 she 52. They were English, and were on a share-boat called *Dorney*, a Dutch Barge but modern, only about 14 years old. We had them aboard for drinks and chat.

I told them how I'd enjoyed an extra shower when their adaptor had popped off the tap.

'Really?' said Bob with surprise. 'When we got back from shopping I used it and it worked perfectly!'

Hmph. Maybe it was my fault after all. Pity Liz didn't have the camera handy for my watery escapade though, it would have been a great photo. (Little did I know it was also a good rehearsal for my getting a lot wetter some time later.)

Bob was a twelfth shareholder in the boat, which sounded to us like an administrative nightmare.

'No, it's fine,' he assured us. 'All the various owners get together once a year for the "AGM" at a farm in England, and we each use the boat for a set amount of time on a rotational basis. It works!'

He and Maureen were towards the end of their three-week stint, heading for Auxerre. Theirs was a bitter-sweet story. Both had lost their partners to illness in the previous two years. They met while visiting at the same hospice, so in a way it was death that brought their lives together. Bob had lots of experience with boats, including racing yachts, and was a mine of information, so we thought, ah-ha! let's get to the bottom of this qualifications thing, and asked him what sort of paperwork we were supposed to have to cruise the French waterways.

However, once again we were given conflicting advice. Bob insisted it was an ICC we needed, an International Certificate of Competency, whereas the brokers we bought *Liberty* from had said none were needed because *Liberty* was French-registered. Others had told us that all we needed to do was re-register *Liberty* as British and we were good to go. So we still didn't know, and even researching the Internet proved inconclusive.

One of these days we'll sort it out, we promised ourselves, 'We'll do a proper boating course in England when we get back,' I said to Liz. 'It might be a bit late, but we'll just have to keep our fingers crossed we don't get asked for any paperwork before the end of the trip.'

There was more to be nervous about. We also heard from Bob of an English boat-owner being fined €500 in France for having an out-of-date fire extinguisher, and others who had been breathalysed by police while in a lock. So despite only one brush with the law to date it seemed we still had lots to worry about. It certainly made us think twice about having wine at lunchtime.

Later, from our aft deck, we watched a French family posing for a group shot on the quayside before we left. As the camera was about to click they all – to our amusement – said 'cheese!' and not '*fromage.*' This took us by surprise somewhat, as the French in general are not quick to adopt English words and phrases, but perhaps it's understandable when you consider that saying '*fromage*' would result in a group photo in which at best everyone would look like goldfish or at worst like angry soccer hooligans. But why don't the French just say '*brie*'? It would be just as effective, and a lot more local.

CHAPTER FORTY-TWO

One of the best things about sailing in lovely warm and calm conditions is that it's easier to see anything unusual on the river. When it's windy the water is ruffled, when it's raining I'd often be steering from inside, peering ahead through fogged and rain-spattered windows, so spotting things in the water was tricky.

But on this particular perfect morning it was a doddle to spot a tiny yet determined disturbance in the water ahead, crossing our bows from left to right.

It was a snake. I throttled back and we leapt into Wildlife Photographer mode, our cameras clicking furiously. The snake was not inclined to pose for photos – it certainly wasn't about to say 'brie' – and continued its cross-river swim unperturbed. Later we looked at the images, and although of no great size it was quite a beautiful thing, with sort-of tiger stripes. Subsequent research revealed we had been scrambling over shooting a harmless common grass snake, rather than something scarier and venomous. Boo, hisssssss.

We had lunch in sweltering sunshine, about 30 degrees according to the thermometer, and regretted that Shaun wasn't with us. From here we intended to continue south partly to search for a place to leave *Liberty* while we nipped back to Merseyside to furnish our new apartment – if indeed we could settle the whole thing by then (lawyers, tchah!) – and partly to look for a suitable wintering-over spot for the boat.

Meanwhile we headed for Cezy, following Bob and Maureen since they were also headed our way. It was only a short journey, and we reached a split in the river. The main route went to the left, but Bob had recommended a nature mooring up the right arm at Cezy. He advised, 'There's an iron suspension bridge across the river beyond which you're not supposed to go, but the mooring is just before then.'

It was a delightful spot, a wooden landing stage with proper bollards, shaded by trees, and with picnic tables on the shore. No buildings around, peaceful, perfect.

The mooring however wasn't very big, so we rafted *Liberty* up against *Dorney*. Rafting-up is not without its issues though.

Being a Saturday the small town of Cezy was closed, apart from a brasserie and the ubiquitous *tabac*. It was gorgeously hot. The Yonne River looked clean and inviting, so I went for my first swim off the back of the boat. That's what a swim platform is for after all. The water was lovely. I wasn't the only one – there were others swimming off the river banks further upstream. And no snakes.

We spent a pleasant lazy day, and then in the late afternoon a hire boat cruised in looking for a mooring. The four crew were Swiss and asked if they could raft up against us, so *Liberty* ended up sandwiched between the two boats. It was okay though, the Swiss were very pleasant, and everyone came on board and we managed to all squeeze onto our aft deck for a few drinks.

The etiquette of rafting up seems to be that if you arrive at moorings and they are full, it is up to you to ask whether you can raft up against someone else's boat. They can then say yes or no, but some marinas and *haltes* don't allow doubling-up. Rafting-up isn't difficult – the new boat simply ties up to the next boat's cleats – but having a boat moored alongside you does block your view, and it means that the second boat's crew has to scramble across the first boat when they want to get ashore.

But it pays to be polite when asked. Wynn, our Kiwi friend who does two months' boating in France every year, told us a story of a rafting-up situation that went horribly wrong. There was one boat already moored, when a man came along in his craft and asked to raft up alongside. However, the first boatie wasn't keen, worrying maybe that two boats together might stick out into the channel too far. This sent the new arrival into a rage, and he roared off angrily at full throttle. Only problem was, he had to slow down to go under a low bridge, at which point his wake caught up with him, lifted his boat up from behind and smashed it against the underside of the bridge. Oops.

Moral of the story – literally and figuratively: don't make waves.

(Another way of looking at it is karma: what goes around comes around. If the water had been karma his boat would have been okay.)

We left Cezy in more hot sunshine (poor Shaun, again!) and cruised only a short distance to the town of Joigny, which provides an attractive backdrop to the river Yonne. The town is built on a hillside, and above it are acres and acres of vines stretching to the hilltop.

Joigny used to be a port from where charcoal was barged, but its waterway commerce days seem to be over, other than having a hire depot for those who want to rent a boat and explore the Nivernais or Bourgogne Canals.

It was a Sunday, so Liz and I didn't expect anything to be open. After tying up we lazed away the afternoon, but about 5pm decided to go for a stroll through town, only to discover we had missed a fête of some sort, which was just packing up. Our

316

first hint of festivities was to see two 'brides' in full wedding dresses walking purposefully along a street chatting animatedly. They didn't seem intent on getting to the church on time, and anyway, one of them wore a satin sash which proclaimed her as Miss Marriageable or some such, so we presumed we had missed a beauty contest. Phew. Close call.

We followed confetti on the cobbled streets to where all the action had taken place, just below where the vineyard belt started. There were still some stalls open, though most were in the process of packing up. A kids' merry-go-round still whirled its way round and round, and the booze tent continued to do good trade. The fête had included a *vide grenier* – the equivalent of a community car boot sale – which annoyed me as I like to browse through junk. Always have done since my Mum and Auntie Muriel used to regularly take me to jumble sales in Liverpool on weekends. They never got any offers for me though.

I've been a fan of rummaging and junk ever since, and have collected a few bargains in my time. However, we were too late for this sale, and what was left was largely tat, so maybe we hadn't missed anything after all.

Liz was greatly relieved that the *vide grenier* was finished. 'We don't have any room for anything anyway darling,' she reminded me gently, noting my disappointment. 'And when we do get the new apartment sorted, it's still not going to be very big.'

She was, as usual, right.

We walked through Joigny's backstreets, admiring yet more four hundred-year-old half-timbered buildings, with charming views down alleyways. Off the town square a soprano accompanied by piano was giving a recital, to enthusiastic applause from the audience. Opera has never been our cup of tea, but she certainly sounded like she knew what she was doing, her lovely voice descanting its way through the streets.

In the Gothic cathedral there was a notice saying that mass had been cancelled due to the fête. We wondered what God thought of that; that merry-go-rounds and shooting galleries should be more important than worship, and that confetti was deemed more urgent than confession. (This might explain why the weather turned from a superbly-warm 30+ degrees on Sunday to miserably cool and rainy the next day.)

After Bob and Maureen's tale of the boatie who'd been fined for having an out-of-date fire extinguisher, we decided to set off to a nearby shopping centre to look for new ones, even though ours didn't have any dates at all on them and had been 'passed' by *les flics* at Saint-Gilles lock back in June. We didn't want to take the risk.

We found some in the *bricolage* (DIY store) but the information on them was confusing, and we couldn't tell if the year was the date of manufacture or expiry, so we left them. Lucky we did, because the *hypermarché* almost next door had cheaper extinguishers with clear manufacture and expiry dates so we bought two and felt smug that we were now compliant for the next four years.

We still however didn't have any official boating qualifications, so we realised we might yet end up in jail. If quizzed by authority we would simply have to shrug and fall back on that good old stand-by, *'Je ne comprends pas, monsieur. Désolé.'*

On the other hand, if the waterway authorities became a flaming nuisance, we'd at least be able to use our new extinguishers on them. Result!

CHAPTER FORTY-THREE

By now we had lived on *Liberty* for around ten months and felt we had come to grips with this boating lark. We'd travelled rivers broad and canals narrow, squeezed under bridges low and cruised across aqueducts aloft. We'd learned how to throw ropes, tie knots, come into a mooring gracefully forwards or backwards, and we'd got better at maintaining and fixing our home.

But there was one thing we still hadn't tackled, and that was the drip from the propeller shaft, down below in that bit of the boat that you could get to only by lifting the carpet, removing floor panels, and squeezing down behind the engine and gearbox in a space designed for yoga practitioners.

I wasn't into yoga, but had been down there often enough to have worked out the best position to wedge myself in when needing to work on the prop flange, or clean the filters and suchlike.

It was down in this steely cell that water had continued to drip into the channel beneath the propeller shaft, water that was coming in through where the shaft exited the boat underwater. This was aft of the gearbox where the prop shaft entered the housing that goes to the stern of the boat. It's like one tube inside another, and where the smaller one enters there's what's called a stern gland, in which some wadding is compressed to stop any water leaking into the boat. It's a very simple thing, and in theory was also simple to replace.

We'd delayed the Day of Fixing though, and instead had fitted an automated bilge pump in the channel, so once the water level reached a couple of inches deep the pump would activate and empty it all overboard through a pipe. It meant we didn't have to worry about the water overflowing the channel and flooding the engine bay, and it gave us more time to research the problem.

Not that that we were sinking or anything; the drip was very slow, and it only worried us from the point of view that it existed and was annoying. But rather like the differing opinions we got about what qualifications were necessary to sail the French waterways, the problem of the drip drew widely differing views.

'You'll have to get the boat hauled out of the water to fix that,' said one. 'Not necessary,' said another, 'Just be prepared to get wet when the water comes flooding in after you take out the old wadding, but as long as you work quickly you should be okay.'

Still others said, 'It's not a problem. Just leave it. All boats leak.'

Slowly but surely we had amassed enough varying opinions and views that we came to a firm decision: we were too scared to tackle it while the boat was in the water, but didn't want to pay up to €400 just to get the boat hauled out only to find that it wasn't really necessary. And it wasn't a conversation we felt confident having in French either.

But, we finally found ourselves in the right place to get a proper professional opinion.

We had arrived at Laroche-Migennes, which is south of Paris and on the Yonne River. It's where the Bourgogne canal begins, and is a busy waterway junction, an ideal place to run a boatyard.

Which is exactly what ex-Navy Englishman Simon Evans was doing. Simon, we discovered, was a no-nonsense bearded bloke in a grimy T-shirt, and a lover of old wooden boats.

He has some vessels over a hundred years old and his yard looked in parts like a boat museum, except not much seemed to be restored. It seemed almost as though a tsunami had swept a whole lot of boats up onto dry land and then receded, leaving them higgledy-piggledy, yet all securely propped up, waiting for repairs or sanding down and repainting. He had a personal liking for old lifeboats, and had even been donated the world's first self-righting lifeboat by the French coastguard.

But we were more concerned with our own boat, and our own lives.

Simon was the first person (and the only professional) to reassure us that the amount of water likely to enter would be minimal, and controllable. He applied a maths equation to it, based on the dimensions of the boat and the quantity of water that it could hold before sinking. He teased Liz about her caution, and offered to lend us his set of bendy corkscrew-type implements to remove the old packing.

And so it came to pass that I spent a hot and unpleasant time wedged between the gearbox and the stern gland, removing brass flanges and worming out the old packing, while Simon sat on the salon steps and talked to Liz about his naval career, his Mum emigrating to New Zealand with a man she'd known for seven years but who left her high and dry within three days of arriving, and about his old wooden boats. I was glad they were having fun.

Meanwhile, Simon had been right; the amount of water that came in was minimal, and actually not much more than the drip itself. It took me a while to realise that I was trying to wedge in the wrong-sized wadding though, and once we'd established it should be 6mm and not 8mm everything went smoothly. In reality, had I started with the correct gauge of packing in the first place the whole process would have taken less than an hour, and we'd have heard a lot less of Simon's life story. But we'd have missed out on it too.

Anyway, the repair worked, and now, for the first time since we bought *Liberty* we didn't have a leaky propeller shaft. Yay! To say that Liz was relieved was an understatement, but at least it wasn't an underwaterstatement. To celebrate, we shared a bottle of bubbly that night, especially as we had in theory just saved about €400, which is what it could have cost if we'd listened to advice a few months earlier down south and had got the boat craned out of the water. Plus my labour was free, and the only thing we paid for was the actual stern gland packing, which looks like a chunky bit of hurricane lamp wick. It's another bit of the boat that we could tick off as 'done,' and could feel a degree of smugness that if it ever leaked again we would at least know how to fix it, and that it definitely absolutely positively could be done with the boat in the water!

Having fixed the drip we made a short excursion onto the Bourgogne Canal and tied up at the town mooring at Laroche-Migennes. Mid-evening we were disturbed by a knocking on the hull. Thinking it was the local marina official wanting payment we were reluctant to respond, but in fact discovered it was boaties Bob and Maureen who had dropped by in their car to say goodbye. They'd finished their three weeks on *Dorney* so came aboard along with Harry their dog for cups of tea (them, not Harry) and it was lovely to be able to round off our recent encounter before they headed back to Blighty.

Later we settled in for the night. The mooring however was directly opposite the railway yards so our sleep was punctuated with passing freight trains, all the more disturbing as it was warm and we wanted to sleep with the windows open. At around 3am I heard Liz closing the windows, muttering, 'I've had enough of trains!' I agreed.

Some days later we learned that the rail yards had been on the hit-list of the Allies during the Second World War, since the yards plus the confluences of the Yonne and the canals made Laroche-Migennes a strategic target. Legend has it that the Allied bombing was spot-on target, even to the point of hitting an ammunition train in the railyards. We were tempted to call in an air strike the night we were there too, as the lack of sleep was to take its toll later.

But morning dawned hot and sunny so we set off in good spirits back along the Yonne River for Auxerre, a pleasant journey in which, for once, all the locks were set in our favour. We reached the former Roman provincial capital mid-afternoon and moored up on the quay alongside the town – a place that everyone had recommended to us.

However, after an interrupted night's sleep we weren't in the mood to instantly explore, so Liz had a nap while I caught up on emails. But late afternoon I set off by bike to have a brief look around town, which lived up to all the recommendations. It was lovely, with winding narrow streets, old houses, churches and (of course) cathedrals, bars and restaurants aplenty, and a general sense of bonhomie and ambience. The fact that it was about 28 degrees helped.

But, once back on the boat Liz and I had a falling-out over how best to resolve our property-buying dilemma in Liverpool. Despite having our offer on an apartment accepted back in the first week of June, here we were on the cusp of August still with no resolution; nothing signed, no agreement, no deposit paid and no completion date agreed.

None of this was our fault – we had been pushing the process as best we could from France, but our conveyancing lawyer in Liverpool was claiming that he was unable to get any responses from the apartment management company, which was holding up the process, plus the vendors' solicitors were 'on holiday.' To say this was increasing our tension levels is an understatement, as we had already booked to fly back to Liverpool on 20 August, feeling sure that by then we would have the keys to 'our' apartment. And yet, with three weeks to go, we still didn't actually own the place.

So, despite being in lovely Auxerre, moored on a quayside with restaurants and even a live jazz band playing virtually right outside our boat, Liz and I spent the early evening vehemently disagreeing on how to manage the process. I wanted to go in guns blazing while she wanted to take a softly-softly approach. She thought I was being a bully, and I thought she was being a marshmallow.

We separated to opposite ends of the boat to fume. Meanwhile on the quayside the whole of Auxerre was in party mood, sitting on the grass or at outdoor restaurant tables, chatting, laughing, listening to the Parisian swing jazz music and having a much better time than we were.

The Dutch are fantastic at designing and building boats – everything has a useful purpose, and there are nooks and crannies for storage in every conceivable space, but there is absolutely no room for an argument.

So within half an hour we made up, and I'm glad we did because the evening was fabulous. We sat on the sharp-end in ringside seats and watched as the band – a family ensemble if our French was correct – played tunes by Stéphane Grapelli and Django Reinhardt, along with other more jazzy numbers to great acclaim from the assembled Auxerroise. It was calm and balmy, one of those out-of-the-box evenings, so to spoil it with a spat would have been unforgivable. Instead we sat companionably with our two hurricane lamps adding ambience, drank wine and chilled out to the live music.

To hell with lawyers. They can wait, we thought. Life, as John Lennon and a few others noted, is what happens to you while you're busy making other plans, and we were here to live, not fight.

The next day we were joined on the quayside by a lovely old boat called *Rival*, and had the pleasure of meeting its crew, Americans Bruce and Yerda. They were in their late sixties, and one of them had a pony-tail. It wasn't Yerda.

They were delightful, and once again we found ourselves in the company of enthusiastic and knowledgeable boaties, with a full tank of stories and buckets of sage advice.

It was these two who'd come under fire for flying a Dutch flag even though they were American, but it didn't faze them.

We travelled in convoy with them the next day after leaving Auxerre, and saw them again further downstream. We regretted not being able to spend more time with them, but we had another deadline.

For the third time we were due to welcome friends on board again, this time Kiwi couple Cleve and Dinah from New Zealand's South Island.

On our way to the rendezvous we came to a very narrow stretch of canal, actually a one-way stretch, and could see another boat was approaching so we pulled over. I looked through the binoculars and said to Darling One, 'I think that's *Alicia*.'

Alicia was a Dutch barge crewed by Australians Phil and Bagusha, who we'd met very early on in our voyage just as they were returning to Saint-Jean-de-Losne to leave their boat to winter-over. At the time we'd said we'd keep an eye out for them the following summer, and sure enough, here they were.

As they got closer Liz yelled 'Is that Phil?' 'Yes...' came a tentative reply from the wheelhouse. Liz jumped up and down on the deck. 'It's Liz and Mike!'

But it was obvious they'd forgotten us. Bagusha emerged, shaded her eyes against the sun and shouted, 'Who?'

Liz pointed to me and shouted, 'Billy Connolly!'

Then it dawned on them who we were and they were all smiles and g'days. We cheered and waved as we passed, and tried to explain we had to keep going, and they seemed to need to continue also. So we exchanged *bon voyages*, and carried on. It was a lovely, if brief, encounter, and another of the quaint and pleasurable aspects about being part of the boating community.

And so we continued, to meet our friends Cleve and Dinah, who were part way through a tour of France and Spain. We'd arranged to meet them at a canalside town called Clamecy, which is where we were now heading after enjoying the live music and the general bonhomie of Auxerre.

We'd continued south in *Liberty*, but knew we wouldn't be able to go any further on the Canal du Nivernais than Clamecy itself because there wasn't enough water.

The Englishman who ran the port office at Auxerre had warned us that *Liberty*'s draft would be too deep for the canal waters beyond Clamecy.

'Even some of the hire boats we've rented out with one-metre drafts have been scraping the canal bottom,' he told us. 'So at 1.2 metres you're not going to get very far unfortunately.' This was a surprise, as we'd thought our *tirant d'eau* would enable us to cruise any of the waterways in France, but apparently not.

As soon as he'd told us this the heavens opened and it rained with a vengeance. We'd both got soaked going back to the boat from the *capitainerie*, but wondered whether the rain would also be falling on the Nivernais and topping it up for us.

It didn't matter too much to us because Clamecy was where we were going to meet Cleve and Dinah anyway, but this now confirmed it as our turnaround point.

Dating back to at least the seventh century, Clamecy was as pretty as everyone had said, and followed the theme of most other places we'd seen – narrow streets, cobbles, some lovely old buildings, and a nice small port. We scored a great mooring on the quayside right beside electricity and water, and actually had Wi-Fi available on board for a change.

Our Kiwi friends turned up as expected in their rental car next day and we installed them on board. They were keen to try out the Bond Lounge, especially the circular sleeping area in the bows, and promptly lay down on it in fits of giggles to see if it would accommodate them. It did, in a roundabout way, and to our surprise they elected to sleep there that night. But they're also veteran campers, so confined spaces don't worry them.

We had a very enjoyable evening catching up, drinking too much and watching the International Space Station as it glided silently overhead in the night sky. It's only a bright dot of light, but is actually the third brightest object in the sky after the sun and moon. It doesn't follow a set orbit, so you need an expert to know where it will be, but you can sign up to a NASA website and they send you alerts telling you when you can see it from your place. It comes as a surprise to many people to discover that the ISS is only about 350 kilometres above the Earth, actually only twice the distance to Paris from where we were moored. With a decent telescope you can even make out its 'H' shape.

Meanwhile, back on Earth, the following day Cleve drove the rental car to the nearest depot at Auxerre and caught the train back. We meanwhile had gone through the lock in town to get a head start, and waited for his return on the other side. The lock is beside a weir that carries some local importance as it was here the *flottage du bois* (floating of wood) was marshalled before the thousands and thousands of logs continued their journey downstream. It was a major industry back in the day.

The timber came from the forests of the Morvan national park. The trees were processed into logs and floated down the river to Paris, a massive undertaking. The *flottage* lasted from the sixteenth century until the early twentieth century, with the last logs being prodded on their way in 1923.

On the quayside were photos showing the heyday of the *flottage* when the river would be just logs from bank to bank. In the end the practice fell out of favour as it restricted too many other commercial users of the river, so today it's just a memory, but one the town of Clamecy proudly clings to.

Cleve returned, and we cruised the afternoon to Châtel-Censoir, a pleasant journey back along the park-like Nivernais. It was lovely countryside. Bucolic is the word, though it's not one I use often. It's always sounded to me like something unpleasant, like a cross between bubonic plague and cholera or colic, yet it means pastoral or countrified. 'This place has got a bad dose of bucolic,' I thought to myself, as the verdant landscape glided by.

We introduced Cleve and Dinah to the foibles of boating and they seemed to enjoy the boat and the rigmarole at the locks. It was nice to have extra 'crew' on board too, to help with the ropes. The weather was quite good, though the forecast wasn't spectacular, and we wondered how long we'd get away with it before we experienced a predicted spell of unsettled weather. We wanted our guests to go away looking tanned, and not miserable like Shaun.

On the Nivernais it appeared it was okay to help the lock-keepers to open and close the gates and paddles, and most seemed grateful for the assistance. Cleve particularly enjoyed helping the female *éclusiers*, who at that time of year were mainly students working during their summer break.

The *éclusiers* ranged from architecture and design students to one who was a violinist and another a cellist, the latter aiming to pull strings and get a job in the French health system.

Performing music on a casual contract basis wasn't conducive to making a living, she explained, but she had been unable to secure any permanent musical position. We didn't mind – her *éclusier* skills were fine.

Most of the locks were quite shallow so didn't take long, which made the journey a lot more satisfactory than having to wait ages for the chambers to fill or empty.

Also, being a cycling fanatic, Cleve offloaded one of the bikes and took full advantage of the smooth towpath to race ahead and help get the locks set for us. This also gave him more time to chat up the *éclusiers*, though I'm sure that was just incidental. Dinah was quite happy to sit forward in business class chatting to Liz.

This might be a good time to mention more about towpaths and cycling, because the two are starting to become synonymous in France. The original concept for the towpath was that it was there for the horses that pulled the barges, but of course once boilers, and later the internal combustion engine came along, the horses became redundant. I doubt they would have gone on strike about it though; they were probably delighted.

Since then the towpaths have remained alongside the canals, though in various states of repair, but now they're being given a whole new lease on life as cycleways, being neatly levelled and cleared, with some even asphalted. Along parts of the Canal du Midi and the Garonne it's possible to ride for many pleasurable kilometres, and other canals are following suit. The beauty of the towpaths is of course that they're basically flat, so cycling is a real pleasure. Cleve certainly enjoyed himself.

At Châtel-Censoir we tied up at the little port and walked into town to stock up at the grocery in the town square. Cleve had read that there was a highly-regarded local restaurant, so that evening we went back and searched for it. It wasn't in the main square, or even anywhere central; it was in a minor side road leading out of town, and, as we approached, it looked – like so much of France – to be closed.

And yet it wasn't. As soon as we stopped outside the front door to read the menu (a great feature of France – most cafés and restaurants have their menus displayed outside) we were greeted with a friendly '*Bonjour messieurs-dames!*' by a smiling dark-haired woman.

The dining room was unpretentious and small, and also empty, but the welcome had been so warm and bright that we went in without a second thought. Within five minutes another group had arrived, followed by two more, and before we'd got our starters we were surrounded by two tables of Australians and one of Germans.

It was (yay!) a lovely meal, and the food was presented with flair, the chef obviously being something of an artist. Liz and I chose an *entrée* called *Cannelloni de Jambon du Morvan et Bavarois Melon*. We found it hard to describe, but agreed it was absolutely superb. It certainly wasn't cannelloni in the Italian pasta sense, it was more like a melon-flavoured cheesecake, with prosciutto rolled into a cannelloni shape, topped with a single delicious parmesan crisp. There was something else too, but we've forgotten what it was. In the photos we took it looks like a mushroom, except it wasn't. Anyway, we raved about it at the time. We'd never make restaurant critics!

Breast of Duck, whole trout, we devoured them, and polished off a couple of bottles of Chablis in the process. The quality and presentation certainly made up for the rather pedestrian ambience, and our waitress couldn't have been nicer. Well done Cleve!

We bumped into the chef outside as he took a break from his kitchen for a smoke, so we shook his hand and told him we'd give him five stars on *Trip Advisor*. He seemed humbly surprised at the fuss.

It was a full and happy group that meandered slowly back to *Liberty* later that evening, as we looked forward to our next challenge: eight million bottles of wine…

CHAPTER FORTY-FOUR

We cruised on back north through the lush Burgundy landscape to Mailly-la-Ville for a lunch stop, then on to a mooring we'd seen in the canal guide book, at a place called Bailly, arriving late afternoon in very warm weather. The mooring was great, with free power and water, and, even better, we were the only boat there.

Even better than that was the nearby wine *cave* of Bailly Lapierre, but in this case it really was a cave rather than just a wine shop. We thought we might be too late to go wine tasting, but as it happened the convenient signpost on the canal bank said they were open till 7pm, so we strolled the short distance up the hill to the *cave* entrance.

The underground limestone caverns are the result of quarrying, the stone originally destined for iconic buildings such as Notre Dame in Paris, Chartres Cathedral, and the Panthéon.

Underground quarrying at the Bailly site continued from the twelfth century right through to the beginning of the twentieth, leaving behind four hectares of cool, dark caverns ideal for the fermentation and storage of wine.

As we approached the huge opening in the limestone rock face we could feel cool air rushing out and over us – a welcome breeze given the sultry warmth of the day. The other thing that took us by surprise was that the road led straight in through the rock, and within seconds we were walking along a wide tunnel, with twinkling lights identifying the edges of the roadway, and a golden glow in the distance around a bend.

It felt like a movie set – the entrance to the villain's underground base from which his evil missiles would be launched at the world's major cities, or in this case more likely the world's major winemakers.

'Good evening Mr Pond, I've been expecting you,' said Goldrinker, twirling a glass of '61 Lafite-Rothschild in his pudgy hand and sniffing its aroma. 'Welcome to my humble wine cellar. I will offer you a glass to celebrate shortly, so you can appreciate that the wine I have stored here will be worth a hundred times what it is today, once I've destroyed all the world's Bordeaux stocks!'

Goldrinker slurped a generous gulp and tilted the glass to consider the contents. 'A good nose and a full yet elegant body,' he proclaimed. 'Rather like myself, eh Mr Pond?' He chuckled at his pathetic joke. 'And also a long farewell, which is quite appropriate, since it is almost time to say goodbye!'

Goldrinker set the glass down on the Louis XIV wine table beside him.

Pond cocked an eyebrow, feigned indifference, and slowly felt for the corkscrew in his pocket…

We reached the source of the golden light – a cavernous tasting room and sales area off to the left, carved out of the limestone. On the right, disappearing into the cool darkness we could see tantalising glimpses of thousands and thousands of bottles resting on their sides. A sign indicated we were not to go adventuring without a guide, so we strolled into the tasting area.

By a stroke of luck we were in time for the last tour of the day, guided by a lovely young *mademoiselle* who spoke good English, and divided her commentary more in our favour (we thought) than the French tourists in our little group. We missed her name, but she looked to me like a Sandrine more than an Amily or a Michelle.

Sandrine led us by her torch along wide underground avenues of bottles, around eight million in all, and stopped at strategically-placed photo displays here and there to explain the fermentation process behind Bailly Lapierre's sparkling wines. Basically it's the *Méthode Champenoise*, where the initial tank fermentation is followed up by a secondary fermentation in the bottle before the dead yeast cells are disgorged, the wine topped-up, and a cork wired on to keep the contents under pressure.

Sandrine was careful not to refer to the process as being the same as Champagne, and only mentioned the word once in the whole tour. Instead, she informed us, Bailly Lapierre makes *crémant* wine, in a range that goes from Extra Brut to Sec and includes a *rosé*. But to all intents and purposes it was Champagne – just not made within the designated Champagne growing area and therefore unable to use or even borrow the appellation. If it did, the chances are a team of Champagne makers would filter south in the dead of night and dynamite the entrance to the caverns, sealing off all eight million bottles and Sandrine with them. At least she would die happy.

But back in reality-land we learned that while the grapes were picked by hand, there's quite a degree of mechanisation in the rest of the method, including a robotic arm to stack multiple bottles at once using a vacuum grip, and that the wines are turned and tilted over a period of three days to bring the dead yeast cells to the neck by a riddling machine. Gone are the days of human riddlers, along with the Occupational Overuse Syndrome that almost certainly went with the job.

Every now and then Sandrine would stop and draw our attention to large carvings in the walls of the subterranean avenues, the result of Bailly Lapierre regularly inviting sculptors to create reliefs in the limestone. These ranged from homages to grape growing and the winemaking process to more *avant garde* carvings at which we were invited to provide our own interpretations. One carving even showed a man sculpting a naked female out of the rock, and we were told this was the sculptor himself, who had said it represented him creating his 'perfect woman.' In the sculpture we could see that he had completed the torso of his goddess and was about to start on her nether regions. He had a look of glee on his face.

We also learned that the constant 12-degree Celsius temperature and darkness were an ideal combination for growing mushrooms, and that the caverns had been used for this prior to their being turned over to the Bailly winemakers' cooperative in 1972. Sandrine used her torch to point out dark fluffy fungi growing on some of the walls and ceilings as evidence. Cleve loves puns as much as I do, and I could see he wanted to tell her he was a fun guy too.

After around forty minutes we arrived back at the tasting area, where we'd left Pond and Goldrinker earlier, and Sandrine announced it was now time to taste the product. Excellent! And it was; just as you'd expect from a wine made from the proper *Champenoise* method; the bead – or bubbles – very fine, the nose yeasty, and the taste a mouth-filling explosion of creamy effervescence. Liz and I like dry bubblies so the Extra Brut was our favourite, and between Cleve and Dinah and ourselves we purchased a dozen. Sandrine gave us our tasting glasses to take away.

I asked her in my halting French whether she was a wine expert and if she particularly liked the Bailly Lapierre *crémant* wines, but disappointingly she said she doesn't drink, and prefers fruit juice.

Ah well, it's hard to find the perfect woman. Maybe that's why the sculptor was carving his own.

Postscript: What happened to Pond…

Pond deftly threw his hat onto the top hook of the coat stand in the corner of the office.

'James! You're back! 'said Pennymoney.

'Couldn't stand being away from you any longer, Pennymoney,' Pond smiled.

'N's waiting. You're to go straight in.'

Pond went through the twin green leather doors. N looked up from a file.

'Ah double-eau-seven, good to have you back. So, what happened? I gather Goldrinker is no longer a threat?'

Pond sat in the proffered chair. 'No sir, he's not.'

'So how did you escape? Your report was sketchy in details…'

Pond relaxed into the leather wingback. 'It wasn't difficult. Goldrinker offered me a final farewell drink – a glass of the '85 Margaux. I took out the corkscrew that P had issued me at the start of the mission, and as Goldrinker set out the glasses I unscrewed both ends of the corkscrew handle. These, as you're no doubt aware, concealed two perfectly-sized earplugs, noise-cancelling too, which I inserted in my ears while Goldrinker's back was turned.

'I then twisted each side of the corkscrew handle to prime the mechanism. Goldrinker turned from the wine glasses. "Ah Mr Pond, I see you have come prepared with your own corkscrew! Excellent! I shall keep it as a souvenir – after you've gone." I handed him the implement.

'Goldrinker blew the dust off the Château Margaux and removed the lead capsule from the bottle. He smiled as he inserted the corkscrew, and I made a final adjustment to the earplugs.

'He gave the corkscrew a hefty twist, which activated the sonic device. The whine began, almost inaudibly at first, but grew in intensity within seconds until it reached maximum pitch. The wineglasses were first to go – they exploded into a million shards. It was only then that Goldrinker realised what was happening.

'The bottle of Margaux began to vibrate in his hands. He looked at it as though he'd never seen a bottle of wine before, and suddenly realised the significance.

'"You have tricked me Mr Pond!" he shouted over the noise, as the bottle exploded in his hand, showering him with glass. Blood and Bordeaux dribbled down in rivulets, as his face turned into a savage Munch-like Scream parody, full realisation finally dawning on him.

'In the nearby cavern Goldrinker heard his entire collection of Bordeaux wines disintegrate into a gorgeously-hued red mass of glass and beautifully-perfumed wine, which ran across the floors, pooling like blood under the dim lights of the cave.'

Pond shot his cuffs and looked at N. 'So his whole reason for destroying the world's Bordeaux stocks was removed in a trice.'

'Didn't he try and launch the missiles?' asked N.

'No sir,' said Pond with a half-smile. 'I don't think he had the bottle.'

CHAPTER FORTY-FIVE

On Sunday 16 August, war was declared between Germany and Britain. What? You think we got the date wrong? No, this was World War *III*, and it started in the small French inland port of Montereau, about an hour south of Paris by train. We were witnesses. We were there. When. It. Happened. And you heard it here first.

This time though, there was no assassination of an Archduke, and no Invasion of Poland. If anything, it could be argued that it was Britain that needed the *lebensraum* on this occasion. Here's what happened…

Liz and I – on our own again now that Cleve and Dinah had carried on with their holiday – had left our mooring at Pont-sur-Yonne early, after a peaceful night moored beside a fun fair. That might sound like a contradiction in terms, but although the fair was indeed adjacent to the mooring – with dodgems, shooting galleries, food stalls, merry-go-rounds and every other attraction designed to lose you money – by about 11pm on Saturday night it was all over bar the shouting, and there wasn't any shouting. The good folk of Pont-sur-Yonne were remarkable by their absence, having stayed away in droves. Sad for the fun fair folk though.

We cruised all morning and approached Montereau where the Yonne River meets the Seine, and eyed the mooring opportunities through the binoculars. Last time we were here a few weeks earlier, there had been only one free space, into which we'd slotted neatly. This time there were two spaces, but both looked quite tight thanks to a small yacht which was poorly moored in the middle. Poorly moored? Yes…

Because, as you know, there's a certain etiquette that goes with mooring boats against a quayside or pontoon. Basically, when you tie up you leave as much room as you can for other boats, which means butting up against any other vessels already there, or moving all the way to the end so you don't hog the middle. However, at Montereau, a little yacht flying a German flag was moored inconsiderately halfway between two other boats, thereby using up valuable space. However, not to be put off we decided that the space in front of him was about 12 metres, and our boat is 11.4 metres, so we figured we could squeeze in.

We did, but not before the burly grey-haired German on *Schweinhund II* had expressed his consternation that we were getting uncomfortably close to his precious bow. By contrast, the Frenchman from the boat in front willingly came to help us moor and between him and Liz they tied *Liberty* up while I stayed at the controls to make sure we didn't back into Herman. I said to the Frenchman, 'All that man has to do is move his boat back a metre.' The Frenchman shrugged and said, 'Yes, but he's German I think.' I, of course, had no opinion.

Alles gut, c'est bien, she'll be right we thought, and tied off, retreating inside for a spot of lunch and to wile away the afternoon watching a DVD (too windy and cool to go exploring. We are wimps…).

Half way through the film we noticed the French boat in front of us had sneaked off, leaving the whole front of the pontoon free, so, to give Herman some breathing space we physically pulled *Liberty* forward as far as possible, leaving a good 13 metres of no-man's land between him and us.

If he sighed in relief it was short-lived, because literally within two minutes another boat arrived to squeeze into the space we'd just vacated – a low-slung older cruiser called *Harmony*, flying a red duster, so she was British, or at least the skipper was. As the boat manoeuvred into place there was sudden Germanic screaming from Herman as he jumped up and down on his boat and turned bright red, pointing to his bow.

Meanwhile, on board *Harmony*, a shortish bearded Englishman muttered something about 'keeping your lid on,' as Liz and I helped him moor. We got him tied up successfully, but Liz whispered to me that it looked like the rear of *Harmony* might possibly have mildly bumped Herman's bows; a glancing blow.

Herman leapt off his boat and shook his fist, turned even brighter red and seemingly declared war. The Brit meanwhile maintained a stiff upper lip and said to the German, 'Speak English or I'm not listening,' then turned to me and said, 'Time for *une tasse de thé* (a cup of tea) and a fag.'

Apoplexy reached Richter scale levels on the German side, and next thing Madame *Capitainerie* arrived asking what was happening: '*Qu'est-ce qui se passe?*'

Herman told her he'd been rammed, in a voice that sounded like he was addressing a Nuremberg rally. Unfortunately the *capitainerie* woman didn't speak German, but we could all understand the word 'police,' and Herman wanted them here and now, preferably armed and descending from helicopters.

Harmony's skipper denied scraping the *Schweinhund*. Madame *Capitainerie* diplomatically told them both to sort it out through their '*assurance*' – which is French for insurance – and then Herman brought out the big guns: his digital camera. He took photos of the alleged scrape, *Harmony*, *Harmony*'s skipper, us standing on the pontoon, and possibly a few sparrows on the bank, but he neglected to get any selfies showing how angry he was that he'd been invaded by Britain.

Mr *Harmony* meanwhile was sitting in his cockpit rolling a cigarette, and assured us all that he would be providing Britain's insurance details to Germany in due course. ('I have in my hand a piece of paper…')

As we know from history, most wars could have been avoided, and the same was true of this one. The German had something like ten metres free space behind him, yet was reluctant to move back to make room for us when we arrived, and made no attempt either when HMS *Harmony* rolled in. Instead he steadfastly clung to the space he had, and paid the price (the price being the tiniest of wavy lines on his starboard bow paintwork, probably no longer than ten centimetres and which would likely come out with a bit of a rub with cutting compound. We had a tin on board, but were disinclined to offer it).

Montereau is no stranger to battles; it was here in 1814 that Napoleon I successfully fought the Austrian Empire and the Kingdom of Würtemburg. Presently Montereau is planning a celebratory theme park, with the incredibly clever name of 'Napoleonland.' Yes, really.

Depending on the outcome of the Battle of the Boats 200 years after Napoleon's skirmish, there might be room for another park: Britland. Or maybe Hermanland. Guess it hinges on who wins the insurance battle.

It had to happen sooner or later; one of us had to fall in the drink.

We were even prepared for the occasion, and had a little silver trophy on board – the Dunkling Cup – which we'd been saving to award to the first person to go overboard. But who would be the inaugural recipient? Liz, me, or one of our guests?

The first of us to 'leave the boat' had been me, but that was when we were moored on the Yonne at Cezy and I went swimming. That was voluntary, so doesn't count.

At other times though there'd been plenty of opportunities for either of us to take an accidental dip. In the 11 months or so since buying the boat we'd tied up to numerous floating pontoons, many narrow and some with even more slender 'fingers' off them. These little floating fingers in particular would bob and sway alarmingly as you walked along them. The prospect of an unexpected dunking had therefore been with us for months, yet we'd both somehow managed to stay dry. Until now.

In the big deep locks on the Rhône, the wearing of life jackets is compulsory, a regulation introduced some years ago following a disastrous barge sinking when the gates at the Bollène *écluse* somehow failed and rapidly flooded the lock, taking a woman and her two dogs to their deaths.

But the rest of the time life jackets and buoyancy aids aren't obligatory, and we'd rarely seen anyone wearing them on the canals or rivers. Nevertheless, every boat is supposed to carry them – one for each crew member – and the maritime authorities can fine you if you fail to produce them during an inspection. We had two on board *Liberty*, along with a life ring, but we'd never worn a floatation aid of any sort while mooring the boat – the big ones are too clumsy and restricting, and anyway, we (naïvely) know we can swim.

So, prior to leaving *Liberty* at Saint-Mammès while we returned to England to buy the apartment, I was tugging on one of the boat's ropes, trying to bring her a bit closer to the floating finger off the main pontoon and make her snug and secure for while we'd be away. Suddenly I went hurtling backwards into the river, and disappeared completely under the green murky water. It happened so quickly – the rope just slipped off the cleat. I'd been pulling hard on it, so the momentum meant I didn't stand a chance, as there was less than a metre of pontoon behind me.

Splash! In, and down, I went. Liz meanwhile was inside the boat working on her CV for a job application, and didn't even hear me go in. I clawed my way back to the surface, spluttering and banging my head on one of the stainless steel floats, but managed to somehow scramble back onto the pontoon, as elegantly as a seal hauling itself onto rocks. I was a bit stunned, but more concerned about getting my watch dry as quickly as possible; it's one of the few things I've ever won in my life, and I didn't want this bit of bad luck to ruin that piece of good one (I'd actually scored it many years previously in a raffle, but it was worth quite a bit).

I called to Liz and when she came out she saw a completely sodden me with blood pouring down my face from a cut in my forehead. Superfluously I said, 'I fell in.' She helped me back on board, dried my precious watch, and helped me clean up and dry off. It's a good job the currency was waterproof as I had seventy Euros in my pocket too. I told Liz I had liquidated our funds. You've got to laugh.

Anyway, within half an hour I was warm and dry, with a plaster on my forehead and some slight bruising to my pride.

By good fortune Cleve and Dinah were heading to Paris to end their trip there and would be passing through, so they kindly offered to take us with them so we could catch our flight to Liverpool.

They picked us up the next day. Somehow it slipped my mind to tell them I'd fallen in the river and won the Dunkling Cup for being completely in-Seine.

CHAPTER FORTY-SIX

'Don't forget to wave to the fish!' Sarah said with a smile as we left her bed and breakfast place in Folkestone. Wave to the fish? Oh right – a joke! Ha, of course; we would be taking our van underwater, so naturally one would want to wave to the fish.

Our mission in England complete, it was time once again to return to France. We needed some light relief, so Sarah's jest (which we were sure she made to everyone heading through the Chunnel) was welcome.

After leaving Liverpool, where we'd finally taken ownership and spent two weeks trying to furnish our new apartment (with only minor success; why does everything take so long to get delivered?) we'd only just survived an eight-hour drive to Folkestone. Appalling traffic on the M25 and 26. Endless delays. Traffic crawling, engine and human temperatures rising; mine included. And to think we used to occasionally complain about the traffic in New Zealand.

We'd arrived in Folkestone so late that we decided to forget the campsite we'd booked – it was dark and anyway the campsite office was already closed. We contemplated sleeping in the back of the van but decided we deserved a better standard of accommodation, so we drove into town and stopped at the first B&B we came to that had a vacancy sign. It was the last available room, Sarah the landlady advised; we were lucky. She showed us the room. It was quaint in that old-fashioned B&B style, and we loved it. Mind you, we'd have loved a garden shed at that point.

Sarah pointed us in the direction of the best of the local fish and chip shops, plus a Tesco, so off we walked and stocked up with a bottle of wine and two cod and chips. Back in the room we opened the windows to dispel the fish smell and gorged ourselves sitting on the bed. Some meals are just the best, and it's nothing to do with Michelin-starred chefs; it's entirely to do with the circumstances. And hunger.

We had a much better night's sleep than we'd have had on a blow-up mattress in a tent or the back of Van Rouge, and woke to a nice day, with breakfast waiting for us downstairs. Sarah was the perfect hostess, and we tucked into eggs, bacon, toast and lashings of coffee. She told us where to find the local Post Office where we needed to dispatch some essential documents back to NZ. Have you any idea how hard it is to buy a single A4 envelope while travelling in the UK? Especially on the motorways, where the so-called 'services' are based entirely around filling your tummy with over-priced food, your tank with overpriced fuel, and definitely not assisting you with your international communication needs.

Having advised us to wave to the fish we told her we were veterans of the Mersey Tunnel, so we knew a thing or two about driving underwater.

But we had time to kill before the train so we drove to Dover to find a boat chandlery to buy some anti-fouling paint for *Liberty*.

The chandlers proved easy to find, as did a parking space a few metres up the road, but this was right outside a so-called 'hobby shop.' Liz looked at it as we parked and said, 'When I saw "hobby shop" I was expecting cottons, buttons, and craft stuff, but,' she said, pointing to the window, 'it's all guns and fishing gear!'

It was. And the owner, who was sitting just inside the door and obviously thought we'd pulled up deliberately outside his place to purchase weapons of mass destruction, tried to sell Liz a rifle. A *pink* rifle. 'I've got pink fishing gear too if you like,' he announced. There followed a brief discussion on whether pink as a colour attracted more fish, but he asserted women were – alas – just better at fishing. And bowling. He needed to talk.

'My daughter, I took her bowling for the first time ever. She was a natural. Like a pro,' he told us, rocking on the back legs of his chair. I told him I'd taken my daughter Catherine clay pigeon shooting as part of her 21st birthday treats and she had beaten me in a competition. The 'hobby shop' owner just shrugged, knowingly. 'There you are, y'see,' he explained, as though it explained something. We weren't sure it did.

We left without buying anything destructive, pink or otherwise, and instead got the anti-fouling paint we needed from the chandlers. The whole wonderful boating supplies shop was run by a woman who was as knowledgeable as she was lovely. She even knew what model of toilet we had on board *Liberty*, which made buying a spare part much easier. But we didn't ask if she had anti-fouling in pink; matt black was fine.

After a pleasant morning sojourn in Dover where we raided the charity shops for some books and DVDs (by far and away the best value way to purchase these things in England) we then headed off to check in for our journey under the English Channel, via that amazing piece of engineering the Eurotunnel.

What a great way to get to France, as long as you don't mind missing out on the nostalgic view of Dover's famous White Cliffs disappearing behind you of course. If it's fresh sea air, screaming toddlers and parties of school kids on so-called 'educational holidays,' or – in rough weather – being surrounded by people barfing into paper bags that you covet, then by all means take one of the ferries. But if you just want to get to France quickly – half an hour in this case – with no waves, worries or the smell of warm sick, then the Eurotunnel (or Chunnel) is the way to go.

It was like being in a science fiction movie. After passing through departure control and assuring them that no, despite being a van we weren't carrying commercial goods, (we were nevertheless questioned and searched; nicely though, no aggro) we followed the signs in the marshalling area and eventually were waved through, following a campervan and two tour buses.

It was fascinating watching the buses drive onto the train ahead of us. They basically just drove down a platform and officials then guided them onto the waiting freight cars, though these were more like long well-lit corridors, seemingly without end. They looked vaguely spaceship-like inside: bright, long and squarishly-tube-ish, if you can imagine such a shape. 2014: A Rail Odyssey. *'Hello Dave…'*

Our turn came and we did the same, apparently driving along the train all the way to France but eventually we stopped and parked behind the campervan. Engine off, handbrake on, first gear engaged… and that was it. All we did from there on was sit in the van for the 'crossing.' Behind us was a Land Rover, so the three of us filled one freight car, which, once we were all in and secure, was sealed off by roller doors from the rest of the train.

The Eurotunnel is fifty kilometres long, and with the trains able to travel up to 160kph it doesn't take long to go through. Sure beats any of the ferry offerings, though there's nothing to see of course. There are windows, but apart from the odd light flashing past there were no fish to wave to. Good thing too, when you think about it.

The Channel Tunnel opened for business in 1994, just over 190 years since the first proposal to build it. Surprisingly, the original idea came from the French, but why? They had spent years trying to avoid the English, so... *je ne comprend pas!*

Quaintly, the original proposal by Monsieur Albert Mathieu included an artificial 'island' midway for the changing of horses. In the early years of the nineteenth century, viable passenger trains were still some years in the future, so horse-drawn transport was envisaged, with illumination provided by oil lamps. Had it been achieved it would have been a dark and exciting ride, and certainly one of the Wonders of the World.

However, the threat of enemies and unseemly characters swarming through the tunnel unchecked, or later, of Hitler using it to stroll into Britain, meant it took until 1988 for any meaningful work to begin, and – six years, ten lives and a cost overrun of eighty percent later – it was finally opened. When I say 'it,' I really mean *them*, because in fact there are three tunnels: two for trains and a central service tunnel.

Of course you see nothing of this as you are swept under the Channel; it's just one seamless operation, drive-on, drive-off. There is no sense of awe, no feeling of being at a depth of 75 metres under the seabed, or that you have travelled almost 38 of the fifty-kilometre distance underwater.

The Eurotunnel authorities have missed an opportunity to provide passengers with large flat-screen TVs showing what to expect on driving off at the other side, where to buy fuel, and wine (!), and a reminder of which side of the road to drive on. They also missed out on showing us what's beneath the waves: fish and other marine life (cod and chips), shipwrecks, and so on. Or even a history of the Eurotunnel itself. All this is, alas, left to the imagination.

The train's windows remained featureless, until suddenly we emerged in broad daylight near Calais, having travelled under the Channel and forward in time by one hour.

A quick fill-up with cheap diesel (much, *much* cheaper than the UK) and we were on the autoroute heading back to *Liberty*. From here we had only about three weeks left of the cruising season, and with luck maybe we'd finish in style with an autumnal cruise to Paris. I say maybe because we'd been told there wasn't much chance of a mooring there this time of the year. But previously, whenever anyone had told us we might have trouble finding a mooring somewhere, we'd always found one, so we remained optimistic.

We returned to find *Liberty* still afloat and seemingly undamaged. Apart from the TV having fallen over, and some cups and glasses tumbled about in the cupboards – evidence of the wash generated by boats large and small passing by on the Petite Seine – there was nothing to worry about.

Laurie, the young woman in the *capitainerie* office, said she had been concerned a couple of times when she saw how much *Liberty* was rocked by the boat wakes, so she too was relieved to discover there was no damage.

'Ze boat, eet was going like zis!' (waving of hands). 'I was worried in case it would get damaged; eet ees such a pretty boat!'

How sweet.

We stayed for an extra couple of days on board in Saint-Mammès itself, and took the opportunity to walk into neighbouring Moret-sur-Loing, across the Briare canal, a much prettier town than Saint-Mammès. Saint-M is a bit downmarket, a bit down-at-heel, whereas Moret is charming, with the requisite half-timbered five hundred-year-old houses, stone towers, cobbled streets and some lovely parkland bordering the river, with willows trailing their fingers in the water. Being a Sunday, people were promenading, or having *pique-niques* on the grassy banks beside the water, children were running around and laughing, and everyone seemed in late-summer good humour.

On the river, kayakers paddled about, making the most of the weather. We wished we'd been able to moor closer, but all the available local moorings (unsurprisingly) were taken.

Back at our mooring we suddenly found ourselves with neighbours – Klaus and June from Britain on one side, and Tony and Sue from New Zealand on the other. We had them all over for drinks in the evening and did the usual swapping of boating stories. Klaus was German but spoke with a broad north-of-England accent, a curious and entertaining blend that was Pythonesque at times.

He was very knowledgeable and called himself 'an old sea dog,' loudly proclaiming he had been sailing since the age of nine. Tony, from Auckland, trumped him, having started boating at the age of six. This is normal if you come from certain parts of Auckland – you learn to trim sails before you know your five-times table.

Either way, their combined total knowledge of boating was useful to us, especially as both couples had recently stayed in Paris, which is where we were determined to end our adventure for the year, if possible.

And possible it was, they insisted. Despite our having been told by the Arsenal Marina in Paris that there were no spaces available, Klaus and Tony asserted that all we had to do was turn up anyway and the *capitainerie* would find us a mooring, even if it meant rafting up against another boat. Liz and I decided there and then that Paris it would be, and we resolved to set off the following morning.

Meanwhile though, much wine and beer was consumed, and boating knowledge imparted. Fate perhaps, because if we hadn't got the encouragement we did we'd planned instead of Paris to go up the Petite Seine to a place called Bray, which had been recommended to us by another boatie, and which sounded lovely. But who could resist Paris, romantic Paris, as a final chapter? Not us. We needed a good ending to the cruising year.

CHAPTER FORTY-SEVEN

The next morning Liz and I did our pre-voyage checks and *Liberty*'s engine started first time. We farewelled our neighbours, promising to keep in touch, and by mid-morning we cruised out of the marina and turned left down the Haute Seine in the direction of the French capital.

Kiwi friends Wynn and Anne on their boat *Waiheke* had said it had taken them about four days to reach Paris from Saint-Mammès, but with *Liberty*'s engine being more than twice the size of theirs, and armed with the more recent wisdom of Klaus, June, Tony and Sue, we estimated it would be only a two-day jaunt, though beginning with a relatively long first day, which at around seven hours, it was.

But the Seine was lovely, the weather kind, and the trees on the river banks were only just beginning to realise that autumn had arrived, turning embarrassed blushes of pale oranges and yellows, knowing that winter starkness would soon be upon them, though for the most part the leaves were still green. With the sun shining brightly at times our hopes of an Indian summer looked like being fulfilled. Liz even alerted me at one point to a topless woman sunbathing on the riverbank.

'Where?' I said, turning to scan the river's edge, and inadvertently steering the boat towards the bank. 'No need to look!' Liz admonished. 'And watch where you're going!'

'Then why tell me?' I asked, perfectly reasonably. I thought it was a little unfair as these were likely to be the last bare breasts of the season. The woman probably had no idea how important a role she was playing, and I felt it my duty to at least provide an appreciative audience. I straightened the wheel and stared straight ahead, as instructed, teeth clenched.

Other impressive sights on the banks included some fabulous homes, mini-*châteaux* almost, with turrets and towers, steeply-sloping slate roofs, patterned brickwork; many looked like dolls' houses. ('Permission to look at the houses Number One?')

Most had manicured lawns sloping down to the water, with their own private moorings, though we saw few boats. We wondered if we just bobbed up to one whether the owners would take kindly to a request for an overnight stay, but we decided not to push *entente cordiale* too far.

Klaus had written us a detailed itinerary of the route to Paris but despite his instructions we failed to find his recommended mooring, and fetched up close to a lock called Evry and tied up beside a sports field and complex. It wasn't a marina, just a concrete quayside with no security, so we were a little concerned, especially by the number of people walking and driving by. In talking with Tony and Klaus the previous evening we'd heard some horrific tales, including one about a couple whose boat was stolen, and then held to ransom. Obviously they weren't on board at the time, and in the end they did manage to get it back without having to pay, but it unnerved us. Most boats can easily be released from their moorings by untying or cutting the mooring ropes, after which they'd be left to the mercy of the current. With luck a boat might just run gently aground in mud, but where we had moored, just upstream from the lock, there was also a weir, and our concern was that if someone did release the boat in the night we might not know about it until *Liberty* tumbled over the edge, plummeting two metres or so and possibly capsizing with us on board. Not the best scenario to have playing in your mind as you try to get to sleep.

We discussed how to minimise the risk, and Liz came up with the solution. 'Drop the anchor!' she suggested. Brilliant! So we did, in the hope that if the ropes were stealthily cut in the night and the boat was swept into the current the anchor would dig into the river bed and stop us from drifting helplessly and going over the weir.

It gave us some peace of mind, and so we drifted... off to sleep.

We arrived in Paris through the arse end, so it was appropriate that we moored at a marina called Port de l'Arsenal. Fate sometimes does that.

When I say 'arse end,' I don't mean to be unkind to the city, but it is by all accounts much prettier and more awesome to cruise into Paris on the Seine from the north. Which of course we couldn't do, since our position meant we were forced to approach the city from the south.

It wasn't all bad by any means, but it was hardly romantic. With around ten kilometres left before reaching the marina the environment on both banks became more and more industrial, to the point where I – in my naïvety – asked Liz where the landmarks were. 'When do we get to see the Eiffel Tower, Notre Dame, and so on?'

'We probably won't,' she replied, not taking her eyes off the river ahead. 'We're entering the wrong way for that.'

This was said through mildly-clenched teeth, because for the first time in almost a full year of cruising the waterways of France we didn't have a *guide fluviale*, the canal and river bible for this particular stretch. I wasn't too worried since we were definitely heading in the right direction, but Liz likes to know exactly where we're going in detail, and the final approach to Paris was a bit more complicated than we'd expected. 'If we overshoot the entrance to the Arsenal we end up in a complicated one-way system, which we don't want to do,' Liz explained. (The interpretation of 'which we don't want to do' was: 'Don't make any mistakes or we'll be in deep shit.')

She was right. The river was increasingly busy with commercial boat traffic – large *peniches*, sometimes two barges end to end pushed by a big tug, passenger boats (*bateaux mouches*), fast little RIBs – as well as boats more our size. There was no room for error.

As it happened, Number One spotted the entrance to the marina and the visitors' waiting pontoon beside the lock without too much trouble, and by early afternoon we were moored safely in the Arsenal Marina. The advice of Klaus, June, Tony and Sue had been correct – there were indeed places available, and even better, at a reduced cost now that the peak season was over. Where else could you stay in central Paris, within coo-ee of the Bastille, for €33 a night, including showers, WCs, Wi-Fi and security? It was a bargain, and we cheerily booked in for three nights.

There have been many times in our year-long voyage when the pop of a Champagne cork had been heard on our aft deck: birthdays, welcoming friends on board, reaching journey milestones, surviving hazards, or just because we felt like it, but no occasion had seemed quite so appropriate as arriving in Paris, so within a very short time of tying up we were toasting our successful arrival with the clink of Champagne flutes.

To add to our welcome, two cats came on board to check us out, one white with no ears, the other a cute but wary tabby. Being cat people we felt even more at home. They didn't stay long, though whitey was brazen enough to go below and check out the accommodation. It was nice to be trusted. We felt special; a warm welcome to Paris.

Even better, the sun was shining and it really was warm, with a sunny outlook for the next few days. We decided to explore the local environment, so set off late afternoon on foot, without a map, and wandered ad-lib through the hectic rush-hour streets, drinking in the sights, sounds and smells.

As evening descended our meanderings took us through the Place des Voges where we spent a happy half hour browsing art shop windows, wondering how much some of the works cost. (There were no prices, presumably on the premise that if you have to ask then you can't afford them. We couldn't anyway, we knew that. Having spent twice as much as planned on buying *Liberty*, and a third more than budgeted on the new apartment, our money was starting to run out, and we both knew that within a month we would have to be looking for work.)

But we weren't destitute yet and were determined to have dinner out on our first night in Paris. In the Le Marais district, where we'd stayed *en famille* in 2007, we found a little Thai restaurant, so capped off our arrival with a nice meal.

Returning to *Liberty* – our cheap inner-city accommodation – we settled down for the night, feeling very satisfied that we'd made the decision to come to Paris, and that it was a lovely way to end the year's boating.

As we went to sleep we had no indication that the next day would involve a thief, armed police and worse: a French language test…

CHAPTER FORTY-EIGHT

On the morning of 11 September there was a man wearing a blue tracksuit top in the Pigalle area of Paris. It's a somewhat sleazy area, known for its sex shops as much as its art nouveau connections, but this man was thinking only of the art of pickpocketing.

He looked around, as he had been for a while, and spotted an obviously-touristy couple going into a café. He observed them order coffees and croissants in halting French, though he cared not for their dietary requirements or their linguistic limitations.

They moved to a table at the back of the *salon* to escape the noise of road works outside. He watched – though pretended not to – as the man sat at the back facing outwards and the woman slung her handbag on the back of her chair and sat facing her partner, her back to the room.

After a couple of minutes the shortish swarthy man made his way to the table behind the woman and sat behind her, his back to her. He was careful to be quiet, and avoided scraping his chair on the tiled floor as he sat. Maybe he wondered if they'd seen the sign at the till, warning patrons to be careful of pickpockets.

He listened as the tourist couple spoke in English, and at a point when their conversation was at a peak he casually and without turning slipped his hand into the woman's unzipped handbag. His fingers searched for the red leather wallet he'd watched her use at the counter, found it, and deftly withdrew it from the bag, slipping it into his tracksuit pocket.

He got up and left without haste. Nobody noticed him go. He was the invisible man.

Five minutes later Liz and I finished our croissants and coffee and got up to leave. Liz, as usual, checked her bag and discovered her wallet was missing. It took only seconds to realise that the man in the tracksuit top sitting behind her had taken it. It couldn't have been anyone else – the café was basically empty, and there was nobody else nearby.

As happens in situations like this, you go into shock initially, then try to think what was in the wallet, then what to do about it. We alerted the people behind the counter and they called the manager from the back. We explained as best we could what had happened. Liz pointed to the security cameras on the ceiling and asked, '*Peut-être, vous avez le video?*' The manager said he did. The police were called, and the boss went off to check the video recording.

I meanwhile went outside, having decided that the thief would most likely ditch the wallet after ransacking it for anything valuable. He would have found only two Euros in coins and eight single *métro* tickets, but also Liz's New Zealand and English credit cards, and her driver's licence. I looked in five nearby rubbish bins, thoughtfully provided in clear plastic by the Paris council, but found nothing. On returning to the café I discovered Liz surrounded by three police officers on their bicycles. They were all devastatingly handsome, and armed (which I thought was a good thing, and hoped for the thief to be spotted fleeing, then falling in a hail of bullets...)

The security image of the *voleur* turned out to be very clear, so while the handsomest cop took details of the theft from Liz and me, the other two *flics* cycled off to check out the area.

To cut to the chase, there wasn't one. No pursuit down the main street of the 18th *arrondisement*, no leaping off bicycles and pinning the suspect to the pavement in a headlock, and no

French S.W.A.T. team with snipers and megaphones. But the three cops did well and took the situation seriously. They even seemed to know who the suspect was, and confirmed he was a professional.

We were advised to make a 'complaint' at a nearby police station for insurance purposes, so, leaving the pedalling policemen to the task of running the scumbag to ground, Liz and I trudged to the small local constabulary, where we were turned away and sent to another one not far away where, we were assured, there were more staff and they spoke English.

It was at this point the circumstances took a bizarre twist. We went into the police station and up to the counter staffed by a woman in civilian clothes and a young policeman in uniform. I said in French that we were sorry but we didn't speak French very well and that maybe they had someone there who spoke English. The young French cop, whose name turned out to be Olivier, then said that I spoke very good French, that he could understand me perfectly and that I should make my declaration/complaint in French.

I protested that the circumstances were such that English would be easier for us, but again he congratulated me on my French, saying that the only way to learn French was to use it. I agreed, in principle, but managed to persuade him that his English sounded much better than my French. I must have made an arresting case because he in turn reluctantly agreed and asked us to wait for a few moments on the bench nearby.

He then surreptitiously appeared from around the counter and whispered, 'I will be with you in just a few minutes, but first I must go outside for a cigarette.'

What could we say? It was so amusing all we could do was agree, and in fact he was back within about four minutes. I said, *'Vous fumez trés rapidement!'* which he agreed was the case, and again complimented me on my French. Tchah. Let's get on with it…

Liz told him the story, he typed the whole lot into his computer (in French), read it back to us (in English, apologising for his interpretation), and printed it out for Liz to sign. Our conversation was a curious blend of Franglais, but we all seemed to cope quite well.

And that was it as far as the police were concerned. Annoyingly, our next task – advising the banks in New Zealand and England of the theft of the credit cards – was complicated by the fact that for the first time in weeks we had left our mobiles on charge on the boat, and had no back-up, no phone cards, and no SIM in the iPad. So it was a worrying journey back to the boat on the *métro* before Liz could get on the phone and cancel the cards. But luck was with us and none of them had been used in the intervening couple of hours since the theft.

In fact, we hadn't been back on the boat more than an hour when we got a call from a French woman who spoke excellent English to tell us she had been about to throw a sandwich wrapper into a rubbish bin in the 18th *arrondisement* when she spotted what she called 'a nice leather purse,' inside of which she'd found one of our *Liberty* business cards with our names and phone number on. *Quel* relief!

However, she confirmed there were no credit cards or driving licence, and no money, but offered to return the purse to us before we left Paris. Wonderful. We made arrangements, and Liz and I decided we deserved to at least rescue some of the day so went on the *métro* to the Orangerie by the Jardins de Tuilerie to view some of Monet's iconic water lily paintings. We figured it would be a nice, quiet, therapeutic thing to do – a million metaphorical miles away from sneaky scumbag thieves and sordid doings.

It was. I had never seen any of Monet's lily paintings in real life before, though since Liz had been to the Orangerie many years ago, she knew what to expect. I certainly didn't, and was gobsmacked. What grabs you at first is the sheer enormity of them: some are 12 metres long by two metres tall. They predate Cinemascope and curved widescreen HDTVs by decades, yet capture in glorious panorama the lilies of Giverny.

Even better, because we arrived at the museum less than an hour before closing we were charged only half the usual admission price. Which seemed appropriate given the events of the day; it was a steal.

Our third day in Paris started with a near-drowning. We were sitting in bed having our first coffee of the morning when we heard splashing outside the boat. It sounded like someone was swimming right beside *Liberty*, but you'd have to be mad to swim in the marina water. And yet we could definitely hear vigorous splashing and bubbling.

We went on deck in our dressing gowns and leaned over the rail. There on the swim platform, having just managed to drag itself to safety, was a very wet and bedraggled tabby cat, possibly the same one who'd come aboard to explore when we arrived. He looked up at us and gave the most heart-wrenching meow you've ever heard. You didn't need to speak Cat to know it meant 'I fell in!' And looking at the drenched animal we didn't need to be told.

The cat repeated its plight loudly, in fact with such volume its howls echoed around the marina and we were worried lest someone thought we were abusing the poor animal. I climbed down the ladder to the platform and tried to lift the soggy moggy but he kept digging his claws into the rope that was coiled there, probably fearing I was going to throw him back in.

I tugged, he clung, I tugged more, he howled louder, and then I realised I was standing on his tail, so I was actually trying to lift him while keeping him trapped, and trying not to fall in the water myself. Between the two of us we were making a dog's breakfast of the whole affair. It was a tragic yet comical situation. Liz went to get the camera but couldn't find it. She returned instead with something far more useful – a towel – and having de-clung the cat and released its tail I passed the dripping moggy up to her.

She had no sooner got him in the towel than he leapt away and disappeared, presumably back to wherever he lived, to shake himself dry and maybe lie low for a while to hide his acute embarrassment – and count how many lives he had left. He didn't even stay long enough to be awarded the silver trophy, The Dunkling Cup. I would happily have passed it on.

Shame we didn't get a photo though – the image could have become the mainstay of a water safety campaign, with posters showing the half-drowned cat with the message underneath: 'Always, ALWAYS, wear a life jacket.'

Having saved one life we then took the *métro* to see a selection of still lifes, in Rodin's garden. It was lovely warm sunny weather for wandering around the gorgeous lawns in the grounds of the hotel where he lived in his dotage and which is now a museum to his life and works.

Rodin seemed to have spent much of his career battling critics, some of whom thought he was a fraud and some who simply didn't like his commissioned works when they were completed. He appears to have carved a niche for himself as the tortured artist, and many of his subjects seem somewhat at odds with the world too.

The Thinker, for example, ponders on his plinth amid cone-shaped shrubbery, tourists striking a similar pose in front for photos. (Seriously, can't they think of something less *cliché*? It's like those people who pose themselves pushing against the Leaning Tower of Pisa to 'stop it falling over.' Yawn.) The statue of The Thinker is actually Dante contemplating hell and mankind's fall – serious thoughts indeed – though looking at him I suspect he was actually thinking, 'Can't these bloody tourists come up with something new for a change?!'

Rodin died in 1917, apparently ending his days not making bronze statues but instead sketching attractive young naked women. When I read this in the guide, I said to Liz, 'Finally I have a plan for my retirement...'

We then went to the Parc des Buttes Chaumont which we'd read about online. We'd Googled phrases such as 'Hidden Paris,' 'Secret Paris,' etc., to see what came up. One suggestion was to take a tour of the Paris sewers, but we decided to save that for another visit. The above-ground *parc* appealed a lot more.

Anyway, the park is an old quarry in the 19th *arrondissement*, which has been landscaped with sloping lawns, lots of trees, snaking paths, a lake, streams and even a waterfall. We saved exploring fully until we'd had a picnic lunch on a sunny grassy slope.

There was another couple sitting down the bank not far from us who looked like actors from a Woody Allen movie – the man looking Jewish with rimless glasses, collarless shirt, beard and dark hat, and the young woman dressed in almost 1920s clothing. They were drinking wine, but he seemed uneasy about it and kept looking round at us perched further up the hill, either hoping for a nod of approval or that we hadn't seen the alcohol. We generated an air of nonchalance (which was easy since we didn't care what they were doing), and sipped from our own wine glasses in the hope it sent a message of support. *L'chaim!*

We then set off to explore this 'secret' piece if Paris, but were a bit underwhelmed at first as it seemed just like many other parks. But that was only because the entrance we'd come in was at the opposite end of the quarry bit, and once we discovered the park proper it was lovely, though hardly a secret given the number of people there: hundreds... singles, couples, groups, families, picnics, sunbathers, and (of course) dogs. Always dogs. *Chaque jour il y a toujours les chiens.*

We found the lake, the waterfall, the meandering paths, and a classical gazebo on the hill from where you can get good views over Paris. The old quarried cliffs added to the drama of the landscape, and it was easy to forget you were in the centre of the French capital. It was a little piece of paradise, and while not as secret or hidden as the web might suggest, it was still worth discovering.

Later in the evening we were back on the boat and the woman who had found Liz's stolen wallet, Anne, came on board to return it. Her English was way better than our French, and we chatted for a long time. We were very grateful to her for noticing the wallet even if the thief had already taken the credit cards and driver's licence. It was the licence that worried us most as it could be used as fake ID to open accounts and which, if they fell overdue for payment, could result in Liz being given a bad credit rating. Identity theft is a serious matter. We were keeping our fingers crossed the thief didn't have any English or Kiwi connections to fence the licence to.

Next day we headed for the Arc de Triomphe by driverless train. We wondered how the *métro* people knew where their trains were without drivers, or how fast they were going, or when to stop them, but assumed it was all done from a central control room and operated in the same way as a model railway. 'The controller's probably a nine-year-old,' I suggested to Liz.

Whatever, it worked, and without a driver's compartment up front we had a great view of the underground journey as we were swept along the shining rails, the tunnel lights rushing towards us, and brightly-lit stations emerging like distant lanterns from the darkness ahead. Not such a great view for the unemployed train drivers though.

From the underground to way above-ground; we slogged our way up the more than 280-step spiral staircase in the Arc de Triomphe, to finally emerge at the top in brilliantly sunny weather. Gorgeous – and great views over Paris. We were mesmerised by the traffic jockeying for position below as it flowed bacteria-like around the arch: braking, starting, pausing, slowing, speeding and – in one instance – colliding, though it was a very minor bump with no fisticuffs or thrown gauntlets. Shame, because we could have recommended a great park nearby as the ideal location for a duel at dawn.

Everyone somehow seemed to know what to do, despite the complete absence of road markings or traffic lights, and it all seemed to be based on giving way to the right.

We strolled down the Avenue de Champs Élysées, stopping in at the Mercedes shop (as you do) to ogle some vintage Merc sports cars. They were absolutely pristine – literally in showroom condition – and had obviously never been driven round the Arc de Triomphe.

There was all manner of three-pronged star merchandise for sale too, from polo shirts and belt buckles to model cars and cigarette lighters. I sprayed myself with some Mercedes man-smell stuff but was disappointed to find it wasn't *Eau de Gazole* and didn't smell of diesel. Needless to say we didn't buy a car, model or otherwise.

Maybe it's because the Champs Élysées is a posh avenue, but the *métro* stations don't have any big signs showing where they are. Instead you just stumble across steps disappearing into the ground every now and then, and only then do you see a discreet *Métro* carved into the stonework. But once we'd found a station we took a train and sat people-watching on the slopes of Montmartre with the cathedral as our backdrop, gleaming white in the sun. There were hundreds of people, including a wedding couple being photographed on the steps, though it would take someone a lot of time to Photoshop all the tourists out of the frame.

Liz and I had both been to Montmartre before so didn't feel the need to go inside the cathedral, and instead strolled around the artists' quarter where artists were busy painting, sketching and otherwise rendering their sitting subjects, or depicting famous Parisian scenes. Some of them were absolutely fantastic, but we decided not to have our portraits done. Instead Liz spotted a monochromatic watercolour of boats on the Seine. 'I like that,' she said, pointing to it. 'I *really* like that.'

We continued strolling, impressed by so much talent crammed into one small square, and eventually found ourselves back at the watercolour. 'I really *really* like that,' Liz said, in case I hadn't got the message.

It had been painted by a nice young man who didn't have much English and seemed quite shy, so we made his day by not haggling too much. Cynically I suspected he was just a superb showman and had duped us with his performance; a genuinely skilled artist. But still, Liz really *really* liked the painting, and I have to admit I did too.

And then, a most un-touristy thing to do – we strolled down the hill to the curtain and material shops, which is what we had originally planned to do on Pickpocket Day.

There are a few streets just at the bottom of the Montmartre steps with multiple stores selling all sorts of material from faux furs and polka dots to the finest linens and cottons. This was haberdashery heaven, and we finally found the materials we'd been searching for for our new kitchen and lounge curtains, yay! We would even be able to say, 'But of course we had to go to *Paris* to find what we wanted, darling!' Yes, we do live in a material world, even if it was one with a 20% discount, but at 49 Euros per metre that was much appreciated.

Even better, this time we managed to avoid the pickpockets.

CHAPTER FORTY-NINE

Sunday 14 September was our last day in Paris, and getting close to the end of the voyage. We paid our mooring bill at the *capitainerie* and set off through the Port de l'Arsenal lock, turning right onto the Seine for our lap of honour of the capital.

We just had to do this – our own *Last Tango* – to cruise down the Seine and past the icons: Notre Dame, the Musée d'Orsay, under the Pont Neuf, and past the Eiffel Tower. We had to finish on a high note, and we did.

It was fabulous. The weather was gorgeous, the trees just beginning to tinge gold and orange, the sky a watercolour blue, and there was a general air of bonhomie in the morning sunshine. The streets alongside the Seine were an explosion of colour as a major running race threaded its way beside and over the river. Music pumped out of speakers to encourage the participants (we both agreed we'd have run faster just to get away from it) and drummers provided further audio incentive, a primal beat, driving the runners onwards. Commentators screamed over the PA system, their words loud, distorted and meaningless, but full of encouragement.

I called out to Liz, 'I guess that's what they mean by a running commentary!' She rolled her eyes and got back to scanning the river, still probably hoping to spot a new husband.

We would have liked to pull over and watch, take in more of the action, and shout '*Bon courage!*' but the Seine was the busiest stretch of waterway we'd encountered in the whole year, with many commercial boats laden with sand, gravel and other cargoes, as well as *beaucoup de bateaux mouches* – tourist boats that are like waterway buses. They were everywhere, constantly stopping and starting as they dropped off and picked up passengers. In time-lapse from a distance they'd have looked like worker ants.

We had to keep our wits about us. Liz was tense, I could tell, but she did a superb job as lookout and kept me fully informed of everything in the water ahead, astern, and to port and starboard, reminding me which arches of the bridges to go under, and so on. It would have been far more relaxing just being a passenger on one of the tourist boats, but we felt we were a part of the river, we felt integrated, actually *in* the postcard and not just looking at it. But we couldn't relax – there was too much to be wary of, too many decisions to make – yet it was exciting.

We annoyed only one Parisian boat skipper, with a Mexican stand-off, so considering the density of the river traffic we did quite well. The problem was his boat didn't have an obvious bow or stern – it was squared-off at both ends, and the position of his wheelhouse was no indication of which way he was facing either, so we waited mid-stream for a hint as to what he was doing as he came away from the quayside. All we could tell was that he was easing away slowly, but whether it was to move towards us or away from us we hadn't a clue. So we figured it was safer to just bob mid-stream till we knew for sure.

However, it turned out he was doing the same – waiting for us to do something before *he* moved. As we finally pushed our throttle forward he gave Liz a glare and an angry shrug of the shoulders (at least we were spared any gestures more serious). *Zees English, zay 'ave no idea!*

Désolé Monsieur, désolé. C'est vrai, we 'ave no idea 'ow to soil a bat.

We sailed under the Pont des Arts – the lovers' bridge – where it has long been a tradition to attach a padlock to the railings to 'lock in your love' with your partner, then together throw the key into the Seine, declaring everlasting devotion that cannot be undone (except with bolt-cutters). Some couples even go to the trouble of getting their padlocks engraved with their initials or names. Cute maybe, but the problem is the padlock practice has become so popular that some of the railings had begun to break away from their mountings due to the sheer number of locks, posing a danger to anyone leaning on them and a risk to river traffic below.

As we cruised under the bridge we could see sheets of plywood in places where railings had succumbed to the sheer weight of the locks. The entire span was so clogged with padlocks that from a distance they presented a solid wall of glinting steel, and you could only make out the true nature of the mass as you got close. We held our breaths but managed to pass underneath without incident. We've no idea how much each piece of love-locked railing weighs but it must be significant, and certainly heavy enough to cause serious damage to anyone or anything passing beneath at the wrong moment.

Seeing Paris from the Seine was special – as millions of tourists each year must realise when they catch one of the *bateaux mouches*, or the river cruise boats offering lunchtime and dinner trips. We felt very special being able to see the city from our own boat, even if it was in broad daylight. (Tony and Sue had told us at Saint-Mammès that they'd enjoyed a voyage on their boat through Paris at night, but given that Liz had been on a knife's edge even just thinking about the busy water traffic, that wasn't something we'd contemplated!)

Paris is a city that begs to be viewed from the air too, so it was no surprise to see a tethered helium balloon on the skyline, its gondola underneath full of people wanting a bird's eye perspective. Of course you can get a fine view from the top of the Eiffel Tower or the Arc de Triomphe, but the balloon enabled you to get an aerial view of those icons as well. The Montgolfier brothers would have been proud.

As we cruised towards the Eiffel Tower it looked like a painted backdrop in a stage play, slightly faded in the morning autumn light. But how fantastic to cruise almost under its sweeping ironwork, and watch its elevators climbing and descending. It was mesmerising, which is not a good thing when you've got a barge-load of gravel bearing down on you from the north!

We saw riverside markets, thousands more runners, families out strolling, the police diving near one of the bridges (why?), and as we passed under one bridge I caught a glimpse of what appeared to be a sea creature, but couldn't have been. Yet it looked like gleaming wet black scaly skin, curving gracefully as though it had just swum up to the surface then turned and dived down again. Is there a Seine equivalent of the Loch Ness monster?

And so we came to the northernmost point of the journey, which proved to be poetically appropriate as we slowed *Liberty* to a stop just past the replica Statue of Liberty. There she was, holding her flaming torch aloft as if saluting our achievement, as fine a finishing line as one could wish for.

Liz scoffed at the statue's relative miniature size having been to New York and seen Eiffel's original, but agreed it was a Good Moment. I swung the wheel hard to port and our own *Liberty* responded, turning an elegant 180 degrees to face back the way we'd come; not so much a tango as a modest twirl.

But neither of us wanted to leave immediately, even though the river was busy and we needed to keep moving. I slowed the engine to tick-over again, and we took a moment to consider the significance of what we'd achieved in the past year: finding *Liberty* (and having to double our budget to buy her!), almost killing our first on-board guests with toxic battery fumes, heading off down the Saône and Rhône rivers with no experience and at a time of the year when everyone else was stopping for winter, getting rocked and rolled while moored as passing boats created wakes of tsunami proportions, almost losing the boat at Avignon as the current tried to wrest the mooring ropes from our hands, travelling on the Rhône à Sète canal with snow falling, marvelling at Roman ruins, and being gobsmacked by the magnificent and not-ruined Pont du Gard, having the *Place in the Sun* TV camera on board at Beaucaire, losing all propulsion (but right outside a boatyard), setting off along the Canal du Midi in spring and providing entertainment for the locals on the scary six-lock Fonserannes staircase, crashing stern-first into the lock gates at Bram, playing dodgems with hire boats, weeping at the felling of diseased plane trees on the Midi, sitting on the back deck on a sultry night listening to a nightingale, drinking far too much wine, enjoying the company of friends visiting, rescuing a yachtie with a broken engine, witnessing a baby deer swimming across the canal, mooring on the Midi miles from civilisation and watching a bird poking its head out from a hole in a tree, sleeping in complete darkness and silence (as well as next to noisy railway lines), finding the bilge full of water one morning, fixing multiple problems with the boat (v satisfactory), causing multiple problems on the boat (v annoying), arguing, fighting, laughing and loving, speaking almost fluent French and at other times talking complete gibberish, meeting some wonderful boat people as well as some pompous bastards, taking far too many photos of herons, eating far too many baguettes and croissants, cooing at ducklings, cygnets (Liz calls them 'swanlings') and other springtime baby wildlife, being swallowed by the cathedral-like Bollène lock, befriending dogs and being adopted (occasionally) by cats, honing our rope-throwing skills as well as making complete fools of ourselves trying to lasso bollards, and, of course, finally conquering Paris.

I reluctantly pushed the throttle forward and we left, going south again to head to our *hivernage*, our wintering-over spot.

We had only about two weeks left, and then we would have to find jobs back in England. Back to reality, and to Liverpool; back to where I once belonged.

As we cruised through and out of the industrial banks of the Seine and into the pretty French countryside again we were going back up-river. It was appropriate; we'd started the adventure by selling up and cutting loose from our corporate lives in New Zealand, 'abandoned' three of our four children there, 'risked' not having any income, 'thrown' caution to the wind, and gone against current thinking by living on a boat for a year, unemployed and of no fixed abode.

We hadn't waited till retirement, and we hadn't left it too late.

We'd had a ton of fun, learned a lot more about France and even some more French, learned that we can live comfortably together in close confinement, and learned that there was nothing at all silly or foolish about what we'd done.

And here we were, heading up the Seine, once more against the current.

Seuls les poissons morts suivent le courant.

POSTSCRIPT

A nd so to the end. Three hundred and sixty-four days after starting the journey, *Liberty* was unceremoniously hauled out of the water by an old yellow crane belching smoke, and placed, as they say in nautical-speak, on the hard.

It all went without a hitch. We had moseyed back up the Seine from Paris and onto the Yonne, taking our time and enjoying the autumn sunshine, aiming to arrive at Simon's boatyard at Migennes towards the end of the third week in September.

We actually arrived a couple of days early, so moored up along the quayside at the local marina, finding ourselves with about four other boats all waiting for Simon's attention. But it was a nice relaxed end to everything, and – even better – Migennes had a launderette so we were able to do some long overdue washing and become socially acceptable again.

At the end of the quay was a lovely boat called *Puddlestone*, an obvious live-aboard as there were lots of plants, and multiple 'things' scattered on the roof and deck, such as bicycles, crockery, and other necessities that are the sure giveaways of a full-time residence. We met the skipper, John, who is a musician 'in the wings' waiting to be discovered. In the lead-up to this situation he'd been a police officer, a full-time doll's house builder, and a general handyman, but when we met him he was waiting for his YouTube songs to go viral, and lamenting the fact that they hadn't.

'Why is it some people get millions of hits and I get nothing?!' he complained.

He played us his original *Jihadi Blues*, which was both clever and very funny, and we too had to wonder why it hadn't taken off.

We met his cat Patrice, who he took for walks on a lead; 'Too many dogs round 'ere,' he explained – and we enjoyed some late afternoon wines and shared boating stories on the upper deck of *Puddlestone*.

All along the sunny quayside there were other boats preparing for lift-out when their turn would come, and the basin was busy with hire boats, their new crews taking advantage of the Indian summer.

In between trips to the *laverie*, the *supermarché* and the *boulangerie* we slowly loaded up Van Rouge with all the items we thought we'd need back in England, as well as any valuable stuff we didn't want to leave on board over winter.

And then it was our turn. We went through the lock and descended to the Yonne, turned the corner and all too quickly arrived at the boatyard.

Simon and his mate Mark had the crane in place and were just lowering the big slings into the water ready for us.

Liz went ashore, while I guided *Liberty* through the straps and then, entrusting her to Simon and his crane, I too hopped ashore to watch our boat take flight.

At the controls of the old crane, Simon was in his element as he revved the engine, twiddled the levers, and slowly, slowly lifted *Liberty* out of her element and onto the cradle waiting on shore.

This was the first time we'd seen our boat, our home, out of the water; she looked enormous, hanging there in the straps, swinging gently, water dripping from her dark hull. We were pleased to see her underside looked as good as we thought it did when we'd filmed it using the GoPro back in June.

Mark cut away some old fishing line from around the prop shaft, nothing to worry about he assured us, and then set about water-blasting the hull to remove the slime and build-up of the past year or more.

Next morning Simon found us a nook in his almost-full boatyard and *Liberty* was moved on a special low-loader and settled onto supports, where she would stay for the winter.

We spent the next three days working on the dents, scratches and gouges on the hull, some of which we were to blame for but others looked much older. The dent in the stern from backing into the lock gates wasn't as bad as we'd thought, and Simon said he'd be able to fix the damaged davit without any trouble.

Meanwhile the weather was gorgeous, 26 degrees each day, and we wondered whether we shouldn't have kept sailing.

But we'd gone for a whole year living a dream, and watching our bank balance reduce, so we knew it was time to return to Liverpool, to our new home. To write this book, to find jobs, and earn money. And then maybe we'd have the liberty to do it all again.